Disciplining Freud on Religion

Disciplining Freud on Religion

Perspectives from the Humanities and Social Sciences

Edited by
Gregory Kaplan and
William B. Parsons

LEXINGTON BOOKS

A division of
ROWMAN & LITTLEFIELD PUBLISHERS, INC.
Lanham • Boulder • New York • Toronto • Plymouth, UK

Published by Lexington Books
A division of Rowman & Littlefield Publishers, Inc.
A wholly owned subsidiary of The Rowman & Littlefield Publishing Group, Inc.
4501 Forbes Boulevard, Suite 200, Lanham, Maryland 20706
http://www.lexingtonbooks.com

Estover Road, Plymouth PL6 7PY, United Kingdom

British Library Cataloguing in Publication Information Available

Library of Congress Cataloging-in-Publication Data

Disciplining Freud on religion : perspectives from the humanities and social sciences / edited by Gregory Kaplan and William B. Parsons.
p. cm.
Includes bibliographical references and index.
ISBN 978-0-7391-4212-7 (cloth : alk. paper) — ISBN 978-0-7391-4214-1 (electronic)
1. Psychoanalysis and religion. 2. Freud, Sigmund, 1856-1939. I. Kaplan, Gregory, 1968- II. Parsons, William Barclay, 1955-
BF175.4.R44D57 2010
200.92—dc22 2010015505

∞™ The paper used in this publication meets the minimum requirements of American National Standard for Information Sciences—Permanence of Paper for Printed Library Materials, ANSI/NISO Z39.48-1992.

Printed in the United States of America

Contents

Introduction	Framing Freud on Religion *Gregory Kaplan and William B. Parsons*	vii
	Part I: On Freud, Religion, and Religious Studies	
Chapter 1	Desiderata and Possibilities for the Psychological Study of Religion: How to Enlarge the Place of Freudian Thought in Religious Studies *Jacob A. Belzen, The University of Amsterdam*	3
Chapter 2	When Throne and Altar Are in Danger: Freud, Mourning, and Religion in Modernity *Diane Jonte-Pace, Santa Clara University*	59
	Part II: Perspectives from the Natural and Social Sciences	
Chapter 3	Love the Mother, Hate the Father: Understanding Sociology's Vehement Rejection of Freud on Religion *Michael P. Carroll, University of Western Ontario*	87

Chapter 4 Of Chariots, Navels, and Winged Steeds: The Dialogue between Psychoanalysis and Buddhism 107
William B. Parsons, Rice University

Chapter 5 Freud and Neuroscience: A Return to Origins 147
Kelly Bulkeley, The Graduate Theological Union, John F. Kennedy University

Part III: Philosophical Reconsiderations

Chapter 6 Freud and Philosophy of Religion after Metaphysics 169
Gregory Kaplan, Rice University

Chapter 7 "The Jewish People Does Not Dream": The Paradoxes of Identification, or Martin Buber and Sigmund Freud on the Meaning of Judaism 181
Bettina Bergo, Université de Montréal

Chapter 8 Freudian Unconscious and Secularization of Judaism 217
Jean-Joseph Goux, Rice University

Index 225

About the Contributors 231

Introduction: Framing Freud on Religion

Gregory Kaplan and William B. Parsons

It is well known that in formulating his general theoretical framework and views on religion Freud drew on multiple disciplines within the natural and social sciences, as well as from the humanities. It is not surprising, then, that the theory Freud gave birth to, once the province of psychology, has migrated to multiple disciplinary sites in the Academy. While the list is long, contemporary studies of Freud from such disciplinary perspectives include, for example, new biographies of Freud;[1] sociohistorical studies of the birth of his ideas;[2] critiques of his appropriation of the biological, neurological, and social sciences;[3] of his views on race and gender;[4] of his relation to philosophy, politics, culture, and ethics;[5] relevance to pastoral education and theology;[6] and his relation to Judaism and atheism.[7] Each of these studies draw on methodological and theoretical advances within their respective fields to reevaluate Freud. These advances have enabled researchers to reject, accept, contextualize, and integrate selected aspects of his theories. Freud is viewed alternately as hopelessly outdated and still relevant, if not prescient.

Our volume adds to this continued multidisciplinary interest in Freud by focusing on his understanding and interpretation of, as well as his relationship to, religion. Ernest Jones famously observed that Freud's views on religion had not only provoked "many books and a spate of essays," but also "evoked more controversy and condemnation than any of his other writings" (Jones 1957,

349). Certainly Freud "on religion" has continued to have as much impact on tradition and culture as any of his other provocative theses. Many of the central themes of religion that Freud addressed like ritual and obsession, Oedipus and the common man, totemism and patricide, civilization and guilt, oceanic feelings and maternal awe have been acknowledged and, as Freud would have it, "worked through." Our volume adds to these voices by bringing together multidisciplinary perspectives which assess, critique, and offer new avenues of exploration for Freud on religion.

The chapters in this volume acknowledge that Freud drew on multiple disciplines (e.g., neurocognitive science, evolutionary theory, biology, anthropological and sociological thought) on formulating not simply his general theory but the application of that theory to religious phenomena. More importantly, we acknowledge that the knowledge base of these various disciplines has evolved, and that any evaluation and utilization of Freud "on religion" must take account of such advances. What distinguishes this volume, then, is that it strives to go beyond what is of immediate concern, namely, the impact of Freud for those in religious studies, to include perspectives from other disciplines in the humanities and sciences. It acknowledges that Freud on religion is no longer the sole province of those working in religious studies for it has migrated to diverse disciplines in the Academy. It "disciplines" Freud by situating his work on religion from the methodological interests and theoretical advances found in diverse disciplinary contexts. Fittingly, the contributors to this volume hail from a variety of disciplines.

In unpacking the ramifications of Freud on religion the contributors have engaged a wide variety of questions, among which are: Where do Freud and his views on religion belong in the Academy? What was Freud's relationship to religion, and how can we make sense of the many and often contradictory scholarly evaluations of him? How has the increased knowledge base within different disciplines affected the evaluation of Freud? What, if any, are the barriers involved in utilizing Freud within particular disciplines? How can Freud's views on religion be most fruitfully used within diverse disciplines to promote a more nuanced understanding of religious phenomena? Are Freud's views on religion still relevant? If not, why not, and if so, in what way?

The various responses of the contributors to these and other questions are found in three interrelated sections. Part 1 details responses to Freud on religion from scholars within the field of religious studies; part 2 offers perspectives on Freud and religion from the natural and social sciences; and part 3 engages the concerns of philosophers. In bringing together these diverse voices, this volume seeks to heighten the academic understanding of Freud on religion, with the associated aim of establishing closer and more direct interdisciplinary communication and collaboration with regard to Freud studies.

Jacob Belzen starts the proceedings by inquiring about Freud's place in religious studies. After presenting an understanding of terms like religion, religious studies and psychology, Belzen proceeds to discuss the psychology of religion, pointing out particularly its all too often forgotten interdisciplinary nature. Cultural psychology is then introduced as a preferred option within the different possible psychological approaches to religion and three variants are lined out. One example of a cultural psychological, interdisciplinary approach to the study of religion ("psychohistory") is dealt with at greater length, and it is shown that psychoanalysis contributes organically to this branch of scholarship. It is argued that for this type of research departments of religious studies may at present be a more fitting "niche" than departments of psychology.

Diane Jonte-Pace continues the discussion by asking, "What is the relation between psychoanalysis and religion?" Her chapter challenges polarized perspectives claiming that Freud is either an opponent of religion or a covert defender of religion. Rather, Freud is a thinker with a deep ambivalence about religion and its loss, an ambivalence that is both personal and theoretical. His ambivalence is expressed in conflicting statements and formulations: he constructs a dominant masterplot critical of religion and a less visible counterthesis that defends religion. More importantly, however, the counterthesis opens up to an analysis of the loss of religion, generating a theory of how we mourn and fail to mourn in relation to "dangers to altars." Drawing from some of Freud's texts that are rarely brought into conversation with religion, and from some contemporary psychoanalytic thinkers such as Peter Homans, Julia Kristeva, and Judith Butler, the chapter suggests that Freud's own contradictory positions on religion represent an analysis of how individuals and cultures respond to the loss of religion: Freud can best be understood as a theorist who analyzes the loss of religion in cultures and individuals by exploring the dynamics of mourning and melancholia.

Michael Carroll begins part 2 by noting that although there is no dearth of investigators who use psychoanalysis to study religion, very few are sociologists. Indeed, the explicit rejection of psychoanalysis by American sociologists studying religion has been vehement. The goal of his essay is to explain why. Some obvious answers, in particular the claim that American sociology is too positivistic, turn out to be problematic given that several subtraditions in sociology have long been concerned with the study of subjective meaning. Similarly, the claim that Freud is "too psychological" is undermined by the ease with which a psychoanalytic perspective on religion can take into account those macrosociological processes—involving social class and social change—so important to sociologists. In the end, American sociology's strong rejection of psychoanalysis derives, argued Carroll, from a rejection of the figure of Freud himself, which in turn derives from a cultural "disdain for hierarchical authority" embedded in the essentially Protestant worldview that continues to shape the study of religion by American sociologists.

The chapter by William Parsons proceeds by contextualizing psychoanalytic studies of religion as part of a broader intellectual enterprise called the "psychology and religion movement," the latter characterized as spanning the years from 1880 to the present, incorporating a diversity of psychological models, being essentially interdisciplinary, and analyzing a broad array of religious phenomena. The essay then turns specifically to the psychoanalytic engagement with Buddhism, providing a brief analysis of the history of the dialogue from 1880–1970, then seizing on the most recent studies for analysis and evaluation. In so doing, Parsons turns to anthropology in treating both psychoanalysis and Buddhism as ethnopsychological systems with varying views of self, world, and other. Each system promotes diverse mental techniques for introspection and champions normative views of development and mental health. Parsons investigates the Western social soil which made this dialogue possible (i.e., the cultural dissemination of an inner-worldly mysticism and the rise of spirituality) and the issues and debates such an encounter raises. In so doing, Parsons shows how such a dialogue must include not only psychoanalysis and Buddhism but related social sciences and the broad array of resources offered by the academic study of religion and the substantial issues and debates this discipline has introduced and worked through.

Kelly Bulkeley wraps up this section by engaging Freud's place in contemporary brain science. It is well known that Freud developed psychoanalysis on the basis of a neurological model of human mental functioning. Scholars and clinicians who value Freud's theories but disagree with his materialist reductionism have generally tried to downplay the neurological roots of psychoanalysis by suggesting that his scientific rhetoric merely reflects a nineteenth-century worldview that Freud's own ideas were destined to transform. Meanwhile, critics of psychoanalysis have insisted on the inseparability of Freud's later theories from their earlier medical context, the better to reject psychoanalysis as outmoded pseudoscience. In neither case are Freud's original interests in the neural underpinnings of psychological life examined with a fair and respectful eye. Bulkeley's chapter aims to recover and update the neurological foundations of psychoanalysis, with a special focus on the implications for Freudian theories and methods in the study of religion.

Part 3 is devoted to some of the many philosophical engagements with Freud. Gregory Kaplan's chapter reopens the philosophical questions of whether Freud's account of religion presupposes naturalism and engages in reductionism. Yet Kaplan suggests that the interesting answers suggest a both . . . and/neither . . . nor situation. Taking Spinoza's naturalism and Husserl's reductionism as touchstones, a comparison to Freud's own conception—and critique—of philosophy indicates that psychoanalysis may not qualify as a "rigorous science," but nor does it abandon the provisional explanation. Likewise, Freud's own appeals to nature hardly disqualify a "progress in spirituality." A close examination of Freud's transference concept will yield tentative conclusions about how something "More" both expresses and institutes psychic life and the social dynamic.

In her comparative chapter Bettina Bergo points out how the uniqueness of God and the ban on idols results in the foreclosure of representation and identity that, like the unconscious, affects change or difference without presenting itself to reason. Martin Buber's reading of Genesis 2–3 suggests that human mortality that ensues from Eve and Adam's eating of the Tree of Good and Evil is not a punishment for sin, but a condition for making the free choices in life which inaugurate history. The sin, or demonry, begins with the human quest to live forever, to become infinite, like us, says God, by eating of the Tree of Life. Instead, the work of finitude entails continual interpretation, marking temporal passages, and promising future redress. The incorporation of the other into the same is a kind of murder, Freud surmises, that brings the perpetrators, a band of brothers, members of a tribe into coordination. The shame and exposure they feel expresses the anxiety of responsibility. The source and result of anxiety is death, both physical and imaginary: death is final, and it is what happens to others, leaving behind it the survivors. The father killed at the hands of the sons whom he had banished especially threatens to return, weighing heavily with judgment over mortality. Moses is distinguished from Oedipus by the irony, the Witz or joke, which Israelites recapitulates of how society emerges with the expulsion from the scene of violence (incorporation, murder). The distance which separates identity from drives thus explains the repetition of time that has no starting point. Without the son-avatar of Christianity, the Father's approach is proscribed by repeating ritual discriminations. Those who survive seek only renewal of the traumatic death which carries no historical assurances.

Jean-Joseph Goux's chapter traces a parallel development of the Mosaic God of Israel and the unconscious of Freud. What Goux calls a second exodus from Egypt, or a secularization of Judaism, is evinced in the Freudian hermeneutic which seeks to bring fantasies and fears into the bright light of day, to dispel illusions before the clear light of reason. Goux shows how the proscription of idols in Jewish iconoclasm reflects a ban against symbolic incest with the great mother goddess in order to obtain fertility. Psychoanalysis mirrors the second commandment by putting a stop to proliferating images and imaginations, dissolving them into a denotative language. Like Moses, the analyst shatters idols. Like monotheism, psychoanalysis transposes hieroglyphs into letters, for such is the movement, the exodus, and the emancipation.

Notes

1. Gay, P., *Freud: A Life for our Times* (New York: W.W. Norton, 1988).
2. McGrath, W., *Freud's Discovery of Psychoanalysis* (Ithaca: Cornell, 1986); Homans, P., *The Ability to Mourn* (Chicago: The University of Chicago Press, 1989).
3. Hobson, J., *The Dreaming Brain* (New York: Basic Books, 1988); Sulloway, F., *Freud: Biologist of the Mind* (New York: Basic Books, 1979); Wallace, E., *Freud and Anthropology* (New York: International Universities Press, 1983).
4. Van Herik, J., *Freud on Femininity and Faith* (Berkeley: California, 1982); Jonte-Pace, D., *Speaking the Unspeakable* (Berkeley: California, 2001); Brickman, C., *Aboriginal Populations in the Mind* (New York: Columbia, 2003).
5. Santner, E., *On the Psychotheology of Everyday Life* (Chicago: The University of Chicago Press, 2001); Mills, J., ed., *Rereading Freud* (Albany: State University of New York Press, 2004); Wallwork, E., *Psychoanalysis and Ethics* (New Haven: Yale, 1991); DiCenso, J., *The Other Freud* (New York: Routledge, 1999).
6. Bingaman, K., *Freud and Faith* (Albany: State University of New York Press, 2004).
7. Klein, D., *Jewish Origins of the Psychoanalytic Movement* (New York: Praeger, 1981); Rizzuto, A., *Why Did Freud Reject God?* (New Haven: Yale, 1998); Yerushalmi, Y., *Judaism Terminable and Interminable* (New Haven: Yale, 1991).

References

Bingaman, K. *Freud and Faith*. Albany: State University of New York Press, 2004.
Brickman, C. *Aboriginal Populations in the Mind*. New York: Columbia, 2003.
DiCenso, J. *The Other Freud*. New York: Routledge, 1999.
Erikson, E. *Young Man Luther*. New York: W.W. Norton, 1958.
Gay, P. *Freud: A Life for our Times*. New York: W.W. Norton, 1988.
Hobson, J. *The Dreaming Brain*. New York: Basic Books, 1988.
Homans, P. *The Ability to Mourn*. Chicago: The University of Chicago Press, 1989.
Jones, E. *The Life and Work of Sigmund Freud*, vol. 3. New York: Basic Books, 1957.
Jonte-Pace, D. *Speaking the Unspeakable*. Berkeley: California, 2001.
———. *Teaching Freud*. New York: Oxford, 2003.

Klein, D. *Jewish Origins of the Psychoanalytic Movement*. New York: Praeger, 1981.
McGrath, W. *Freud's Discovery of Psychoanalysis*. Ithaca: Cornell, 1986.
Mills, J., ed. *Rereading Freud*. Albany: State University of New York Press, 2004.
Rieff, P. *The Triumph of the Therapeutic*. New York: Harpers, 1966.
Rizzuto, A. *Why Did Freud Reject God?* New Haven: Yale, 1998.
Santner, E. *On the Psychotheology of Everyday Life*. Chicago: The University of Chicago Press, 2001.
Sulloway, F. *Freud: Biologist of the Mind*. New York: Basic Books, 1979.
Van Herik, J. *Freud on Femininity and Faith*. Berkeley: California, 1982.
Wallace, E. *Freud and Anthropology*. New York: International Universities Press, 1983.
Wallwork, E. *Psychoanalysis and Ethics*. New Haven: Yale, 1991.
Yerushalmi, Y. *Judaism Terminable and Interminable*. New Haven: Yale, 1991.

PART ONE

ON FREUD, RELIGION, AND RELIGIOUS STUDIES

CHAPTER ONE

Desiderata and Possibilities for the Psychological Study of Religion: How to Enlarge the Place of Freudian Thought in Religious Studies

Jacob A. Belzen

Psychoanalysis, Psychology of Religion and Religious Studies: Prelude

If what we call religious studies can be described as the place within academia where the scientific analysis of religion is taken up and taught, then parts of the psychology of religion, in all its varieties, should also be considered part of this branch of learning. And indeed, in a great many places there are specialists who give courses such as Psychology and Religion and who also publish on the same theme. Texts by the founding fathers of the psychology of religion—such as James, Jung, and Freud—are carefully read. Studies are carried out (usually historical ones) on the backgrounds of such authors and their written works, and they are brought into dialogue with what other thinkers on religion had to say.[1] As important as this work is, however, it is not a specimen of the psychology of religion in the proper sense. It approaches foundational research and is therefore often more philosophical than scientific in nature, and it certainly also belongs to the psychology of religion, but not as a core element. It is only mentioned here as one of the ways in which Freud comes up for discussion within religious studies.

Another way, with many more examples to show for it, is in the use of psychological ideas in the analysis and interpretation of a certain religious work (such as the *Confessions* of Augustine)[2] or of a certain religious celebrity (such as Ramakrishna or Jesus of Nazareth)[3] or religious thinkers.[4] This category employs psychoanalysis as well as the analytical psychology of Carl Gustav Jung, but it does tend to ignore other important aspects of the psychology of religion, especially the so-called empirical psychology of religion.[5] The work alluded to here is nevertheless of great importance, not only in terms of content but also for its "market politics": the many fine studies this category has produced have engendered a great deal of good will (as well as animosity, however) with regard to the psychological analysis of religion. But this is still not the core of the psychology of religion. It is even doubtful whether this core can be found within religious studies at all. I will argue here that the core of the psychology of religion ought to be discernable in religious studies as well, that indeed it ought to be one of the pillars of religious studies. Although Freudian thought can already be encountered as an element within religious studies in many places, I will make an argument for the proposal that more psychoanalytical research should be undertaken in religious studies, precisely so as to bring religious studies into closer contact with the psychology of religion.

Let me first explain what—in my not too humble opinion—should be understood by religious studies and by the psychology of religion. I am assuming that within the framework of the present volume it will not be necessary to introduce psychoanalysis in all its varied forms. The fact that Freud, and the thinking he has inaugurated, already occupies an important position within religious studies no longer needs to be demonstrated. From the perspective of the psychology of religion, which is the perspective I am taking, I will therefore not be presenting a historical overview of the many psychoanalytical contributions to this discipline, whether they were made from the institutional context of religious studies or not.[6] In conformity with the aims of the present project, I will not present a technical example of the application of Freudian psychoanalysis. Rather, I will reflect on the way in which and the conditions under which psychoanalysis can be employed within religious studies, perhaps more widely than it has been. I will try to argue that a cultural psychological approach (of which psychoanalysis does form an important part) is the most appropriate within the psychology of religion. Within this cultural psychological approach three variants can be detected, two of which are already represented in religious studies and the more empirical of which is mainly to be found in institutions for the study of psychology. By integrating the empirical variant also, religious studies will be able to incorporate more of the core of the psychology of religion, and, in turn, more of a contribution will be possible from religious studies to the core of the psychology of religion, a situation that is desirable to both the psychology of religion and to religious studies. And it is psychoanalysis that will serve as a link in this process. Yet, let me first introduce a number of terms and concepts.

On What Is Known as Religious Studies

In many places[7] religious studies presents itself as a conceptually vague undertaking: it is not theology, but it is not *Religionswissenschaft*[8] either. All too often, it is an institute that is born of need, or rather it seems to have developed by manipulation of nomenclature. As a consequence of secularization, and especially of the emptying out of the churches, the need for ecclesiastical office holders has been reduced in numerous Western countries, and at the same time the eagerness of young people to follow professional training in this area has sharply dropped. The result is that many theological faculties (which in many cases offered such professional training) are without clientele, and their survival is at risk. Diligent efforts are made to draw in possible students, either for an entire degree program (with a degree in something other than theology) or for a number of specific courses of a general nature (such as knowledge of the Bible and Christianity or, perhaps, recent developments in the area of churches or religious groups). In many cases and at many places, therefore, religious studies is a derivation of what used to be a theological education.

At some universities it is also possible to study *Religionswissenschaft*; sometimes it has been so for many years. Such a curriculum is usually part of the theology faculty or the faculty of letters. Placing it there is not logical, but there is a historical explanation for it. I will comment first on the situation in the theology faculty. It is often thought that everything in the university that has to do with religion (or might have to do with religion) should be placed within this faculty. (Often theological faculties themselves have claimed this as well.) *Religionswissenschaft* is not theology, however, and cannot simply be made an element of it.[9] Theology is a reflection on the contents of confessed religion, usually Christian; this reflection is rational in nature, can base itself on many different forms of scientific investigation, and may even be critical of religion itself. But whatever the case, theology remains tied to the premises of the religion it is studying—and usually of the specific denomination within Christianity—and relates to those premises in a variety of ways. *Religionswissenschaft*, however, tries to be neutral with respect to the truth claims put forward by the religions being studied. Naturally, no one is ever fully indifferent with respect to the object of her or his study, nor is it desirable to be indifferent; the interest of the scholar, regardless of how it developed or is motivated, opens the eyes, provides a horizon of understanding, and can be of fruitful use.[10] Yet the *Religionswissenschaftler* methodically tries to remain impartial—even if choosing her or his own religion as the object of study—and does not work on the basis of any personally confessed truth. Such a methodical agnosticism[11] is difficult, and it takes a considerable amount of effort to acquire and cultivate the necessary attitude. (This difficulty is certainly one of the main reasons why *Religionswissenschaftler* generally do not study their own religion but one that is foreign to them: it is much easier to speak objectively about it.) Naturally, theology can also make use of the results of research from *Religionswissenschaft*. Often, however, *Religionswissenschaft* is either a merely tolerated element within the faculty of theology or has been assigned a service function within the faculty, such as providing information about foreign religions, so that theology students will be better equipped to reach the followers of those religions with information about their own religion (in such a case, the science of religion is little more than an ancilla of missiology).

The other location for *Religionswissenschaft* is the faculty of letters. The simplest definition of *Religionswissenschaft* might be the scientific study of religion.[12] In principle, all scientists who study religion could be regarded as *Religionswissenschaftler*; this makes the science of religion a multidisciplinary enterprise in principle, and for this reason it would be better (because it is more consistent) to speak of it in the plural: the sciences of religion. In the course of its rather brief history, its situation—or, to put it better, its character—has changed drastically. The forerunners and roots of *Religionswissenschaft* are many and diverse, of course, but in general it can be said that when the West was confronted by religions other than Christianity, and when the followers of those religions were no longer regarded as just objects for conversion, interest arose to describe and study those religions more systematically. With this impulse, which took place in the 1860s and 1870s, the sciences of religion were born.[13] *Religionswissenschaft* is difficult; it requires learning the language in which the followers of the particular religion express themselves, studying the sources of that religion and systematically identifying and analyzing rituals, convictions and customs, codes of behavior, and so forth. What is required, therefore, is philological, historical, and anthropological research. In order to explain the empirically discovered information, scholars soon found themselves turning to disciplines such as psychology, sociology, and anthropology. The latter fields were a permanent part of the enterprise of the science of religion about a hundred years ago. They were also able to study religion independently—that is, to make it an object of study from their own original academic context (from the context of sociology, for instance)—which is what was done by almost all the founders of these disciplines. Each one of these disciplines underwent spectacular growth during the twentieth century, including those segments devoted to religion. Often, the advancing specialization within each of these disciplines and within the recently developed sciences of religion came to a division of territory: the sociological study of religion took place in the institutes for sociology, the anthropological research found a home in anthropology, and so forth, while the scientists of religion usually specialized in fields other than the social and human sciences (although the historical perspective was usually maintained). In so doing, the social scientists concentrated mostly on the religion they observed around them—Christianity—and the *Religionswissenschaftler*, once they had managed to secure a separate place within academia, concentrated on the scriptures of non-Christian religions. This development led to what is actually a totally illogical situation, in which *Religionswissenschaftler* often devote themselves mainly to philological and historical research (in many places their discipline is actually called "history of religion"; even the relevant international organization uses this designation in its name), without regard to the perspectives of the social and human sciences. Given the embedding within a faculty of letters, this seems to be logical. This situation, which is historically understandable, is actually undesirable and needs to be changed and improved.

In addition to theology and *Religionswissenschaft*, religious studies is a third and more recent phenomenon to appear. As a field of study, in comparison with the sciences of religion, it still seems to resemble theology, of which it is a derivative in many cases: there is often an accent on Christendom; the disciplines being taught are often precisely those that one would encounter in a theological faculty (i.e., philosophical or systematic-reflexive in nature), with very little empirical research. The emergence of religious studies, however, could or even should make it possible to restore a number of historical deficiencies. Pairing up with *Religionswissenschaft* could turn religious studies into an institution that does honor to its name; religious studies could become a full-fledged manifestation of what *Religionswissenschaft* originally stood for: being the place in the university where nontheological, multidisciplinary research and teaching in the area of religion was taking place or, at least, was being coordinated. All forms of religion could be addressed (not exclusively or mainly Christianity), and all relevant disciplines could be at home there (not just history, philosophy, Bible studies, ethics, and the like, but also archaeology, economics, history, sociology, and anthropology specializing in religion in all its forms). A distinctive feature of religious studies would, therefore, be the object: phenomena called religious and, to a certain extent, the conscious multidisciplinary approach. Yet religious studies is not a logically necessary part of a full-fledged, comprehensive university. It is not a separate discipline like economics or philosophy. It is a course of study because it is characterized either by a certain area of special attention or by orientation toward a social need. In and of itself—as already stated—the material object, religion, could be studied from any of the disciplines represented within religious studies, and ideally this would be the case, and would remain so. Indeed, there are a great many academics today—philosophers, historians, and psychologists, for example—whose research and teaching is mainly focused on religious phenomena, and they are not connected to an institute of religious studies. Yet a separate institution, such as an institute of religious studies, does make sense if it helps in maintaining the purity of the focus on the singular object of its study: religion (no matter how it is understood). I will explain this, hopefully even demonstrate it, based on the situation in the psychology of religion.

On the Psychology of Religion: General Remarks

When it comes to a definition of the psychology of religion, there is anything but agreement.[14] Yet in conformity with the simple definition of *Religionswissenschaft* given above, it might be defined as the psychological study of religion or as the research of that which is psychological in religion (which is not exactly the same thing). I admit that this definition sounds almost tautological, but I hope to demonstrate that it is definitely not. As I have already noted: for the sake of convenience the problem of the definition of religion will be set aside; we will act as if we knew what "religion" is. For the psychology of religion, the definition of religion is not the main problem; that job can be left to others. Just as art psychologists do not have to determine what art is and sports psychologist do not have to come up with their own definition of sports, so psychologists of religion do not have to furnish a definition of religion. Psychologists are expected to produce definitions of psychic phenomena, to come up with strategies to study them and theories to explain them and with definitions of what psychology is or should be—in all its diversity of activities. This is where the biggest problem lies: there is no agreement at all among psychologists as to what is to be understood by the word "psychology," and as a result there is no agreement as to what specific area psychologists are to focus their attention on in their research.[15] There are still some psychologists who believe that "behavior" is the object of their discipline (yet they usually do not specify the perspective from which they undertake their research). Others, conversely, speak of intentional actions, and others of subjectivity. The number of schools or clusters of perspectives in psychology today is greater than anyone can view comprehensively: besides the psychoanalytical approaches there are cognitive psychology, ecological psychology, social constructionism, rhetoric-responsive approaches, physiological psychology, evolutionary psychology, and more. Almost all of these perspectives, and many others, have something to say about religion, so the diversity (and rivalry!) within the psychology of religion is in principle just as great as that within psychology in general.

This means that the psychology of religion is not a basic discipline of psychology, in the way that developmental psychology, cognitive psychology, or social psychology are; it is a field of application: it is that segment of psychology in which religion is the material object of research. As a genuine component of psychology in general, the psychology of religion therefore shares the advantages or disadvantages of psychology in general. We do not have to devote a great deal of time to the advantages. The fact that there is a widespread interest in psychology is obvious, and so is the fact that psychology is regarded as relevant even in the realm of religious studies. But, understandably, not everyone in religious studies is equally aware of the current state of affairs in psychology. Let us therefore take a look at two of the problems with contemporary psychology.

The first problem is that much of psychology appears to be trivial. The vast amount of research being carried out in the world of psychology does not usually produce more insight into the human being or into human existence, while psychology is expected to provide a certain amount of clarification on this point (which is exactly why there is such a profuse supply of popular psychology material: in book shops one can find shelves and entire corners full of books about happiness, love, relationship, spirituality, etc.). The paradox is that much of what is specific to human beings is not being addressed in academic psychology. The "crisis in psychology," which seems to have been a topic of discussion ever since Karl Bühler's publication by the same name,[16] exists in the psychology of religion as well. This crisis has been delineated by Amedeo Giorgi as a lack of unity, a lack of relevance, and a problematic self-understanding as a science.[17] Even if, in a postmodern era, one might be inclined to hail the plurality in psychology, Giorgi's second and third reproaches still seem to hold true. The many lamentations from various sides—about psychology's restricted value for a fundamental understanding of human beings, its loss of sight on the peculiarities of the individual, the nongeneralizability of its results obtained from middle-class white students, and many more—are well known. They also pertain to the psychology of religion and need not be repeated here. In spite of (or perhaps because of) the small-scale questions, concepts, and manipulated variables being dealt with, and in spite of its ever increasing refinement of scales and sophisticated statistical techniques, psychology is being criticized for not observing sufficiently, not going deep enough into the phenomena it wants to explore, especially when it is constructing its "measuring instruments." One of the main reasons for this lack of relevance, according to Georgi, is psychology's problematic self-understanding. Because it chose to emulate the natural sciences, it could not solve this fundamental dilemma: when it remained faithful to the demands of the life world, it could not do justice to science; and when it remained faithful to the requirements of science, it could not, for this very reason, do justice to the life world. To Georgi, phenomena have to be approached as they present themselves in the world, and therefore "the kind of science psychology should be must be constructed from within the viewpoint of the 'world.' For the world of man, psychology must be a human science."[18]

This criticism, or this requirement, also—perhaps especially—holds true when psychology turns to religion as an object of research. If religion is not studied in its full richness (including its aberrations), if it is not studied in vivo and in situ, no academic discipline is likely to come up with meaningful results.[19] But psychology in particular has developed the habit of naturalizing its object of study; its modus operandi is marked by de-subjectivization and de-contextualization. Although I fully subscribe to the thesis that religion can be researched from many branches of psychology, I believe that religion is best served by a cultural psychological approach, or by any approach that regards psychology as a social or a human science, since these approach the phenomenon in the fullness of life. (Presently I will take a closer look at the cultural psychological approach within the psychology of religion.) To reiterate: I do not deny the possibility and desirability of other psychological approaches. But I have my doubts when it comes to a narrowed presentation of the object of research, as is commonly done in much psychological research (not only in research on religion).

I would also like to point out a second, not entirely independent problem. At the moment, things are going very well with the psychology of religion. After having been something of a taboo theme for decades,[20] religion and spirituality have suddenly become the objects of increasing attention in many places—including the realm of general psychology. But this positive impression is rather deceptive: most of the increase in psychological research related to religion has been in the field of what we traditionally call "religion and mental health." As with psychology at large, the field devoted to questions of mental health has always been one of the largest within the psychology of religion, not because it is most important but because it seems to have the highest relevance for society. The applications of psychological knowledge, attitudes, and skills in clinical situations have been numerous, but this has never meant that all research focusing on mental health or mental health services has contributed most to the development of psychology as a scholarly enterprise. The part of psychology oriented toward clinical work or dealing with well-being is largest because most psychologists find their jobs there, not because it has generated the best research or the best theories. The same can be observed for the field of "religion and mental health": there is a lot of activity going on there—which is good, and I am not criticizing that at all—but much of the research being done in this field has not enhanced the general psychological insight into religious phenomena. A larger part of the research being reported is definitely not aimed at the exploration of religious phenomena as such, but is focused on some other issue (whether life satisfaction and subjective well-being, stress, adjustment, affective disorders, trauma and intervention, addiction, care of the disabled elderly, abuse, blood pressure, burnout, etc.).[21] And whereas we should be happy, perhaps even grateful, that research on religion related to these issues is now being published in journals that have no relation to the psychology of religion at all,[22] we also should realize that this kind of research serves goals other than the ones that are primary to the psychology of religion. These publications, worthwhile as they may be in their own right, belong to the periphery of the psychology of religion—at best.[23]

We are confronted here with an old problem in the psychology of religion. Even in the first decade of its existence, it found itself faced with criticism: many publications in the psychology of religion did not focus on religion at all; their authors strove to be fully recognized psychologists but had little to say about religion as such. The problem has to do with the academic context, among other things, which is why it is being addressed here. Anyone working as a psychologist in an institute or on a faculty of psychology will be under great pressure to adapt to the prevailing corporate culture. While today there is a tendency within psychology to concentrate on a particular variable considered psychological and to pay little or no attention to the cultural context or even the nature of the phenomenon, psychologists desiring to move in this direction run into problems: their style of doing research deviates from that which is customary and desirable within psychology at large, and they have more trouble getting their work published in peer-reviewed journals. An analogous problem is confronted, however, when attention is paid to the psychological analysis of religion within the so-called religious studies: there the pressure comes from the prevailing theological or philosophical corporate culture, and almost no empirical research is undertaken. Here, too, we see that the institutional context keeps the psychology of religion from developing its full potential. But let us now consider this phrase "The psychology of religion in its full potential": what might we understand that to mean?

Brief Sketch of the Psychology of Religion: First Definition

First, in conformity with the practice in academic circles, let us speak about what should *not* be understood by the psychology of religion. First of all, we must maintain that the psychology of religion is not religious psychology (a term that was still generally current a half century ago), and that this qualification covers a variety of aspects. The psychology that is utilized in the psychology of religion (though almost never independently developed) is not religious as such. The psychology of religion uses conventional secular psychology, which is applied to examine religious phenomena from a conventional secular point of view.[24] The rise of the psychological study of religion had a great deal in common with the rise of so-called scriptural criticism and other historical research on the religious traditions or doctrines of various religious groups, whose proponents believed that the phenomena they held dear were not historically conditioned. There are still people who think that the "human" factor plays no role in religion and that, therefore, they do not need the insights of a human science like psychology in the study of religion. But for all the material differences of opinion present in it, the formal axiom governing the psychology of religion is—in the words of the title of a now well-known publication—"it doesn't fall down from Heaven."[25] Whatever the origin, essence, and value of religion may be, earthly human factors such as emotions, learning, psychodynamics, social-cultural class, motivation, gender, and many more play a weighty role in the functioning of religion. Within a given religious tradition it is often these factors that are primarily responsible for the differences between individuals and groups, more than doctrinal differences. Just as "sacred Scriptures" become no less "sacred" as a result of philological analyses, so also religious conduct, perception, and experience become no less religious as a result of psychological investigation. In whatever measure they may always be dependent on religious meanings and intentions, in religious conduct, perception, and experience there are always countless factors at work that can be examined by psychology (and that have often long been recognized by "judges of human nature" among believers or religious professionals).

However, whereas a scholarly discipline like history is often no longer expected to furnish evidence for the truth of a given doctrine, this is frequently still the case when it comes to the psychology of religion. While in the psychology of religion there are scarcely any authors left who attempt to demonstrate the superiority of Christianity, for example, such authors have been superceded by others who are perfectly willing to proceed from the premise that humans are by nature religious beings and that being religious is therefore better, healthier, or more natural than not being religious. To what extent, given this apologetic interest, they do not finally end up with a kind of reductionism (when in the case of clearly nonreligious persons, for example, "something" still has to be described as religious, even if it is something like meaning-bestowal) is a matter on which we must postpone judgment.[26] One also encounters apologetics where—in Allport[27] or Batson and Ventis,[28] for example—technical-statistical procedures are used to document the superiority of one's own religious views or disposition. It is important at this point, however, to maintain that even in such cases the psychology of religion works with the theories, methods, and techniques of conventional secular psychology: it does *not* develop a psychology that only concerns religion, and that is necessary because in religious matters people would function differently than they do in everyday matters.

In addition, in English or French the terms for the discipline are "psychology of religion" and "psychologie de la religion"; what matters in this "of" (or "de la") is an objective, not a subjective, genitive. What is being referred to is a psychology that deals with religion, not one that belongs to religion. The latter, of course, also exists. Buddhist traditions, for example, have highly differentiated psychologies that are inherent in them.[29] Although Western psychology (for it is this that is applied as a rule in the psychology of religion) has certainly been influenced by Christian ideas (but even much more still by Greek ideas), it is, nevertheless, not an intrinsic part of any religion, not even of Christianity or of any of its denominations. The psychology of religion is, in principle, neutral with respect to the religion it examines (even though individual studies may or could be inspired or guided by antipathies or sympathies toward religion).

One finds a rapidly growing number of psychological publications on "religion" in esoteric and New Age–related circles. Here the authors frequently fall back on so-called transpersonal psychology (with its influential author Ken Wilber). Inspired by C. G. Jung, an author like Corbett views the psyche as intrinsically religious.[30] In his opinion the divine and the human belong to a single indivisible consciousness continuum. In this view so-called depth psychology replaces religion, inasmuch as it would be in a better position than traditional religious or theological categories to articulate and conceptualize the experiences that used to be called religious. While frequently interesting, publications of this sort are not, however, considered part of the psychology of religion. Hence Corbett himself expressly distinguishes his work (and other Jung-inspired schools) from the psychology of religion. In his opinion he represents a religious understanding of a certain dimension of the individual psyche (which is roughly the opposite of psychology of religion).

Psychology of Religion as Interdisciplinary Science

When, then, does psychological work that is focused on religion actually belong to the psychology of religion? In keeping with the previously given, rather liberal definition, one might reason as follows. Psychologists for the most part examine persons in the here and now. When, in whatever fashion, they investigate the religious conduct, perception, and experience of today's subjects, they are practicing the psychology of religion. Up until this point the proposed definition will probably provoke little resistance. The psychology of religion would then be the attempt to investigate what is "psychic" about a given form of religious conduct, perception, and experience, and this investigation of the psychic moment or aspect would then take place by way of the theoretical, methodical-technical instrumentarium of psychology. In this sense, then, the psychology of religion is an area of application of psychology in general. One must not, however, view this simplistically. An area of application in psychology is something very different from what it would be, say, in the natural sciences, which find their application in technology. Since psychic reality is always shaped by changing cultural-historically given factors, it is never identical in different persons and groups (as may be—to put it simply—presupposed concerning the empirical reality examined by the natural sciences). Religion, too, is a structuring factor in psychic functioning as it manifests itself in dreams, longings, emotions, cognitive activity, and so forth. Psychology, therefore, is never a deposit of knowledge and techniques that can just be "applied" to any person or group. Psychology in its various characteristic forms, however, makes available a heuristic and hermeneutic instrumentarium that enables its practitioners to determine the extent to which certain previously investigated structures can also be found in the persons or groups to be studied or invoked for the purpose of investigation. This also holds true for the study of religion.[31]

The proposed definition of the psychology of religion can, however, be understood more broadly. Religion, however defined, almost always contains, peripherally or centrally, elements like ideas (doctrine), ethics and morality, cultic and/or liturgical action, images and conceptions, spirituality, organization, tradition, scriptures, and many others. With regard to each of these categories one can similarly examine whatever is or has been psychic about their rise, persistence, and functioning. The moment one becomes aware that religion, however defined, is always something that involves a supporting human subject, the (potentially) relevant domain of research takes on almost immense proportions; psychology is one of the weightiest points of entry for this research. If one realizes that there is no such thing as religion without people, then all its manifestations can be explored in terms of the aspect of human involvement in it. Since all liturgy, dogmas, symbols, conceptions, and so forth are always formulated by people, the human factor inherent in them can be examined. With all these phenomena it is naturally the case that much more can be said about them than has been formulated by human beings. Texts, symbolic representations, and actions are and have been influenced by so many distinct factors that it will not do to leave their exploration solely to psychologists. History, anthropology, semiotics, economics, and many more disciplines have their own legitimate role to play here. This may sound like a platitude, but it is manifestly true that problems always arise when either (a) one of these discipline-based viewpoints becomes the all-determining one or (b) a certain viewpoint must be suppressed at any cost (perhaps even out of fear of the reductionism indicated under [a]).

Despite its modesty, the proposed definition therefore nevertheless implies a broad conception of the psychology of religion. By implication, the psychology of religion must necessarily be interdisciplinary in its practice. If, for example, a given person, speaking as a psychologist, wanted to say something about a mystic like Ramakrishna, he or she would have to have a thorough knowledge of the variants of Hinduism known to Ramakrishna. Additionally, one would also have to have a history-of-culture-based knowledge of the individual being studied and about his or her social environment. Another example: those who might want to say something about the psychic processes involved in the production, reading, interiorization, and enacting of holy scriptures could consult literary scholars, including exegetes. And so forth. In addition, those who might want to study the religious conduct, perception, and experience of people of our own time would be dependent on theological or science-of-religion-based knowledge concerning the religious tradition to which the people being studied belong, on knowledge concerning their culture, their time, and so forth. In the examination or treatment of the psychic dysfunctioning of a religious person, medical-psychiatric knowledge may be relevant. Here, again, the reality is to be found in the "and so forth."

On the Disciplinary Classification of the Psychology of Religion

The psychology of religion, accordingly, is basically an interdisciplinary enterprise, and it is in this capacity that it is in the best position to do justice to the diversity found in the psychology of religion and to render discussions about which discipline it may belong to patently irrelevant. When we accept the premise that contributions can be made to the psychology of religion from within psychiatry, academic psychology, psychoanalysis, the sciences of religion, history, anthropology, and other disciplines, it is rather meaningless to discuss the questions about what kind of discipline the psychology of religion is and where it should be academically situated. However, this understanding—so liberally put forth here—does *not* imply that psychiatrists, historians, theologians, and so forth, can simply *be* psychologists of religion or practice the psychology of religion. On the contrary, the instrumentarium of the psychologists of religion is psychology in general (a statement that hopefully no longer sounds tautological at this point), and it must be practiced adequately, but this does not mean that such practice is necessarily and exclusively reserved for those who are officially registered as psychologists or active in a faculty (or department) of psychology.[32]

Just as the psychology of literature works with the instrumentarium of psychology but is most often localized in a faculty of letters or of humanities, so the psychology of religion is a branch of psychology that is often found in institutes other than that of psychology. Most frequently one finds it in the sciences of religion (though still too rarely), in religious studies, and in theology (also far from everywhere). It is self-evident that the psychology of religion, even when it is localized, say, in a faculty of theology, must remain an independent form of psychology (hence not subordinate to systematic or practical theology), but one that will nevertheless be influenced by the particular objectives of its context. This also means that psychologists of religion on faculties of theology will pursue research of a different kind from that of colleagues on a faculty of psychology. More fruitful than debates about the question who does "real" psychology of religion, however, is picturing this situation in terms of the principle of "family resemblances" (Wittgenstein) and bearing in mind that, for all their differences, the representatives of the psychology of religion are united in the attempt to determine what is psychic in or about religion.

The understanding presented here, while sounding quite irenic, should not tempt us to think that everything that presents itself as the psychology of religion is equally valuable, or, perhaps better said, equally central. Metaphorically speaking, one can picture the psychology of religion as a number of concentric circles that intersect with other (probably equally concentric) circles that represent other academic disciplines or areas of specialization (which are therefore not identical!). In this metaphor, the central focus would be the development of a psychology that is or would be capable of analyzing a subjectivity that has become religious. Centered around it there would be a circle for basic research (including methodology); around that again a circle with theories, methods, and techniques from related psychologies. A further circle would represent the numerous applications, or praxis orientation, of psychology of religion. Each of these circles would intersect with circles representing disciplines such as history, sociology, or anthropology or areas of specialization such as psychotherapy, pastoral care, or exegesis. It is not the label that is used as a term for the research or praxis but the nature of the work performed that determines whether one can speak of psychology of religion and whether one is dealing with a central or a more peripheral element in the field. There are many publications in which the term "psychology of religion" (in whatever language it is used) does not occur or hardly ever occurs, but which, nevertheless, belong to the core of this discipline.[33] Other publications may clearly have been written from the perspective of another discipline, like history[34] or systematic theology,[35] but are psychology-of-religion in character. Others, though they have been defended at some faculty of theology, are clearly not theology but psychology of religion.[36] And other academic achievements in theology, though they employ psychological theories or techniques, clearly remain theological in nature.[37] Those who want to actually draw the picture presented here will probably not find this portrayal very clear, but it is likely to do justice to the rather complex structure of the psychology of religion (as well as to the empirical reality to which it refers). Like most things that have a certain significance in human life, it does not readily fit into simple schemes and formulas.

Cultural-Psychological Psychology of Religion

So the psychology of religion covers a broad area to which contributions can be made from many different backgrounds and which can be classified under quite different academic locations. The heart of the whole matter has to do with the development of new theory: the development of psychological theory that is also capable of addressing and analyzing religion. In all fairness, however, it must be said that, as a rule, psychologists of religion do not develop new psychological theories. There have been great psychologists who have developed new theories and have adapted them to religion (such as Allport, Freud, Jung, and Maslow), and others who have tried to adapt existing psychological theories to benefit the empirical study of religion,[38] yet the vast majority turn to existing psychological theory to interpret religious phenomena. Let us then regard the core of the psychology of religion in this triplicate way, always as a combination of empirical research and psychological theory formation. Obviously, such work is usually carried out at institutes of psychology by psychologists. This is the most logical situation, although it is not the only one possible.[39] Naturally, those who contribute to clinically oriented psychology of religion are mainly clinical psychologists.[40] Personality psychologists are the ones who are interested in motivations,[41] and social psychologists have developed scales of mysticism.[42] Yet empirical clinical research within the realm of religion is also being done by psychiatrists[43] and psychoanalysts[44] whose institutional basis is not rooted in a faculty of psychology. Numerous contributions to the psychology of religion are also being made from religious studies, as was mentioned earlier, yet usually not on the basis of empirical research. *If this were to be the case*—and here is one of the main theses of this chapter—religious studies would be able to incorporate more *from* the core of the psychology of religion and to contribute more *to* the core of the psychology of religion. I believe the renewed rise of cultural psychology clearly has something to offer in this area.

This cultural psychology that has been mentioned here several times—what exactly is it? Like psychology in general, cultural psychology is a rather broad, heterogeneous enterprise to which many well-known psychologists have made significant contributions. It is important to realize from the onset that cultural psychology is not a psychology entirely different from other kinds of psychology that have developed throughout the discipline's past; neither is it one of its separate subdisciplines or simply a field of application. Broadly stated, and at this point without much specification, cultural psychology is an approach within psychology that is trying to describe, to investigate and to interpret the interrelatedness of culture and human psychic functioning.[45] It is the part of psychology that tries to take seriously the perhaps seemingly trivial observation that one would not exist without the other, that, therefore, culture is a major factor in all meaningful human conduct, and that, likewise, traces of human involvement can be found in all expressions of culture. It may be instructive to divide cultural psychology as a whole into different variants, which are obviously not entirely independent of one another and cannot all be dealt with in depth in this text.[46]

First of all, and vital to the development of psychology as a body of knowledge, attitudes, and skills, cultural psychology investigates how culture constitutes, facilitates, and regulates human subjectivity and its expression in diverse psychic functions and processes (e.g., perception, memory, mental health, the self, the unconscious, etc.), as postulated and conceptualized by different psychological schools and theories. It is important to note that the concept of culture employed here is a dynamic one (it does not just mean "context" or "situation") and goes beyond the common understanding of culture in psychology as a whole. Whereas contemporary psychology generally recognizes that not only human interactions are influenced by culture but the feeling, thinking, experiences, and behavior of individuals are constituted by it as well. Cultural psychology conceives of these as being inherently cultural: as being the result of human embeddedness in culture, which is therefore to be considered a genuine element of all human functioning relevant to psychology.[47] Culture is here understood as a system of signs, rules, symbols, and practices that both structures the human realm of action and is being (re)constructed and transformed by human action and praxis. This form of cultural psychology is usually developed by psychologists.

This first variant of cultural psychology consists, roughly, of two forms: synchronic and diachronic.[48] In both forms there is a realization of the historical nature of culture (in its various manifestations) and, therefore, of human psychic functioning. Yet in the first form the emphasis is on psychic functions and processes in contemporary subjects; there is an abstraction of historical variation. In the second form, however, the historic changes in human psychic functioning are investigated and explained on the basis of modifications in cultural conditions and determinations. Cultural psychology as a whole is an interdisciplinary approach, as will be readily understood with the first of its variants: in both forms distinguished here, cultural psychology is in need of collaboration with other disciplines from the social and human sciences. In the synchronic form, psychology relies on information and sometimes theories, concepts, and skills from disciplines like anthropology, sociology, and the political sciences. In the second form, historiography and sometimes even evolutionary biology are among the obvious partners in theorizing and research.

Secondly, numerous publications have traditionally been devoted to the effort to detect and determine the human involvement in all kinds of cultural artifacts. Whereas in the first variant the understanding of culture is more or less anthropological, on a macro-level, in the second variant of cultural psychology a much more elitist and restricted concept of culture is usually employed. Attention is given to products of so-called high culture like novels, movies, operas, and the other arts as well as to entire areas like peace and war, sports, advertising, organizations, international affairs, and important domains like socialization, sexuality and courting, labor, death, and dying. Each of these subjects is also studied by other scholarly disciplines to which psychology in such cases often relates as an auxiliary discipline. In fields (to be distinguished from disciplines) like cultural studies, education, and the arts, the discipline of psychology is often called upon to explore the human involvement in the phenomena studied. In these cases some kind of psychology (very often psychoanalysis) is typically applied. Although this may and has been done by psychologists themselves (again, psychoanalysts in particular), frequently in these cases it is done by researchers and authors who are not trained in psychology.[49] If psychologists are, in fact, hired in these contexts, they are obviously serving a goal other than the development of (new) psychological theory.

In this variant of cultural psychology, considerable attention has been given to a variety of religious phenomena, which contributes substantially to the literature of the psychology of religion. Not only have numerous "great" psychologists, especially from the psychoanalytic tradition, written explicitly on religion from the perspective of the psychological approach or theory they themselves have developed (e.g., Freud, Jung, Erikson, Allport, Maslow, Fromm), but their psychological approaches or theories have also often been utilized by others to analyze religious phenomena. The latter has been done both by authors with psychological (and psychopathological) training[50] and frequently also by scholars with a (primary) background in theology, sciences of religion, or religious studies in general.[51]

A third variant of cultural psychology will be mentioned even more briefly only. It is common to find an understanding among cultural psychologists that different cultural contexts, different times, and different places bring about different psychologies, partly as a result of their being developed with/on subjects who are psychically differently constituted,[52] so that the history of psychology is not about natural facts but about socially generated constructions.[53] Therefore, within cultural psychology there is attention to so-called indigenous psychologies, on the one hand: the psychologies as developed by "ordinary people" (as distinguished from Euro-American psychologists, who produced almost all of the present "academic" psychological knowledge), on both sides of the Atlantic and in other parts of the world;[54] on the other hand, there is also a fair amount of attention to the history of psychology as a Western enterprise. As will be clear, in this third variant there is collaboration once again with experts on local cultures (whether academically trained in the Western tradition, like anthropologists, or not) or with historians, especially intellectual historians, or with historicizing philosophers and theologians.[55]

Revealingly, a great deal of the psychology of religion is already sensitive to or compatible with a cultural psychological approach, especially in the second and third variants just mentioned. It will also be clear that much of this very work is being carried out today in places other than the institutes for psychology. In these institutes, where psychology should be developed as the "mother discipline," distressingly little attention is being paid to important life domains that could be adopted as areas of application for psychology—such as art, love, war, and peace. Insofar as psychologists are active in these areas, they are usually appointed to other academic institutes such as art academies, faculties of letters, sports schools, and training facilities for the armed forces. For a long time religion has shared the same fate and has been greatly ignored by academic psychology. If religion from a psychological perspective was dealt with at the university, it was in the departments of theology and sometimes *Religionswissenschaft* and religious studies. Yet, as far as I know, this was usually not done by psychologists.[56] Now, as we have seen, the last condition is not a conditio sine qua non: the psychology of religion does not necessarily have to be pursued by psychologists, and work belonging to the second and third variants of cultural psychology within the psychology of religion is often done by people other than psychologists. Yet—and this is one of the main points I am making in this chapter, which up until now has primarily been an exposé of basic concepts—in order to contribute to the first form of a cultural-psychologically oriented psychology of religion, it is not necessary to be on a faculty of psychology as such. Working in such a faculty should undoubtedly be an advantage for anyone wanting to do research in the cultural psychology of religion, but, as we have already noted, these faculties are often pursuing a very different theoretical and methodological approach.[57] It is quite conceivable that cultural psychological research could be carried out with even greater ease at a more multi- or interdisciplinary-oriented institute than at an institute for psychology. This can definitely be asserted with regard to the cultural psychological study of religion. An obvious problem with a great deal of psychology of religion research pursued by professional psychologists is that it does not examine the religious phenomenon in its fullness. After studying this kind of research, readers often do not feel that they are learning something about religion or about the religious phenomenon actually being researched. Whenever psychologists work in a context that is especially aimed at research on religion, as in *Religionswissenschaft* or religious studies, they will come under pressure from the corporate culture to stick with the phenomenon being studied as much as possible and to present it as fully as possible. A cultural psychological approach is perfectly compatible with this and could be pursued (including in its first variant distinguished above) at just such an institute, probably less problematically than at a strictly psychological institute.

The obvious counterquestion concerning the equipment of those who desire to do cultural psychological research localized at places other than psychological institutes need not result in a rejection of this proposal. Naturally, the application of psychological insights and theories demands thorough schooling, including a mastery of the prevailing research methods and techniques. Yet, as pointed out, there are large areas of psychology in general that seem irrelevant to the study of religion. Although it may be stretching it a bit, a person desiring to become a psychologist of religion might make a decent claim for omitting a substantial part of the training in positivistic and mechanistic psychology. Anyone who concentrates on the theories and research methods that have taken and are taking root in cultural psychology will probably come up with significant results anyway. Research as practiced by cultural psychologists shares a great deal of common ground with that of sociologists, historians, and anthropologists, for instance, precisely because of its interdisciplinary character. Any setting that brings these disciplines together in their concentration on religion, such as religious studies, may certainly be regarded as fruitful for a cultural psychologically oriented psychology of religion.

An Example of Interdisciplinary Research: Psychohistory

Although this chapter is supposed to be meta-theoretical, it might be a good idea to try to elucidate a few things on the basis of a single example. Let us look at a possible interdisciplinary field, a field that has already produced many studies but that is still fiercely controversial: the combination of psychology and the writing of history. I am choosing this subject because psychoanalysis has so frequently been employed here (although I will try to show that, in principle, the following reflections can be applied to all forms of psychology).

The use of psychology in research having to do with persons or groups, events, and situations in the past has been criticized not only in research in the religious realm but also in general. Some considerations, very generally speaking, are correct: the past is not something that can be simply approached, let alone explained, by using theories from today's human and social sciences. In fact, many examples can be shown of this kind of anachronistic, unnuanced, and even incorrectly executed research, in which modern psychological categories are "pasted" onto persons and events from the past. But if we do try to be more nuanced, do we find that psychohistory, in the sense intended here, is also an essential impossibility? The answer is no; psychohistory may not and cannot be regarded as being an essentially impossible field because that would mean declaring impossible, not only most of the historical research in which a psychological component can be detected, but all historical research in general. Indeed, every study of the past begins with questions that were developed at a later point in time and makes use of contemporary terms and concepts in order to enable discussion of the past. Doing history is always a matter of asking questions about a past that did not and could not ask such questions. In theory this need not result in anachronism, not even if the historical research in question contains a psychological component or interest: there is an enormous quantity of historical studies in which the personal involvement of historical actors is taken into account or subjected to lavish attention. As soon as motives (for anything: battles, murders, marriages, contracts, initiatives in general, etc.) or feelings or sentiments (of individuals, groups, sometimes even entire nations) or relationships (whether or not of an amorous nature) are discussed, and as soon as such works as biographies or family histories are written, the area of psychology has been entered, even though implicitly. In doing so, the researcher and author always employ an interpretation that is related to psychology, whether it be about Caesar's relationship with Cleopatra or the motives of the members of the House of Orange in the Dutch revolt. Researchers who refrain from all use of explicitly psychological theories will unavoidably resort to the psychology that is part of their "personal equipment." Not every reader will notice it immediately (indeed, some readers may be employing exactly the same lay psychology), but those who are psychologically informed need only read a book such as *Structure and Change in Economic History* to be amazed at the naive psychological presuppositions of the author and where they have apparently led him.[58] Just as incomprehensible is the absence of any question about human motivation in a book of more than eight hundred pages about the waging of war by someone like MacNeill.[59] If human subjectivity in the past was entirely different from that of contemporary historians, then these historians would essentially have no access to the human world of the past—and that, after all, is what the writing of history is generally all about, even economic history or the history of a landscape. So as not to be caught up in unconsidered psychological categories and ideas, it is advisable to avail oneself of a form of scientifically validated psychology, preferably as systematically as possible.

It is important to carefully consider what psychology to turn to and how to put this choice into practice. Obviously, a psychology that explicitly reflects the historical-cultural character of human subjectivity in its theory formation should be chosen over a psychology that is based on the postulate of the psychic unity of the human species.[60] It is also important to consider how such a psychology is to be used. If one allows oneself to be led to too great a degree by the results of any particular psychological research from any particular period, one may run into danger. Those who aim to assert something about mental health (or illness) on the basis of psychological research, for example, should make sure their orientation is broad. Not only do the precise forms of expression and their contexts change, but the way in which such research is carried out and the amount of effort involved are subject to historical changes. Even those who hold to the letter of a hermeneutic psychology cannot be sure their research is valid; probably the opposite is true. It would be much wiser to hold to the spirit, that is, to take psychological theory in the broad sense. Today's hermeneutic psychologies emphasize relationality, the fact that the human being, or the human self, can only be thought of as existing in and owing to relationships, that human subjectivity is socially constructed and is the product of a historic process. Naturally there are differences between these theories, and each one interprets this foundational structure differently. The important thing to remember, however, is that they bring corresponding considerations to the fore with regard to what might be called anthropological constants. The fact that the human subject functions in a way that clearly shows that large and significant portions of individual developmental history are forgotten will be just as true for Roman emperors as it is for people today, whether this is conceptualized by means of the notion of the "unconscious" (Freud) or that of the "habitus" (Bourdieu). That the self should be understood not essentialistically and in terms of reification but as an entity with a narrative structure is no more true for postmodern West Europeans than it was for Charles V. Or turning it around: in all the differences in psychic functioning through the ages there is evidence of sound anthropological constants in the structures of human subjectivity. Taking this into account in studying the past should not be considered problematic. If today's psychological theory formation (or some of it) realizes this more strongly today than it was realized in earlier decades, it does not mean that this was not the case in earlier centuries, or that when researching historical persons it would be a methodological mistake to focus attention on the way their relationships were structured, particularly during their first years. The fact that there are often no sources to be found to document those early relationships does indicate that little attention was paid to such relations in earlier years, but it cannot be made to imply that such relationships did not exist at all and that, therefore, specific searches for such information are useless. It is often new ideas, new explorations (under the direction of new theories), that enable searches to be carried out in unexplored places, and that make it possible to derive new information from sources that have already been dealt with. Along with all the significance that should be attached to careful dealings with sources in any investigation, it should also be realized, first of all, that nothing is a source in and of itself: a trace of the past only becomes a source if the asking of certain questions makes it so. Second, it is not the source that produces the results that the historian reports on; it is the historian's interpretation of those sources, made in a particular light, that leads to the publishable narrative, and not the source in itself. And it is certainly not the past as such. Without an interpretive principle, traces from the past remain as obscure and voiceless as the archeological objects for which Thomsen designed the three-period system.

In other words, contemporary psychology can be used in historical research in two ways: as heuristics and as hermeneutics. No matter what the research, one should decide what it is that one wishes to study. This decision can be directed by traditional questions—such as those concerning the rise of democracy, the monarchy, the railways, or whatever—or by more recent questions concerning the living environment of ordinary individuals; it can be directed by questions that are partly derived from disciplines such as political science, economics, or sociology.[61] Some claim that the introduction of points of view from these disciplines has changed the way history was written in the twentieth century and even turned it into a separate discipline.[62] Whether this is so or not, it is clear that cross-fertilization with other disciplines in the writing of history has led to new questions and points of interest. In the same way, questions and perspectives have been derived from psychology, although often implicitly rather than explicitly. The increased attention to psychological themes and connections, such as those registered in the West in the twentieth century, was not ignored in the writing of history either. In a certain sense, the entire history of mentality (*histoire des mentalités*) is a form of psychologically sensitive history writing, although it seldom uses psychology in a systematic way. When it is used systematically, it gives us a second way psychology (or some other perspective) can be used in the field of history: psychology functioning as hermeneutics. By this we mean in the present context not much more than the creation of an interpretive framework. The insights derived from psychology can be used to assist in understanding facts and situations from the past, and in a few instances they may even partly explain them.[63] The fact that this can go wrong in any number of ways may be admitted a priori, but it is no reason to suppose that contemporary psychological principles that seem applicable should not be used to illuminate or clarify something from the past. Naturally, the contemporary psychological knowledge should be examined to see if it actually is applicable and in what way and under what conditions it is applicable; but this is something that should likewise be done with the perspectives derived from other academic disciplines.

I have spent a bit more time discussing the essential applicability of psychology in the writing of history because it is so fundamental. Most of the objections raised against psychohistory over the years are not concerned with this point but focus on other things which, from a methodological perspective, however, are of a lower order. There is the occasional lashing out at the use of psychoanalysis, for example, which is understandable to a certain extent. The form of psychology that is most often employed in psychohistory is indeed psychoanalytical; some even go so far as to describe psychohistory as psychoanalytical history writing.[64] And now the accusations abound: that psychoanalysis produces only reductionistic observations, that it has no place in real science, and so forth. There are a few remarks that should be made concerning this criticism, however. First, although there may be many examples of poorly applied psychoanalysis in the writing of history—and there can be many reasons why the application is poor: the theory may have been employed improperly, the research may have been carried out badly (something that not a single theory can compensate for), the theory probably should not have been applied at all in a particular case—such examples are no argument against the use of psychoanalysis as such, and certainly not against that of psychology in general. Second, whether psychoanalysis is a full-fledged discipline or not is a question that need not be fought out within the realm of psychohistory. If it were not a full-fledged discipline, it would be better not to use it; in that case, psychohistorians would be advised to consult other psychologies. In no case does this line of thinking result in an argument against the systematic use of psychology in the writing of history. And third, let us note that, in general, it would be desirable to use views other than psychoanalytical ones in psychohistory. Indeed, why should one limit oneself to psychoanalysis? Perhaps because so much psychohistorical research has to do exclusively with individual persons (the so-called psychobiography),[65] and because psychoanalysis offers very detailed forms of individual psychology? The latter is certainly true, yet psychoanalysis is not the only approach to do so. In addition, psychoanalysis is not only an individual psychology but at least a form of psychology that is capable of saying something about groups and cultures (although a close watch should be kept on the limited validity of its perspective). Moreover, it would be desirable to give other themes in psychohistory besides the biographical a chance.[66]

Let us look at and attempt to refute a few other objections. As stated above, most of the psychohistorical efforts up until now have been devoted to psychobiographies. It is said that psychoanalytical psychobiographies are reductionistic, narrow-minded, and disparaging with regard to the subject of the research. Once again: that there are examples where these reproaches are adequate is beyond doubt, yet psychoanalytical literature is just as full of warnings against such practices. Naturally, the point is not to trace everything back to one or a few psychological factors. Mozart's music is manifestly not the result of his personality, nor can the Second World War be blamed on Hitler's relationship with his mother. Yet that is not to say that Mozart's psychic disposition played no role in his composing. (To suggest such a thing would actually be much more absurd: Mozart evidently was a human being of flesh and blood, but he was also an individual with a certain life history at the moment he was composing.) That the Second World War was not caused by Hitler's relationship with his mother is also not to say that Hitler's person, his history, and his way of associating with others—including the German people—would not have been important in the outbreak of that conflict. Psychology does not shed light on and explain everything, but in a mosaic that represents the whole it should not be absent. It is also not true that a psychobiographer's aim is to explain everything based on infancy, as if the entire person could be determined from those years alone. (Remember Erikson's well-known challenge of this assertion, which he called the "originological fallacy.") There are always numerous factors at work in the present that determine the outcome of a process. Yet not a single historian may be given to doubt that the history (and prehistory) of any person or any event is a factor that both creates limitations and supplies possibilities. It is also not true that psychobiography only pathologizes. Certainly psychoanalysis is a psychology that has developed from clinical work, and it supplies a fully elaborated psychopathology. Yet that is not to say that every individual who is subjected to psychoanalysis will be declared mentally disturbed. On the contrary, psychoanalysis shows that the differences between illness and health (or normality) cannot be sharply drawn, that in all subjects there are similar psychic processes at work, and that that which is revealed in the so-called pathology are enlargements of conflicts, injuries, and desires that are manifested in healthy persons in other, less derailed, and sometimes even socially valued ways. Finally, it may be obvious that the mere "pasting on" of psychopathological or other psychological terminology does not as such clarify or explain anything. A sensible use of psychology within the discipline of history involves a form of application as put forward by Gadamer: it has to do with the movement of the hermeneutic cycle in which the *Vorverständnis* (preliminary understanding) is repeatedly appealed to and broken open. On occasion this may even lead to the conclusion that with regard to a particular situation certain forms of *Vorverständnis* must be entirely rejected.[67]

Almost all the remedies that someone like Anderson enumerates for avoiding the kinds of blunders mentioned here in terms of psychobiographical research are quite obvious and are a matter of great concern in other areas of research as well:[68] basing one's work on thorough original research (instead of basing one's work on secondary literature alone), using restraint in the use of psychological terminology, recognizing that events are almost always the result of many different factors, and realizing that every person is too complex to be comprehended by a single theory. He also advises carrying out extensive historical research in order to enable the building up of a cultural basis for the development of empathy with a historical person. One point that should not be exclusive to the psychoanalytical psychobiographer is learning to handle one's own countertransference. "Transference" and "countertransference" are terms over which a great deal of psychoanalytical literature has been written.[69] "Transference" means the reexperiencing during treatment of one's childhood emotions or, more broadly, observing and experiencing (outside treatment as well) by means of patterns that developed during childhood. Transference, as such, is a normal and unavoidable phenomenon; in psychoanalytical treatment, however, it is dealt with consciously (it is made possible and thereupon interpreted) so that the patterns referred to can be changed. "Countertransference" is the counterpart exhibited by the psychoanalytical therapist, and is the tendency to see the patient according to unconscious patterns that play a role in the life of the analyst. The term refers especially to how the analyst responds to the transference of the patient. Countertransference can therefore result in a distorted observation of the patient, which means that analysts must learn how to handle their own transference in a systematic way: they should undertake training analysis to become familiar with their own unconscious patterns and to learn to recognize their tendency toward certain forms of countertransference. Countertransference is unavoidable, too, but it can serve as an important instrument in treatment as long as it is consciously reflected on: by analyzing what it is that the patient evokes in him or her, the analyst can obtain clues about the patterns at work in the patient.[70] According to Erikson, the registration and analysis of one's own countertransference can be an important instrument for a psychobiographer as well: it can help the researcher track down the way in which others in the past have reacted to the person who is the focus of the research.[71] It would probably be advisable for a psychobiographer wishing to make use of psychoanalysis to first undergo psychoanalytical training analysis; in fact, even those desiring to use other kinds of insights besides the psychoanalytical will find certain forms of training analysis quite helpful. In conclusion, Anderson points out that despite the disadvantage that comes with the fact that the psychobiographer, unlike the psychotherapist, can derive no information from direct communication with the patient, it has its advantages.[72] First of all, the therapist usually has nothing to go on but the information that the patient provides, while the psychobiographer can derive information from many sources of information, even sources that are quite different. Second, the psychobiographer can see the life of the subject as a whole and can thereby place events in a broader (and not just a retrospective) context; she or he can also include the consequences of certain acts and events in making observations. It is easier for the psychobiographer to see a pattern in someone's life than it is for the therapist. Finally, the psychobiographer is not limited by a therapeutic objective. Whereas a therapist—despite the *freischwebende Aufmerksamkeit* (free-floating attention)—will be inclined to pay attention mainly to those aspects in the patient's life that are regarded as dysfunctional or maladjusted, psychobiographers are free to attempt a more balanced portrait of their subjects. We might add here that the psychobiographer, precisely because he or she does not have to respond to a person in vivo during a particular session, usually has more time to reflect on alternatives, which would be regarded as an advantage sooner than as a disadvantage.

Naturally, the methodological observations included in this section are not specific to the combination of psychology and history in religious studies. As has already been noted a few times: the theories, methods, and techniques of the disciplines represented in religious studies are not unique for this academic context. It is the object of research—religion—that holds religious studies together and legitimizes it. Methodological reflections on the nature, the contribution, and the combination of the different disciplines occur independent of this object, but these reflections should be translated in the case of religion. Let us, therefore, take a brief look at how some of these objectives can be realized.

Cultural Psychology of Religion in Religious Studies

In the ideal case religious studies is a broadly conceived institute and a broadly conceived course of study for academic research with regard to religion. It is broader than the traditional *Religionswissenschaft*, and in a certain sense it is as broad as this science of religion was in its early years. It comprises the empirical social and human sciences of religion such as anthropology, sociology, and psychology. It is also broader than *Religionswissenschaft* because it may include the study of literature, art, and culture (as well as new areas such as film and media studies and the like). And it is not exclusively oriented toward non-Christian and/or non-Western religions: Christianity, too, is studied as one of the important religions of mankind. It should initially be taught along disciplinary lines with as much care as possible, for only those who are firmly anchored in one existing discipline or another will be able to properly observe the borders of that discipline as well as to cross them and to carry out multidisciplinary or even interdisciplinary research in a meaningful way. Courses should be offered in which attempts to conceptualize religion and similar metatheoretical questions are addressed, yet the teaching itself should not primarily follow the lines of the different religious traditions but be organized on the basis of the scientific disciplines. Religious studies should strive to focus on the object of research—the various manifestations of "religion"—as correctly as possible, and for this reason the approach followed by religious studies as a whole would be culturological in nature: religion should be discussed as a cultural phenomenon that is understood against and on the basis of its own cultural background. Within the entire range of disciplines that are relevant to the scientific analysis of religion, many forms of religion should be reviewed, but specific introductions to Islam, shamanism, Christianity, and so forth, should not be the primary focus. On the other hand, courses that address these forms of religion from a historicizing perspective are quite conceivable. These courses, too, should not present the phenomenon of "religion" descriptively but should consist of showing and teaching how the history of such a cultural element should be described and analyzed.

After basic instruction in the various disciplines, a two-pronged specialization should occur. On the one hand, in order to acquire theoretical and methodical-technical depth, students should be allowed to pursue further studies in a chosen discipline by taking courses wherever the discipline is anchored to as a mother department in the university (sociology courses in the faculty of social sciences, for example, or courses in archaeology). The methods and techniques of the disciplines by which religion is analyzed are no different from those of the mother discipline and should be applied just as rigorously in research on religion. On the other hand, interdisciplinary and comparative education should be promoted by focusing special attention on certain themes that are relevant to the study of religions (such as martyrs, idolatry, mysticism, conversion, stigmata, pilgrimages, liturgy, etc.).

The situation is the same for the psychology of religion in religious studies: courses in the psychology of religion should be courses *in psychology*, in its applications within the analysis of religion. (As a rule, most examples or illustrations are taken from the main forms of Christianity because up until now the psychology of religion has had almost nothing to do with other religious lifestyles, unfortunately.) For the reasons set forth above, it would be most appropriate to choose an orientation in line with cultural psychology. This means that students would not have to be introduced to all the branches of psychology that have had anything to do with religion (that would hardly be possible anyway within a religious studies curriculum in which the amount of room for the psychology of religion is always limited); little attention, if any at all, would need to be paid to physiological psychology, comparative psychology, and general psychology, and methods such as experimentation and various statistical techniques would not necessarily have to be taught. Students who might want to specialize in the psychology of religion would take such courses, which are useful for cultural psychological research, in the psychology department: the various forms of hermeneutic psychology including psychoanalysis, for example, and interpretive research methods in the social and human sciences (which can also be useful in the study of other disciplines such as sociology, anthropology, political science, and the like). For further specialization, such as the training that might be expected of psychology of religion staff members, the ideal plan would be for the student to earn a full degree as a psychologist in addition to a degree in religious studies or *Religionswissenschaft*, or otherwise to acquire qualifications in psychology. This would be not only desirable for operating as a full-fledged colleague in the company of other psychologists of religion, especially outside religious studies, but it also would be beneficial for research and would—once again, the main point that I make in this chapter—make it possible to carry out empirical research as well.

Many people who have worked in the psychology of religion but were based in a nonpsychological institute have sought additional schooling in some form of psychology, very often in psychoanalysis (next to their primary training in such fields as theology, *Religionswissenschaft*, or religious studies). In many respects, psychoanalysis is, indeed, a form of psychology that can be compatible with the multidisciplinary context of such fields as theology or religious studies. It is also a form of psychology that can combine very well with the prevailing insights in cultural psychology and, in fact, forms a necessary element in those insights. The reasons that the thinking inaugurated by Freud cannot be disregarded if there is a desire to engage in psychological reflection (whether applied to religion or not) are actually very simple. Psychoanalysis is that form of psychology that allows for the most nuanced conceptualization of the irrational, unconscious dimension of psychic functioning, relying on or determined by the pulsion-driven body.

This dimension was not something that remained unrecognized until the twentieth century: religions, in fact, have always referred to it and have had their own ways of dealing with it. It is true that this dimension became more generally recognized in the most recent past, thanks to but not mainly owing to psychoanalysis (whose emergence and growth are more a symptom than a cause). Naturally, watching out for this dimension initially led to one-sidedness and exaggeration in psychoanalytical observations as well. Yet psychoanalysts who only see this dimension in the phenomena they themselves recognize, or who limit their search to this dimension when treating a patient or when applying psychoanalytic thinking in some kind of cultural analysis, are obviously being reductionistic. This problem has been adequately corrected and does not have to be addressed here. In addition, psychoanalysis is that form of psychology that thinks most radically historically with regard to psychic functioning: that is, from the very earliest, primordial corporeal experiences. By the nature of our corporeal being, the child's first recurring experiences are hunger and thirst. This primordial experience of lack and of contact with an object of satisfaction (usually the mother's breast or its substitute) imprints upon the psychic apparatus the whole matrix of desires and strengths that support a subject's ideals of happiness and his sexual fantasies (also in the pathological forms), and it also forms the supportive basis for the symbolic discourse of religious desiring. Psychoanalysis calls this enduring primordial form of desire "orality" and emphasizes that, insofar as it is a foundation of experience, the oral stage is not a transitory "phase." Rather, it is a grounding experience that once and for all provides desire with an oral disposition.[73] Desire, insofar as it is both a radical opening and a bond established on the basis of attachment, is shaped and deployed within the context of language into which human beings are born and which they inhabit. Language enables the human being to enter the realm of meanings and to reach beyond the self to a world that is not limited to the observable. The human being would not be a creature of desire if the foundational experiences, orality, and attachment did not take place within the opening and the promise that constitute the entry into language. These considerations are also important for an analysis of religion in human life. Indeed, it is one of the characteristics of religion that it is a discourse about the world and about human existence, articulated in terms of a universal and ultimate dimension. Rituals as well as propositions on origins, on good and evil, on destiny, and so forth—all organize existence with reference to the whole of being by linking all to whatever the particular religion calls or conceives of as the divine.[74]

So it seems to be psychoanalysis that is in a position to make inquiries of every manifestation of religion in terms of the psychic, that is (according to this way of interpreting), life-historical dynamic. It is striking, however, that most studies in the psychology of religion of a psychoanalytical nature that take place within the context of religious studies usually fall in the previously mentioned categories 2 and 3 of cultural psychology. In other words, they deal with the psychoanalytical psychology of religion (category 3) or are applications thereof (category 2). This is not being criticized here, but explicit mention is made of the possibility offered by the psychoanalytical theoretical framework to attempt empirical research in religious studies. In many respects, psychoanalysis coincides with cultural psychological perspectives. The formation of that which will later be designated the "subject" was already conceived by Freud as dependent on culture, dependent on that which is not-me. The human being, in his vision, is a passionate creature who at birth and for a long time afterward relies on the care provided by others. As a *neonatus*, the human being is not yet a "subject" and does not yet possess an "I." The pulsion, by which the human being is primarily and chiefly characterized, must be directed and refuted; it must be guided in culturally asserted channels (this is what is called "sublimation"). A central element of the process that the subject-in-progress must follow is the so-called triangular constellation: human beings must abandon certain pursuits (such as the desire to possess the mother entirely for themselves) and to focus on culturally acquired ideals (such as taking the father as a model). In this way, the subject-in-progress internalizes the surrounding culture (from language to norms and values), and psychic structures arise: besides the *Es*, seat of pulsion, there now appears the *Ich* and the *Über-Ich*. Because the treatment of the *neonatus* and of the developing child differs from culture to culture and age to age, and even from individual to individual, the nature of the *Ich* and the *Über-Ich* will also always be different. In his work, Freud paid increasing attention to culture in its constitutive relevance for the development of the personality and the growth to adulthood.[75] This trend has continued in later developments in psychoanalytical theory formation, such as object-relationship theories, self-psychology, and the Lacanian school. In each of these schools of thought, human existence is seen as socially constituted and symbolically mediated.

In these circles there is an awareness of the impact of culture that seems contrary to much vulgarized psychoanalytic reasoning found so often. There is a recognition that supraindividual entities like societies and/or entire cultures are not just repeating the phases and mechanisms that psychoanalytic theorizing claims to have discovered when studying patients. Instead, structurally informed psychoanalysts emphasize the importance of what Jacques Lacan called the "symbolic order" or the *discours de l'Autre*. This symbolic order exists prior to the individual and will persist when the individual has left it. Yet the individual is already represented in this order before birth, even if only by the name she or he will be given. Lacan clearly gave primacy to cultural order when he invented his dictum: "man talks, yet because the symbol has made him man."[76] Psychic development is the result of culture. There is no natural—in the sense of innately preconceived—growth, according to Lacan. The structure of the psyche as such (not just its culturally variable contents) is dependent on culture, on forces from "the outside." The constitution of the subject, the "psychic birth" (which occurs later than the *partus* from the womb) is dependent on (awareness of the separateness of) "other" (usually the mother); in order to achieve a first (imaginary) image of itself, the child (in the so-called mirror-phase) needs someone else to pass down this image. Most important for cultural psychology: self-consciousness, in Lacan's view, only emerges thanks to language. It is because of identification with the "discourse of the other" that the human being becomes a participant in culture, able to say "I" and, later, to speak in its own name. Subjectivity is constituted and marked by cultural givens. Because of the entrance into the cultural symbolic order (preeminently language), needs are transformed into desires, which are, therefore, not naturally given but are a product of culture. In this sense, it is impossible to conceive of a human instinct that would not be marked by cultural references that define it. Even sexual instincts are never merely natural forces: the strata of meanings deposited in them invariably condition the strategies of satisfaction as well as the pitfalls of suffering and discontents. That human beings desire, and the way in which they want to satisfy that desire, is the consequence of cultural signifiers that direct human desire. Thus, as Freud defined the drive as psychic *labor* because of the intrinsic unity with the corporeal, so culture similarly imposes labor; it shapes the psychic realm.

Ricoeur also tried to show extensively that "desire" cannot be conceived of without an "other," and that Freud developed his second topical model precisely because of his realization that libido is confronted with a nonlibidinal variable that manifests itself as culture.[77] Although it must be admitted that in this branch of psychoanalysis the emphasis is perhaps one-sided in terms of language, stories, and symbols, there is recognition of the cultural embeddedness of the individual life history and awareness that for a psychological understanding of meaningful action and experience it is, therefore, necessary to apply a double perspective: the perspective of the meaning shared by a cultural community in general as well as that of the personal meaning that can only be understood in terms of the individual life history. Even a deviation can be thus interrogated as to its meaning, since in deviating from the surrounding order it can be seen as a manifestation of the psychic conflict underlying it. I deliberately say "can be" since not every deviation points to psychopathology and, conversely, the (apparent) absence of conflict need not indicate psychic health. A psychologist cannot say a thing in advance about a person's health and sickness and will only make statements after having examined a concrete individual against the background of his or her culture and life history.

Within the "return to Freud" inaugurated by Lacan, a great deal of attention is paid to the impact of culture on the subject-in-progress. Yet since Freud there have been other psychoanalytical schools that have made just as many attempts to conceptualize the "cultural" character of human subjectivity and thereby to strip psychoanalysis of the solipsistic character that sometimes adhered to it. According to the object-relationship theoreticians, for example, the *neonatus* is not only dependent on the other but also relates to the other as to his goal. They argue that the human being does indeed pursue his or her desires, but they emphasize the fact that those desires must be gained from an object that, technically speaking, might be one's own body but is usually the body of someone else. The human being, they submit, is born with a fundamental need for alliance.[78] Influenced by this object-relationship way of thinking, and attempting to build on Freud's classical ideas, Heinz Kohut designed a theory in which the term "self" is explicitly introduced to designate a construct intended to indicate the place where one acquires one's experiences with oneself and one's whole environment.[79] In order for the self to emerge and continue, so-called self-objects are needed. Not only are these self-objects necessary for the child, but every adult needs them, too, in order to keep her or his psychic balance and to avoid fragmentation of the self.

Examples of Empirical Cultural Psychology of Religion along Psychoanalytical Lines

These theories were not developed within the psychology of religion, nor do they have to be developed there. As stated earlier, the core of the psychology of religion does not exclusively or necessarily consist of the formulation of new, original psychological theories. What the core does include is the adaptation of new theories in psychological research on various forms of religion. Unlike Freud, psychoanalysts such as Lacan, Mitchell, and Kohut did not make religion the object of their research or reflection. Other contemporary nonpsychoanalytically oriented cultural psychologists do not do that, either, and they are often just as unable to translate their work to the psychology of religion.[80] That kind of translation requires additional expertise—expertise concerning religious forms of life (and probably also concerning research in the psychology of religion in general). Such expertise, in fact, can be found in religious studies and provides an argument for expecting that contemporary cultural psychological theories often adapt themselves to religion in such an institute better than they do in a psychology faculty, as is often the case in the relatively few nonpsychoanalytically grounded attempts to do so.[81] We do not have to discuss such examples in the framework of this chapter, however. To conclude, and by way of substantiation, let us briefly look at a few examples of research conducted with the help of psychoanalytical theories. I will briefly discuss a classical study as well as a few more recent studies dealing with various traditions in Western Christianity.

One of the most important texts from the psychology of religion in Europe in the last decades is probably *Dette et désir* by Vergote.[82] This study is a monumental combination of philosophical and psychological insights that excels in considering the epistemological and methodological borders in general in the area of religion and science. Radical in his psychoanalytical interpretations (and therefore misunderstood by many theologians),[83] he is never reductive, thanks to his thorough knowledge of the religious tradition to which the phenomena he discusses belong (Roman Catholicism). From the point of view of the psychology of religion, Vergote's enterprise is an attempt to submit a number of religious phenomena to psychological analysis on the basis of extensive clinical-psychoanalytical experience. Following on Freud, he postulates as a guiding principle that the ground where religion and psychoanalysis meet is a psychic depth dimension. Psychoanalysis traces important anthropological themes that also occur in religion (such as desire, guilt, the meaning of the father) back to the primordial experiences of the human being, whereas religion raises them to a relationship with God, which may be conditioned by the psychic depth dimension but is not determined by it. In fact, psychoanalysis always follows the same working method in this regard, a method it has made its own through use in clinical work: it begins in the present and goes back to the causes that lie in the past. But it cannot reconstruct the present by beginning with the causes; psychic causes only determine conditionally. (This is why Vergote speaks of conditioned determinism.[84]) Religious desire, as desire, also has its origins in the pulsional wishes of the human creature, helplessly cast into the world, who depends on primary caregivers to satisfy her or his needs. But according to Vergote, psychoanalysis also observes that in this situation a relationship is established that transforms the neediness to a beginning love and recognition, and also that the memory of the satisfaction becomes an enjoyment that gives rise to the erotic inclination in the psyche:

> That mutation, by which the human being is elevated above the vital cycle of need and satisfaction without abolishing it, brings about a working openness that penetrates the reality on which scientific reason is focused. The arrival of language, with its capacity to ignore the captivity in the here and now and with its never completed expression of reality, provides desire with an unending dynamism. Religious language grafts new terms with new meanings onto that unending desire, which open it even further by directing it precisely towards that which it imagines to be more real than the reality understood by scientific reason.[85]

These psychoanalytical insights furnish us with the possibility of analyzing the connection between eroticism, for example, and religious desire. Naturally, psychoanalysis cannot make any statements about the nature or adequacy of religious desire. Following in the footsteps of Freud, who argued that the capacity to love is a characteristic of psychic health, psychoanalysis can only investigate with regard to religious desire-love to see if it, indeed, is witnessing that capacity. Assisted by the psychoanalytical conceptual framework, Vergote studies in *Dette et désir* a great many Christian mystics and the similarities and differences between sublimated desire-love and the hidden, shifted eroticism of religious hysteria or erotomania. By listening carefully to documented witnesses and observing the particular religious frame of reference, he is able to arrive at nuanced judgments. He draws a strict distinction between a religious and a psychopathological judgment, and he strives to avoid a hasty imposition of contemporary Western categories. According to him, the vision of St. Teresa's transverberation can—once situated in its context and elucidated by a psychology of sublimation—be taken as a sign of the psychic health and lucid judgment of that woman: "She indeed mortified her body, not out of a horror of sexuality but because of her project to grow into a love that might be worthy of him whom she believed herself destined to love in the depths of her identity."[86] Although doubting,[87] Vergote interprets the preoccupation of the "venerable" Agnes Blannbekin (born in Vienna toward the end of the thirteenth century and died 1315) with the question of what became of Christ's "Holy Foreskin" as a perversion (in the clinical sense of the word, with neurosis being the negative[88]), and the experiences (especially the torments she reported) of Marie Alacoque (1647–1690; celebrated apostle of devotion to the Sacred Heart) as hysterical.

Entirely apart from whether Vergote's interpretations are correct or not, it is important to note that they only reach any depth by employing clinical-psychoanalytical study combined with a solid knowledge of Roman Catholic mysticism. All in all, a work such as that presented by Vergote is not representative of the kind of psychology of religion practiced at psychological institutes (he himself taught philosophy, theology, and psychology at the University of Leuven in Belgium), but it would fit very well at an institute for religious studies. In many respects, his study is psychohistorical (because it often discusses historical examples), but in many other respects it is a systematic exploration of the desire dimension in religion, based on clinical study with contemporary subjects.

In her *Faith Born of Seduction: Sexual Trauma, Body Image and Religion*, Jennifer L. Manlowe provides an example of a study of contemporary subjects with interpretations from a psychoanalytical perspective.[89] She chiefly used the interview as an empirical social-scientific method. The book brings together three themes: sexual abuse (in family situations), preoccupations (or disorders) having to do with food and weight, and patriarchal religious structures. Manlowe notes a high correlation between incest and anorexia. She argues that for a survivor of incest, food is a "double-edged" defense against becoming overwhelmed by a painful past and a nonaffirming present. Often religious belief does not lighten the trauma but functions as a kind of second cause of the trauma by making it possible to spiritualize the traumatic past and the symptoms. Manlowe also uses the Bible and tradition to show to what extent texts and other data refer to incest, which can then be used to legitimize or at least to cover up. According to her, survivors who remain dependent on a paternalistic and transcendent deliverance run the risk of being seduced once again and ending up in the paradigm of the "helpless victim—powerful father." Manlowe's study is critical with regard to religion—whether her conclusions are always correct and whether her positions are not sometimes too audacious is beside the point here. What is important is to note that she combines basic information about religion with empirical fieldwork and psychoanalytical interpretations of her research subjects. (She works mostly with Winnicott and Kohut.) This is an example of a study that could have taken place in a psychological faculty but was probably less welcome there because of its interpretive and psychoanalytical bias than in an institute for religious studies. It is another example of empirical research in the field of religion along cultural-psychological lines and conducted at an institute for religious studies.

I believe I can make the same kinds of claims for some of my own work. To give but one recent example: in my study *Religie, melancholie en zelf* (Religion, melancholia and self), the focus is on a nineteenth-century religious autobiography, in and of itself a subject of research that would cause astonishment at a psychology faculty. One of the questions that I attempted to answer in the study is what function this autobiography served for its author—Mrs. Reinsberg, a former psychiatric patient who testified that she had been healed by God's intervention. In one of the chapters I try, assisted by a combination of psychopathological instruments, past and present, to acquire certain insights into the sickness and personality of the author. Various attempts were made to classify her condition and symptoms by using a contemporary instrument, such as the *Diagnostic and Statistical Manual* (*DSM*), published by the American Psychiatric Association. This instrument professes to be explicitly atheoretical with regard to the vast majority of mental disorders concerning the etiology and pathophysiological processes of the particular syndromes. By concentrating on a purely descriptive approach (also called descriptive-phenomenological), the *DSM* hopes to be of use to people with a broad range of theoretical orientations (*DSM*-III-(r), 23). The underlying idea is that even if the various clinicians differ in their interpretations of the cause and nature of the disorder, they nevertheless should be able to agree on the classification of the symptoms. Whether the APA succeeded in its plan for the *DSM* need not be discussed here. It only need be noted that this system has now become the most well known and most widely used diagnostic instrument worldwide with regard to mental disorders. Naturally, including such an instrument in the literature for an autobiography is a perilous undertaking because its intended purpose is quite different. So I only used it in order to present and discuss the symptoms reported by Mrs. Reinsberg in an ordered fashion. The results of the exercise may be seen as reasonably reliable for at least two reasons. First of all, while this attempt at "diagnosis" was undertaken by various researchers independent of each other, they all came to the same conclusions: that Mrs. Reinsberg apparently suffered from depression and that there was evidence of a narcissistic personality disorder. Second, these results are in full agreement with the diagnostic attempts made by her physicians at the time: in the archive of the former Veldwijk psychiatric hospital in Ermelo, the Netherlands, there is still a patient file for Mrs. Reinsberg complete with medical annotations. The diagnosis recorded in the file is "melancholia agitans." When one considers what was understood by psychiatry at the end of the nineteenth century, the symptoms exhibited by Mrs. Reinsberg are in almost full agreement with the clinical picture described by Kraepelin.[90]

But because the *DSM*, consistent with its own pretensions, can only be used as a descriptive instrument, it was necessary to attempt some theoretically grounded interpretations of Mrs. Reinsberg's disease and personality. According to contemporary psychopathology, it is generally true that with the emergence and persistence of a depressive period factors of a sociological (or sociopsychiatric), psychological, and biological nature can be identified. As obvious as this may seem, there is still no clarity at all as to the weight and possible interaction of these factors. That there was a combination of external stress factors and individual vulnerability at work was even recognized by the psychiatry of Mrs. Reinsberg's time, although the classifications were identified differently in each case or given a different name.[91] The available information on her case contains virtually no basis for any reflection on Mrs. Reinsberg's biological-physical condition and hardly any for her sociopsychiatric condition. There was also very little information in her case history concerning psychological factors, which was certainly regrettable. Yet over against this we do have her own self-presentation in the form of an extensive autobiography. On the basis of what she herself reports—in combination, wherever possible, with information from other sources—we can extract many things that bring us closer to an answer as to why Mrs. Reinsberg developed a depressive disorder. With the assistance of psychoanalytical insights such as those presented by Freud, Vergote, and Kohut, I then attempted to develop some insight into the possible stress factors that may have played a role in the origins of Mrs. Reinsberg's depressive disorder and into the kind of individual vulnerability that could have existed in her case. These theoretically guided reflections produced a number of hypotheses that could be tested in additional empirical-historical research and that allowed for a theoretically based interpretation of the psychic function the writing of an autobiography may have had for her. In order to interpret her psychic condition at the time her book was written, it was also necessary, of course, to reconstruct Mrs. Reinsberg's religious background and development (a reconstruction that also made it possible to distinguish the various voices constituting her self, in the sense of Hermans and Kempen).[92] Obviously, her autobiography had to be placed in the relevant genre, context, and so forth.[93] Although the study as a whole is psychological in nature, it is so strongly based on empirical-historical research and on information from literary theory and the history of church and spirituality that it can by no means be regarded as a specimen of research in the psychology of religion at a psychology faculty. That it is cultural-psychological and empirical is beyond any doubt, although conducted from an institute for religious studies.

Thus, a few examples of cultural-psychological research, both clinical and socioscientific, with contemporary and historical subjects, that might have been conducted at a psychology faculty but, because of the heavy accent and dependence on knowledge of the relevant religious traditions, would more easily—or more effectively—have been carried out in religious studies (which in fact they were). My chapter has been aimed at encouraging more of this kind of research in religious studies. Religious studies should be (or become) the place within the university for the full-fledged disciplinary, multidisciplinary and interdisciplinary study of religious forms of life. These studies should be fully acceptable within the disciplines on which they are based, and it should also be possible to conduct them within what might be called the "mother institutes." As for the psychology of religion, for religious studies it is obvious that it should mainly apply a cultural-psychological working method, of which empirical research conducted along psychoanalytical lines also presents a specimen. A great deal of good and high-quality research having to do with psychoanalytical psychology of religion or an application thereof is already being conducted in religious studies. The palette would be broadened even further if psychoanalytical psychology of religion itself were taken on: by conducting original and empirical research within a cultural-psychological framework.

Notes

1. For a few outstanding examples of these kinds of studies, see D. S. Browning, *Religious Thought and the Modern Psychologies: A Critical Conversation in the Theology of Culture* (Philadelphia: Fortress Press, 1988); P. Homans, *Jung in Context: Modernity and the Making of a Psychology* (Chicago: University of Chicago Press, 1979), *The Ability to Mourn: Disillusionment and the Social Origins of Psychoanalysis* (Chicago: University of Chicago Press, 1989); D. Jonte-Pace, *Teaching Freud* (New York: Oxford University Press/American Academy of Religion, 2003); D. Jonte-Pace and W. B. Parsons, eds., *Religion and Psychology: Mapping the Terrain* (New York: Routledge, 2001); W. B. Parsons, *The Enigma of the Oceanic Feeling: Revisioning the Psychoanalytic Theory of Mysticism* (New York/Oxford: Oxford University Press, 1999). See also J. A. Belzen, *Changing the Scientific Study of Religion: Beyond Freud?* (Boston: Springer, 2009).

2. D. Capps and J. E. Dittes, eds., *The Hunger of the Heart: Reflections on the Confessions of Augustine* (West Lafayette, IN: Society for the Scientific Study of Religion, 1990); S. L. Dixon, *Augustine: The Scattered and Gathered Self* (St. Louis: Chalice Press, 1999).

3. See for example, D. Capps, *Jesus: A Psychological Biography* (St. Louis: Chalice, 2000); S. Kakar, *The Analyst and the Mystic: Psychoanalytic Reflections on Religion and Mysticism* (Chicago: University of Chicago Press, 1991); J. J. Kripal, *Kali's Child: The Mystical and the Erotic in the Life and Teaching of Ramakrishna* (Chicago: University of Chicago Press, 1995); N. P. Sil, *Ramakrsna Paramahamsa: A Psychological Profile* (Leiden: Bril, 1991).

4. D. Capps, Men, *Religion and Melancholia: James, Otto, Jung and Erikson* (New Haven/London: Yale University Press, 1997); J. J. Kripal, *Roads of Excess, Palaces of Wisdom: Eroticism and Reflexivity in the Study of Mysticism* (Chicago: University of Chicago Press, 2001).

5. For an excellent overview, see R. W. Hood, P. C. Hill, and B. Spilka, *The Psychology of Religion: An Empirical Approach*, 4th ed. (New York: Guilford, 2009).

6. For such an overview, see D. M. Wulff, *Psychology of Religion: Classic and Contemporary* (New York: Wiley, 1997).

7. In the section that follows (as well as in the whole of the text), the initiated reader will be able to detect the strong influence of the European academic context, especially the situation in the Netherlands. I do not attempt to depart from this context, but I do attempt to transcend it (and even to criticize it). In fact, because this text is a form of "essay," I allow a personally colored treatment.

8. This German term literally means "science on religion," but is often too narrowly translated or understood as "history of religion(s)" or "comparative religion." As I shall show in the text, I advocate a broader, multidisciplinary concept of "sciences on religion" (to be distinguished from religious studies, which I understand to be an ever broader but also vaguer scholarly enterprise). In the text I use the German expression, as a kind of *terminus technicus*, but sometimes I also refer to "sciences of religion."

9. J. A. Belzen, *Der kulturpsychologische Ansatz in der Theologie, insbesondere in der Religionswissenschaft* (Turku, Fin.: Åbo Akademi University Press, 2001), esp. chap. 1.

10. H.-G. Gadamer, *Hermeneutik I: Wahrheit und Methode. Grundzüge einer philosophischen Hermeneutik* (Tübingen: Mohr, 1960).

11. This is not to be confused with atheism, which in itself is a religious standpoint.

12. For the sake of convenience, we will carry on as if we knew what "religion" is. In fact, there is no agreement at all as to what should be understood by this term, nor is there agreement as to its empirical denotation. *Religionswissenschaftler* as well as representatives of religious studies are increasingly pointing out that it is impossible to contain the worldwide multitude of phenomena called religion within a single definition or concept that would be valid always and everywhere. They suggest that perhaps it would be most accurate to stop using the term since it is calibrated to Western Christianity; so often using the term means fitting basically different phenomena into a Western category system, which makes it difficult to view the other phenomena clearly (cf. Feil 1986, 1997; Fitzgerald 2000, 2007; Haußig 1999; Kippenberg 2001; McCutcheon 2003).

13. D. J. Hoens, J. H. Kamstra, and D. C. Mulder, *Inleiding tot de studie van godsdiensten* [Introduction to the Study of Religions] (Kampen, Neth: Kok, 1993); E. J. Sharpe, *Comparative Religion. A History* (Illinois: Open Court, 1986).

14. Hence A. Vergote's, "What the Psychology of Religion Is and What It Is Not," *The International Journal for the Psychology of Religion* 3 (1993): 73–86).

15. The classic term for this is the "formal object" of a scientific discipline: the same material object, such as urbanization, morality, or architecture, can be looked at by entirely different disciplines from their own specific perspective (their formal object).

16. Karl Bühler, *Die Krise der Psychologie* (Jena: Fischer, 1927).

17. Amedeo Giorgi, "Phenomenology and the Foundations of Psychology," in *Conceptual Foundations of Psychology*, ed. W. J. (Lincoln/Arnold: Univ. of Nebraska Press, 1976), 281–408.

18. Giorgi, "Phenomenology," 293.

19. J. A. Belzen, "Spirituality, Culture and Mental Health: Prospects and Risks for Contemporary Psychology of Religion," *Journal of Religion and Health* 43 no. 4, (2004): 291–316.

20. J. A. Belzen, "Taboo Religion? A Contextual Analysis of the Marginalization of German Psychology of Religion," *Zeitschrift für Psychologie* 217, no. 2, (2009): 85–94.

21. Cf. Ayele et al. (1999), Bickel et al. (1998), Biggar et al. (1999), Bowman (2000), Braam et al. (2000), Buchanan et al. (2001), Calhoun and Tedeschi (2000), Calhoun et al. (2000), Carone and Barone (2001), Carrol, McGinley, and Mack (2000), Chang, Noonan and Tennstedt (1998), Chang, Skinner, and Boehmer (2001), Ellison et al. (2001), Fabricatore, Handal, and Fenzel (2000), Gall, Miguez de Renart and Boonstra (2000), Giesbrecht and Sevcik (2000), Graham et al. (2001), Hettler and Cohen (1998), Hintikka et al. (1998), Jersild (2001), Joseph (1998), Koenig et al. (1998), Krause, Ellison, and Wulff (1998), Levin and Chatters (1998), Levin and Taylor (1998), Loewenthal et al. (2000), Neumann and Chi (1999), O'Neill (1999), Pargament et al. (2001), Pfeifer and Waelty (1999), Prager (1998), Razali et al. (1998), Schnittker (2001), Shaddock, Hill, and van Limbeek (1998), Tek and Ulug (2001), Tigert (2001), Young, Cashwell, and Shcherbakova (2000), and many, many others.

22. Like *Cognition and Emotion*, *Stress Medicine*, *Journal of Aging and Health*, *International Journal of Psychiatry in Medicine*, *Journal of Community Psychology*, *Journal of Family Violence*, *Journal of Psychosocial Oncology*, *Journal of Family Practice*, *Gerontologist*, *Alcoholism Treatment Quarterly*, *Journal of Traumatic Stress*, *International Journal of Geriatric Psychiatry*, *AIDS-Care*, *Journal of the American Geriatrics Society*, *Clinical Psychology Review*.

23. J. A. Belzen, "Spirituality, Culture, and Mental Health."

24. One must not think that this point of view is entirely undisputed. In the psychology of religion itself there is a small group of authors (often calling themselves "Christian") who think they are able (or even compelled) to construct their psychology (of religion) not only on the basis of an intersubjective processing of generally accessible empirical materials but also on the basis of religious doctrine and/or premises; cf., e.g., Utsch (1998), Benner and Hill (1999).

25. A. Godin, *The Psychological Dynamics of Religious Experience (It Doesn't Fall Down from Heaven)*, (Burmingham: Religious Education Press, 1985).

26. See A. Vergote, *Religion, Belief and Unbelief: Psychological Study* (Amsterdam/Leuven: Rodopi/Leuven University Press, 1983); J. A. Belzen, "The Cultural-Psychological Approach to Religion: Contemporary Debates on the Object of the Discipline," *Theory and Psychology* 9 (1999): 229–56.

27. G. W. Allport, "Religion and Prejudice," in *Personality and Social Encounter*, (Boston: Beacon Press, 1960): 257–67; G. W. Allport, "Prejudice: Is It Societal or Personal? *Journal of Social Issues* 18, (1962): 120–74.

28. C. D. Batson and W. L. Ventis. *The Religious Experience: A Social-Psychological Perspective* (New York: Oxford University Press, 1982).

29. See H. F. de Wit, *De verborgen bloei: over de psychologische achtergronden van spiritualiteit* [The Hidden Flowering: On the Psychological Backgrounds of Spirituality] (Kampen: Kok, 1993).

30. L. Corbett, *The Religious Function of the Psyche* (London/New York: Routledge, 1996).

31. In clinical psychology, which is perhaps the best-known form of "applied" psychology, psychologists usually proceed in this fashion. It is never the case that a syndrome (e.g., anorexia nervosa) found in a person can simply be reduced to some psychosocial complex of problems. On the other hand, knowledge of the relations between psychosocial factors and psychic dysfunction does, generally speaking, facilitate the exploration and eventual treatment of individual complaints.

32. With respect to psychoanalysis, for example, it can be quickly established that it is represented in almost no faculty of psychology. One finds it in all sorts of other faculties, although it is nevertheless manifestly a branch of psychology.

33. Such publications can even be considered classics, such as Rizzuto (1979), a work that begins with the statement: "This is not a book on religion" (3). Such modesty is characteristic of most of the psychology of religion today. There is scarcely a single psychologist of religion who thinks that the psychology of religion has "religion" (in general) as its object or in any way explains it. Usually authors restrict themselves to precisely defined aspects of a given religion (as a rule the Christian religion), which are then exclusively analyzed from a precisely fixed perspective. Thus Rizzuto continues: "It is a clinical study of the possible origins of the individual's private representation of God and its subsequent elaborations."

34. See, for example, L. Breure, *Doodsbeleving en levenshouding: Een historisch-psychologische studie betreffende de Moderne Devotie in het IJsselgebied in de veertiende en vijftiende eeuw*. [Perception of Death of Attitude towards Life: A Historical-Psychological Study Concerning Devotia Moderna in the IJssel Region in the Fourteenth and Fifteenth Centuries] (Hilversum, Neth.: Verloren, 1987).

35. See, for example, G. Dresen, *Onschuldfantasieën: Offerzin en heilsverlangen in feminisme en mystiek* [Fantasies of Innocence: Desire for Sacrifice and Longing for Salvation in Feminism and Mysticism] (Nijmegen: Sun, 1990).

36. See, for example, T. Källstad, *John Wesley and the Bible: A Psychological Study* (Uppsala: Acta Universitatis Upsaliensis, 1974); H. A. Alma, *Identiteit door verbondenheid: Een godsdienstpsychologisch onderzoek naar identificatie en christelijk geloof* [Identity through Solidarity: Research in the Psychology of Religion on Identification and Christian Faith] (Kampen, Neth.: Kok, 1998).

37. See, for example, R. R. Ganzevoort, *Een cruciaal moment: Functie en verandering van geloof in een crisis* [A Crucial Moment: Function and Change of Faith

in a Crisis] (Zoetermeer, Neth.: Boekencentrum, 1994); W. Meng, *Narzißmus und christliche Religion: Selbstliebe Nächstenliebe Gottesliebe* (Zürich: Theologischer Verlag, 1997); E. Nestler, *Pneuma: Außeralltägliche religiöse Erlebnisse und ihre biographische Kontexte* (Konstanz, Germ.: Universitätsverlag Konstanz, 1998).

38. See, for example, A.-M. Rizzuto, *The Birth of the Living God: A Psychoanalytic Study* (Chicago: University of Chicago Press, 1979); A. Vergote, *Guilt and Desire: Religious Attitudes and Their Pathological Derivatives*, trans. M. H. Wood (New Haven: Yale University Press, 1978/1988); A. Vergote, *De sublimatie: Een uitweg uit Freuds impasses* [Sublimation: A Way Out of Freud's Impasses] (Amsterdam: SUN, 1997).

39. A number of the originators of psychological theories (such as James or Freud) never completed a degree in psychology.

40. Such as K. I. Pargament, *The Psychology of Religion and Coping: Theory, Research, Practice* (New York/London: Guilford Press, 1997); K. I. Pargament, *Spiritually Integrated Psychotherapy: Understanding and Addressing the Sacred* (New York: Guilford Press, 2007); K. I. Pargament, K. I. Maton, and R. E. Hess, eds., *Religion and Prevention in Mental Health: Research, Vision, and Action* (New York: Haworth Press, 1992).

41. Such as R. A. Emmons, *The Psychology of Ultimate Concerns: Motivation and Spirituality in Personality* (New York/London: Guilford, 1999).

42. Such as R. W. Hood, *Dimensions of Mystical Experiences: Empirical Studies and Psychological Links* (Amsterdam/New York: Rodopi, 2001).

43. G. Hole, *Der Glaube bei Depressiven: Religionspsychopathologische und klinisch-statistische Untersuchung* (Stuttgart: Enke, 1977); W. W. Meissner, *Ignatius of Loyola: The Psychology of a Saint* (New Haven: Yale University Press, 1995).

44. A.-M. Rizzuto, *The Birth of the Living God.*

45. S. Kitayama and D. Cohen, eds., *Handbook of Cultural Psychology* (New York: Guilford, 2007); J. Valsiner and A. Rosa, *Cambridge Handbook of Sociocultural Psychology* (New York: Cambridge University Press, 2007).

46. J. A. Belzen, *Towards Cultural Psychology of Religion: Principles, Approaches, Applications* (Boston: Springer, 2010).

47. Cultural psychologists usually define meaningful action or conduct as the object of psychology. Obviously, there are also forms of human behavior that are not intentional or not regulated by meaning (like drawing back one's hand from a hot object, although even this involves cultural variation).

48. J. A. Belzen, "The Historicocultural Approach in the Psychology of Religion: Perspectives for Interdisciplinary Research" *Journal for the Scientific Study of Religion* 36, no. 3 (1997): 358–71.

49. M. Bal, *Reading "Rembrandt" Beyond the Word-Image Opposition* (New York: Cambridge University Press, 1991); M. Bal, *Quoting Caravaggio: Contemporary Art, Preposterous History* (Chicago: University of Chicago Press, 1999); C. van Boheemen-Saaf, *Joyce, Derrida, Lacan and the Trauma of History: Reading, Narrative, Postcolonialism* (Cambridge: University of Cambridge Press, 1999).

50. For example, P. W. Pruyser, *The Play of Imagination: Toward a Psychoanalysis of Culture* (New York: International Universities Press, 1983); A.-M. Rizzuto, *Why*

Did Freud Reject God: A Psychodynamic Interpretation (New Haven/London: Yale University Press, 1998); W. W. Meissner, *Ignatius of Loyola*; W. W. Meissner, *Vincent's Religion: The Search for Meaning* (New York: Lang, 1997); S. Kakar, *The Analyst and the Mystic*; W. Stählin, "Experimentelle Untersuchungen über Sprachpsychologie und Religionspsychologie," *Archiv für Religionspsychologie* 1 (1914): 117–194.

51. For example, K. Beth, *Religion und Magie: Ein religionsgeschichtlicher Beitrag zur psychologischen Grundlegung der religiösen Prinzipienlehre* (Berlin: Teubner, 1927); K. Beth, "Religion als Metabiontik. I. Der Fall R. Sch." *Zeitschrift für Religionspsychologie* (Beiträge zur religiösen Seelenforschung und Seelenführung), 4 (1931): 25–37; K. Beth, "Religion als Metabiontik. II. Madeleine Sémer." *Zeitschrift für Religionspsychologie* (Beiträge zur religiösen Seelenforschung und Seelenführung), 4 (1931): 145–56; O. Pfister, *Die Frömmigkeit des Grafen Ludwig von Zinzendorf* (Leipzig: Deuticke, 1910); O. Pfister, *Die Legende Sundar Singhs* (Bern: Haupt, 1926); O. Pfister, *Christianity and Fear* (London: Allen & Unwin, 1944); H. Sundén, *Die Religion und die Rollen* (Berlin: Töpelmann, 1959); K. Girgensohn, *Der seelische Aufbau des religiösen Erlebens* (Leipzig: Hirzel, 1921); N. G. Holm, *Einführung in die Religionspsychologie* (München: Reinhardt, 1990); W. B. Parsons, *The Enigma of the Oceanic Feeling*; Kripal, *Kali's Child*; A. Vergote, *Guilt and Desire*; A. Vergote, *Religion, Belief and Unbelief*.

52. See W. J. Gomperts, *De opkomst van de sociale fobie* (Amsterdam: Bert Bakker, 1992); W. Zeegers, *Andere tijden, andere mensen* (Amsterdam: Bert Bakker, 1988).

53. See K. Danziger, *Constructing the Subject: Historical Origins of Psychological Research*. (Cambridge: Cambridge University Press, 1990); K. Danziger, *Naming the Subject: How Psychology Found Its Language* (London: SAGE, 1997); K. Danziger, *Marking the Mind: A History of Memory* (Cambridge: Cambridge University Press, 2008).

54. See, for example, N. Much, "Cultural Psychology," in J. A. Smith, R. Harré, and L. van Langenhove. eds., *Rethinking Psychology* (London: SAGE, 1995), 97–121.

55. See, for example, J. A. Belzen, *Rümke, religie en godsdienstpsychologie* (Kampen, Neth.: Kok, 1991); J. A. Belzen, *Psychologie en het raadsel van de religie* (Amsterdam: Boom, 2007); U. Laucken, *Sozialpsychologie* (Oldenburg, Germany: BIS, 1998); A. C. Paranjpe, *Self and Identity in Modern Psychology and Indian Thought* (New York: Plenum Press, 1998).

56. The situation in a small country like the Netherlands is quite remarkable in this respect: not only is there a relatively large number of available places for the psychology of religion at a high academic level (far and away the largest number in comparison with other European countries), but at institutes for theology and Religious Studies these positions are usually occupied by persons who have earned a degree (or an additional degree) in psychology. More information can be found in Belzen (1999b).

57. Also note that the academic appointments of a substantial number of leading cultural psychologists have been to places other than institutes of psychology. Michael Cole, for instance, may have been appointed as a professor of communications and psychology, but he is working at the Laboratory of Comparative Human Cognition at the University of California in San Diego; Richard Shweder was primarily

trained as an anthropologist and is working as a professor of human development at the University of Chicago. Jaan Valsinger, editor of the journal *Culture & Psychology*, recently pointed out that there is a whole wave of theoretical constructions (also within anthropology) not usually categorized as "cultural psychology," yet which see the core of making sense of human beings' meaningful construction of themselves as a serious intellectual endeavor (Valsiner 1997, 244).

58. D. C. North, *Structure and Change in Economic History* (New York: Norton, 1981).

59. W. H. MacNeill, *America, Britain and Russia: Their Co-Operation and Conflict 1941–1946* (London: Oxford University Press, 1953).

60. Please note: This by no means implies that mechanistic or organistic psychologies would by definition be of no use in psychohistorical research. Researchers who encounter incidents of hallucinating in their research can benefit a great deal from current insights into, say, physiological psychology. It also does not mean that every form of hermeneutic psychology is unquestionably suitable to the same degree in historic research.

61. See, for example, P. Burke, *Sociology and History* (London: Allen & Unwin, 1980; Smith, 1991).

62. L. Stone, "History and the Social Sciences in the Twentieth Century," in *The Future of History*, ed. Delzell (Nashville: Vanderbilt University Press, 1977), 3–43.

63. In the context of a study whose object is religiosity, it may be useful to note that the modest view of psychohistory presented here is entirely different from that which is intended with terms like "psychohistorical parallelism." In using this term, Abrams was referring to the tradition of explaining the Bible that deals not only with the external events from a sacred history but also with the history of the individual mind (Abrams 1973, 49, 83).

64. As in a recent survey by J. Szaluta, *Psychohistory: Theory and Practice* (New York: Lang, 1999).

65. See W. T. Schultz, *Handbook of Psychobiography* (Oxford/New York: Oxford University Press, 2005).

66. See also J. A. Belzen, *Psychohistory in Psychology of Religion: Interdisciplinary studies* (Amsterdam: Rodopi, 2001); J. A. Belzen, *Religie, melancholie en zelf, Een historische en cultuurpsychologische studie over een psychiatrisch ego-document uit de negentiende eeuw* [Religion, Melancholy and Self: An Historical and Cultural-Psychological Study of a Psychiatric Ego Document from the Nineteenth Century] (Kampen, Neth.: Kok, 2004).

67. Gadamer, *Hermeneutik I*, 281–317.

68. J. W. Anderson, "The Methodology of Psychological Biography," *Journal of Interdisciplinary History* 11 (1981): 455–75. Compare the summary he provides at the end of his article: "The strategies discussed in this essay for minimizing the difficulties in writing psychobiography do not clash; rather, they fit into a coherent approach. This approach requires the psychobiographer to do thorough research and immerse

himself in the source material; to develop an empathic relationship with his subject, a relationship which aids him in 'listening' to the material through his model of the subject's personality; to eschew dogmatic personality theories; and, by continually going back and forth between hypotheses and the data, gradually to build a portrait of the subject" (474). These are recommendations that even an opponent of psychobiography will endorse.

69. See N. Treurniet, "Wat is psychoanalyse nu [What Is Psychoanalysis Now]?" *Tijdschrift voor Psychotherapie* [Journal of Psychotherapy] 19 (1993): 65–84.

70. See J. Sandler, C. Dare, and A. Holder, *The Patient and the Analyst* (London: Hogarth Press, 1992).

71. E. H. Erikson, "On the Nature of Psychohistorical Evidence," in *Life History and the Historical Moment* (New York: Norton, 1971), 113–68.

72. Anderson, "The Methodology of Psychological Biography."

73. Vergote, *Guilt and Desire*, 125.

74. Vergote, *Guilt and Desire*, 128–29.

75. J. DiCenso, *The Other Freud: Religion, Culture and Psychoanalysis* (London/New York: Routledge, 1999).

76. J. Lacan, *Écrits* (Paris: Seuil, 1966), 242.

77. P. Ricoeur, *Freud and Philosophy: An Essay on Interpretation* (New Haven: Yale University Press, 1965), 188.

78. S. Mitchell, *Relational Concepts in Psychoanalysis* (Cambridge: Harvard University Press, 1988).

79. H. Kohut, *The Restoration of the Self* (New York: International Universities Press, 1977); H. Kohut, *The Search for the Self* (New York: International Universities Press, 1978); H. Kohut, *Self Psychology and the Humanities: Reflections on a New Psychoanalytic Approach* (New York: Norton, 1985).

80. See, for example, the somewhat awkward attempts, realized only on request, by Gergen (1993, 2002a, 2002b); cf. also Moosbrugger (1998) for an example of an "ordinary" psychologist who may tolerate research in the psychology of religion by his students yet, apparently, makes no contribution himself.

81. See, for example, J. A. Belzen, "Religion as Embodiment: Cultural-Psychological Concepts and Methods in the Study of Conversion Among 'Bevindelijken,'" *Journal for the Scientific Study of Religion* 38, no. 2, (1999): 236–53; J. A. Belzen, *Der kulturpsychologische*; U. Popp-Baier, *Das Heilige im Profanen: Religiöse Orientierungen im Alltag. Eine qualitative Studie zu religiösen Orientierungen von Frauen aus der charis ma tisch-evangelischen Bewegung* (Amsterdam: Rodopi, 1998); N. H. Hijweege-Smeets, *Bekering in bevindelijke kring. Een psychologische studie* [Conversion Among Bevindelijken: A Psychological Study] (Kampen, Neth: Kok, 2003).

82. Vergote, *Guilt and Desire*.

83. See H. Blankers, "Dilemma's in lichamelijkheid: Interpretatie van het mystieke genieten bij Teresa van Avila" [Dilemmas In Corporeality: Interpretation of Mystical Enjoyment in Teresa of Avila]. *Tijdschrift voor Theologie* [Journal of Theology] 32 (1992): 367–87.

84. Vergote, *Guilt and Desire*, 287.

85. A. Vergote, "Psychoanalyse in contact met religie," in *Psychoanalyse: De mens en zijn lotgevallen*, eds. A. Vergote and P. Moyaert (Kapellen, Belgium: De Nederlandsche Boekhandel, 1988), 287.

86. Vergote, *Guilt and Desire*, 163.

87. Vergote, *Guilt and Desire*, 164.

88. Vergote, *Guilt and Desire*, 165.

89. J. L. Manlowe, *Faith Born of Seduction: Sexual Trauma, Body Image and Religion* (New York/London: New York University Press, 1995).

90. E. Kraepelin, *Psychiatrie: Ein kurzes Lehrbuch für Studierende und Aerzte* (Leipzig: Abel, 1883).

91. R. H. van den Hoofdakker, P. A. Albersnagel, and H. de Cuyper, "Stemmingsstoornissen" [Mood disorders] in *Handboek psychopathologie, deel 1* [Handbook of Psychopathology, part 1], eds. W. Vandereycken, C. A. L. Hoogduin and P. M. G. Emmelkamp (Houten, Neth.: Bohn, Stafleu, Van Loghum, 1990), 166–204.

92. H. J. M. Hermans and H. J. G. Kempen. *The Dialogical Self: Meaning as Movement* (San Diego: Academic Press, 1993).

93. See also J. A. Belzen, "Autobiography, Psychic Functioning and Mental Health: The Role of Religion in Personal Life" in *Autobiography and the Psychological Study of Religious Lives*, eds. J. A. Belzen and A. Geels (Amsterdam: Rodopi, 2008), 117–57.

References

Abrams, M. H. *Natural Supernaturalism*. New York: Norton, 1973.

Allport, G. W. "Religion and Prejudice." Pp. 257–67 in *Personality and Social Encounter*. Boston: Beacon Press, 1960.

———. "Prejudice: Is It Societal or Personal?" *Journal of Social Issues* 18 (1962): 120–74.

Alma, H. A. *Identiteit door verbondenheid: Een godsdienstpsychologisch onderzoek naar identificatie en christelijk geloof* [Identity through Solidarity: Research in the Psychology of Religion on Identification and Christian Faith]. Kampen, Neth.: Kok, 1998.

Anderson, J. W. "The Methodology of Psychological Biography." *Journal of Interdisciplinary History* 11 (1981): 455–75.

Ayele, H., T. Mulligan, S. Gheorghiu, and C. Reyers Ortitz. "Religious Activity Improves Life Satisfaction for Some Physicians and Older Patients." *Journal of the American Geriatrics Society* 47 (1999): 453–55.

Bal, M. *Reading "Rembrandt" beyond the Word-Image Opposition*. New York: Cambridge University Press, 1991.

———. *Quoting Caravaggio: Contemporary Art, Preposterous History*. Chicago: University of Chicago Press, 1999.

Batson, C. D., and W. L. Ventis. *The Religious Experience: A Social-Psychological Perspective*. New York: Oxford University Press, 1982.

Belzen, J. A. *Rümke, religie en godsdienstpsychologie: Achtergronden en vooronderstellingen* [Rümke, Religion and the Psychology of Religion: Backgrounds and Presuppositions]. Kampen, Neth.: Kok, 1991.

———. "The Historicocultural Approach in the Psychology of Religion: Perspectives for Interdisciplinary Research." *Journal for the Scientific Study of Religion* 36, no. 3 (1997): 358–71.

———. "Continuïteit, verlies en vooruitgang in de Nederlandse godsdienstpsychologie" [Continuity, Loss and Progress in the Dutch Psychology of Religion.] Pp. 7–28 in *Van gisteren naar heden: Godsdienstpsychologie in Nederland, teksten 1* [From Yesterday to Today: Pyschology of Religion in the Netherlands, texts I], edited by J. A. Belzen. Kampen, Neth.: Kok, 1999.

———. "The Cultural-Psychological Approach to Religion: Contemporary Debates on the Object of the Discipline." *Theory and Psychology* 9 (1999): 229–56.

———. "Religion as Embodiment: Cultural-Psychological Concepts and Methods in the Study of Conversion among 'Bevindelijken.'" *Journal for the Scientific Study of Religion* 38, no. 2 (1999): 236–53.

———. *Der kulturpsychologische Ansatz in der Theologie, insbesondere in der Religionswissenschaft: Theoretische und empirische Beiträge*. Turku, Fin.: Åbo Akademi University Press, 2001.

———. *Psychohistory in Psychology of Religion: Interdisciplinary Studies*. Amsterdam: Rodopi, 2001.

———. *Religie, melancholie en zelf: Een historische en cultuurpsychologische studie over een psychiatrisch ego-document uit de negentiende eeuw* [Religion, Melancholy and Self: An Historical and Cultural-Psychological Study of a Psychiatric Ego Document from the Nineteenth Century]. Kampen, Neth.: Kok, 2004.

———. "Spirituality, Culture and Mental Health: Prospects and Risks for Contemporary Psychology of Religion." *Journal of Religion and Health* 43, no. 4 (2004): 291–316.

———. *Psychologie en het raadsel van de religie: Beschouwingen bij een eeuw godsdienstpsychologie in Nederland*. [Psychology and the Mystery of Religion: Reflections on a Century of Psychology of Religion in the Netherlands] Amsterdam: Boom, 2007.

———. "Autobiography, Psychic Functioning and Mental Health: The Role of Religion in Personal Life." Pp. 117–57 in *Autobiography and the Psychological Study of Religious Lives*. Edited by J. A. Belzen and A. Geels. Amsterdam: Rodopi, 2008.

———. *Changing the Scientific Study of Religion: Beyond Freud?* Boston: Springer, 2009.

———. "Taboo Religion? A Contextual Analysis of the Marginalization of German Psychology of Religion." *Zeitschrift für Psychologie 217*, no. 2 (2009): 85–94.

———. *Towards Cultural Psychology of Religion: Principles, Approaches, Applications*. Boston: Springer, 2010.

Benner, D. G., and P. C. Hill, eds. *Baker Encyclopedia of Psychology and Counseling*. 2nd ed. Grand Rapids: Baker Books, 1999.

Beth, K. *Religion und Magie: Ein religionsgeschichtlicher Beitrag zur psychologischen Grundlegung der religiösen Prinzipienlehre*. Berlin: Teubner, 1927.

———. "Religion als Metabiontik. I. Der Fall R. Sch." *Zeitschrift für Religionspsychologie* (Beiträge zur religiösen Seelenforschung und Seelenführung) 4 (1931): 25–37.

———. "Religion als Metabiontik. II. Madeleine Sémer." *Zeitschrift für Religionspsychologie* (Beiträge zur religiösen Seelenforschung und Seelenführung) 4 (1931): 145–56.

Bickel, C. O., J. W. Ciarrocchi, N. J. Sheers, B. K. Estadt, D. A. Powell, and K. I. Pargament. "Perceived Stress, Religious Coping Styles, and Depressive Affect." *Journal of Psychology and Christianity* 17 (1998): 33–42.

Biggar, H., R. Forehand, D. Devine, G. Brody, L. Armistead, E. Morse, and P. Simon. "Women Who Are HIV Infected: The Role of Religious Activity in Psychosocial Adjustment." *AIDS-Care* 11 (1999): 195–99.

Blankers, H. "Dilemma's in lichamelijkheid: Interpretatie van het mystieke genieten bij Teresa van Avila" [Dilemmas in Corporeality: Interpretation of Mystical Enjoyment in Teresa of Avila]. *Tijdschrift voor Theologie* [Journal of Theology] 32 (1992): 367–87.

Boheemen-Saaf, C. van. *Joyce, Derrida, Lacan and the Trauma of History: Reading, Narrative, Postcolonialism*. Cambridge: University of Cambridge Press, 1999.

Bowman, E. S. "The Assets and Liabilities of Conservative Religious Faith for Persons with Severe Dissociative Disorders." *Journal of Psychology and Christianity* 19 (2000): 122–38.

Braam, A. W., C. M. Sonnenberg, A. T. F. Beekman, D. J. H. Deeg, and W. van Tilburg. "Religious Denomination as a Symptom-Formation Factor of Depression in Older Dutch Citizens." *International Journal of Geriatric Psychiatry* 15 (2000): 458–66.

Breure, L. *Doodsbeleving en levenshouding: Een historisch-psychologische studie betreffende de Moderne Devotie in het IJsselgebied in de veertiende en vijftiende eeuw*. [Perception of Death of Attitude towards Life: A Historical-Psychological Study Concerning Devotia Moderna in the IJssel Region in the Fourteenth and Fifteenth Centuries] Hilversum, Neth.: Verloren, 1987.

Browning, D. S. *Religious Thought and the Modern Psychologies: A Critical Conversation in the Theology of Culture*. Philadelphia: Fortress Press, 1988.

Buchanan, M., K. Dzelme, D. Harris, and L. Hecker. "Challenge of Being Simultaneously Gay or Lesbian and Spiritual and/or Religious: A Narrative Perspective." *American Journal of Family Therapy* 29 (2001): 435–49.

Bühler, K. *Die Krise der Psychologie*. Jena: Fischer, 1927.

Burke, P. *Sociology and History*. London: Allen & Unwin, 1980.

Calhoun, L. G., and R. G. Tedeschi. "Early Posttraumatic Interventions: Facilitating Possibilities for Growth." Pp. 135–52 in *Posttraumatic Stress Intervention: Challenges, Issues, and Perspectives*. Edited by J. M. Violanti et al. Springfield: Thomas, 2000.

Calhoun, L. G., A. Cann, R. G. Tedeschi, and J. McMillan. "A Correlational Test of the Relationship Between Posttraumatic Growth, Religion, and Cognitive Processing." *Journal of Traumatic Stress* 13 (2000): 521–27.

Capps, D. *Men, Religion and Melancholia: James, Otto, Jung and Erikson*. New Haven/London: Yale University Press, 1997.

———. *Jesus: A Psychological Biography*. St. Louis, Mo.: Chalice, 2000.

Capps, D., and J. E. Dittes, eds. *The Hunger of the Heart: Reflections on the Confessions of Augustine*. West Lafayette, IN: Society for the Scientific Study of Religion, 1990.

Carone, D. A., and D. F. Barone. "A Social Cognitive Perspective on Religious Beliefs: Their Functions and Impact on Coping and Psychotherapy." *Clinical Psychology Review* 21 (2001): 989–1003.

Carrol, J. F. X., J. J. McGinley, and S. E. Mack. "Exploring the Expressed Spiritual Needs and Concerns of Drug-Dependant Males in Modified, Therapeutic Community Treatment." *Alcoholism Treatment Quarterly* 18 (2000): 79–92.

Chang, B. H., A. E. Noonan, and S. Tennstedt. "The Role of Religion/Spirituality in Coping with Caregiving for Disabled Elders." *Gerontologist* 38 (1998): 463–70.

Chang, B. H., K. M. Skinner, and U. Boehmer. "Religion and Mental Health among Women Veterans with Sexual Assault Experience." *International Journal of Psychiatry in Medicine* 31 (2001): 77–95.

Corbett, L. *The Religious Function of the Psyche*. London/New York: Routledge, 1996.

Danziger, K. *Constructing the Subject: Historical Origins of Psychological Research*. Cambridge: Cambridge University Press, 1990.

———. *Naming the Subject: How Psychology Found Its Language*. London: SAGE, 1997.

———. *Marking the Mind: A History of Memory*. Cambridge: Cambridge University Press, 2008.

Diagnostic and Statistical Manual of Mental Disorders. Washington, DC: American Psychiatric Association, 1987.

DiCenso, J. *The Other Freud: Religion, Culture and Psychoanalysis*. London/New York: Routledge, 1999.

Dixon, S. L. *Augustine: The Scattered and Gathered Self*. St. Louis, Mo: Chalice Press, 1999.

Dresen, G. *Onschuldfantasieën: Offerzin en heilsverlangen in feminisme en mystiek* [Fantasies of Innocence: Desire for Sacrifice and Longing for Salvation in Feminism and Mysticism]. Nijmegen: Sun, 1990.

Ellison, C. G., J. D. Boardman, D. R. Williams, and J. S. Jackson. "Religious Involvement, Stress and Mental Health: Findings from the 1995 Detroit Area Study." *Social Forces* 80 (2001): 215–49.

Emmons, R. A. *The Psychology of Ultimate Concerns: Motivation and Spirituality in Personality*. New York/London: Guilford, 1999.

Erikson, E. H. "On the Nature of Psychohistorical Evidence." Pp. 113–68 in *Life History and the Historical Moment*. New York: Norton, 1971.

Fabricatore, A. N., P. J. Handal, and L. M. Fenzel. "Personal Spirituality as a Moderator of the Relationship between Stressors and Subjective Well-Being." *Journal of Psychology and Theology* 28 (2000): 221–28.

Feil, E. *Religio. Band I: Die Geschichte eines neuzeitlichen Grundbegriffs vom Frühchristentum bis zur Reformation*. Göttingen: Vandenhoeck & Ruprecht, 1986.

———. *Religio. Band II: Die Geschichte eines neuzeitlichen Grundbegriffs vom Frühchristentum bis zur Reformation (ca. 1540–1620)*. Göttingen: Vandenhoeck & Ruprecht, 1997.

Fitzgerald, T. *The Ideology of Religious Studies*. New York: Oxford University Press, 2000.

———. *Discourse on Civility and Barbarity*. New York: Oxford University Press, 2007.

Gadamer, H.-G. *Hermeneutik I: Wahrheit und Methode. Gründzüge einer philosophischen Hermeneutik*. Tübingen: Mohr, 1960.

Gall, T. L., R. M. Miguez de Renart, and B. Boonstra. "Religious Resources in Long-Term Adjustment to Breast Cancer." *Journal of Psychosocial Oncology* 18 (2000): 21–37.

Ganzevoort, R. R. *Een cruciaal moment: Functie en verandering van geloof in een crisis* [A Crucial Moment: Function and Change of Faith in a Crisis]. Zoetermeer, Neth.: Boekencentrum, 1994.

Gergen, K. J. "Belief as Relational Resource." *The International Journal for the Psychology of Religion* 3, no. 4 (1993): 231–35.

———. "Social Construction and Theology: The Dance Begins." Pp. 3–21 in *Social Constructionism and Theology*. Edited by C. A. M. Hermans, G. Immink, A. de Jong, and J. van der Lans. Leiden: Brill, 2002.

———. "Reflecting On/With My Companions." Pp. 273–89 in C. A. M. Hermans, G. Immink, A. de Jong, and J. van der Lans, eds., *Social Constructionism and Theology*. Leiden: Brill, 2002.

Giesbrecht, N., and I. Sevcik. "The Process of Recovery and Rebuilding among Abused Women in the Conservative Evangelical Subculture." *Journal of Family Violence* 15 (2000): 229–48.

Girgensohn, K. *Der seelische Aufbau des religiösen Erlebens: Eine religionspsychologische Untersuchung auf experimenteller Grundlage*. Leipzig: Hirzel, 1921.

Giorgi, A. "Phenomenology and the Foundations of Psychology." Pp. 281–408 in *Conceptual Foundations of Psychology: Nebraska Symposium on Motivation 1975*. Edited by W. J. Arnold. Lincoln/London: Univ. of Nebraska Press, 1976.

Gomperts, W. J. *De opkomst van de sociale fobie: Een sociologische en psychologische studie naar de maatschappelijke verandering van psychische verschijnselen* [The Rise of Social Phobia: A Sociological and Psychological Study into the Societal Change of Psychic Phenomena]. Amsterdam: Bert Bakker, 1992.

Graham, S., S. Furr, C. Flowers, and M. T. Burke. "Religion and Spirituality in Coping with Stress." *Counseling and Values* 46 (2001): 2–13.

Haußig, H.-M. *Der Religionsbegriff in den Religionen: Studien zum Selbst-und Religionsverständnis in Hinduismus, Buddhismus, Judentum, Islam*. Berlin/Bodenheim: Philo, 1999.

Hermans, H. J. M., and H. J. G. Kempen. *The Dialogical Self: Meaning as Movement*. San Diego, Calif.: Academic Press, 1993.

Hettler, T. R., and L. H. Cohen. "Intrinsic Religiousness as a Stress-Moderator for Adult Protestant Churchgoers." *Journal of Community Psychology* 26 (1998): 597–609.

Hijweege-Smeets, N. H. *Bekering in bevindelijke kring. Een psychologische studie.* [Conversion among Bevindelijken: A Psychological Study.] Kampen, Neth: Kok, 2003.

Hintikka, J., H. Vinaemaki, K. Honkanen, A. Tanskanen, and J. Lehtonen. "Associations between Religious Attendance, Social Support, and Depression in Psychiatric Patients." *Journal of Psychology and Theology* 26 (1998): 351–57.

Hoens, D. J., J. H. Kamstra, and D. C. Mulder. *Inleiding tot de studie van godsdiensten* [Introduction to the Study of Religions] 2nd edition. Kampen, Neth: Kok, 1993.

Hole, G. *Der Glaube bei Depressiven: Religionspsychopathologische und klinisch-statistische Untersuchung*. Stuttgart: Enke, 1977.

Holm, N. G. *Einführung in die Religionspsychologie*. München/Basel: Reinhardt, 1990.

Homans, P. *Jung in Context: Modernity and the Making of a Psychology*. Chicago: University of Chicago Press, 1979.

———. *The Ability to Mourn: Disillusionment and the Social Origins of Psychoanalysis*. Chicago: University of Chicago Press, 1989.

Hood, R. W. Jr. *Dimensions of Mystical Experiences: Empirical Studies and Psychological Links*. Amsterdam/New York: Rodopi, 2001.

Hood, R. W. Jr., P. C. Hill, and B. Spilka. *The Psychology of Religion: An Empirical Approach*. 4th edition. New York: Guilford, 2009.

Hoofdakker, R. H. van den, P. A. Albersnagel, and H. de Cuyper. "Stemmingsstoornissen" [Mood Disorders]. Pp. 166–204 in *Handboek psychopathologie, deel 1* [Handbook of Psychopathology, Part 1]. Edited by W. Vandereycken, C. A. L. Hoogduin and P. M. G. Emmelkamp. Houten, Neth.: Bohn, Stafleu, Van Loghum, 1990.

Jersild, A. "Field Mice and Mustard Seeds: Approaching Spirituality as a Therapeutic Tool." *Eating Disorders* 9 (2001): 267–73.

Jonte-Pace, D. *Speaking the Unspeakable: Religion, Misogyny and the Uncanny Mother in Freud's Cultural Texts*. Berkeley: University of California Press, 2001.

———. *Teaching Freud*. New York: Oxford University Press/American Academy of Religion, 2003.

Jonte-Pace, D., and W. B. Parsons, eds. *Religion and Psychology: Mapping the Terrain. Contemporary Dialogues, Future Prospects*. London/New York: Routledge, 2001.

Joseph, M. "The Effect of Strong Religious Beliefs on Coping with Stress." *Stress Medicine* 14 (1998): 219–24.

Kakar, S. *The Analyst and the Mystic: Psychoanalytic Reflections on Religion and Mysticism*. Chicago: University of Chicago Press, 1991.

Källstad, T. *John Wesley and the Bible: A Psychological Study*. Uppsala: Acta Universitatis Upsaliensis, 1974.

Kippenberg, H. "Was sucht die Religionswissenschaft unter den Kulturwissenschaften?" Pp. 240–75 in *Kulturwissenschaft: Felder einer prozeßorientierten wissenschaftlichen Praxis*. Edited by H. Appelsmeyer and E. Billman-Mahecha. Weilerswist, Ger.: Velbrück, 2001.

Kitayama, S., and D. Cohen. eds. *Handbook of Cultural Psychology*. New York: Guilford, 2007.

Koenig, H. G., L. K. George, J. C. Hays, D. B. Larson, H. J. Cohen, and D. G. Blazer. "The Relationship between Religious Activities and Blood Pressure in Older Adults." *International Journal of Psychiatry in Medicine* 28 (1998): 189–213.

Kohut, H. *The Restoration of the Self*. New York: International Universities Press, 1977.

———. *The Search for the Self*. New York: International Universities Press, 1978.

———. *Self Psychology and the Humanities: Reflections on a New Psychoanalytic Approach*. Edited by C. Strozier. New York: Norton, 1985.

Kraepelin, E. *Psychiatrie: Ein kurzes Lehrbuch für Studierende und Aerzte*. Leipzig: Abel, 1883.

Krause, N., C. G. Ellison, and K. M. Wulff. "Church-Based Support, Negative Interaction and Psychological Well-Being: Findings from a National Sample of Presbyterians." *Journal for the Scientific Study of Religion* 37 (1998): 725–41.

Kripal, J. J. *Kali's Child: The Mystical and the Erotic in the Life and Teaching of Ramakrishna*. Chicago: University of Chicago Press, 1995.

———. *Roads of Excess, Palaces of Wisdom: Eroticism and Reflexivity in the Study of Mysticism*. Chicago/London: University of Chicago Press, 2001.

Lacan, J. *Écrits*. Paris: Seuil, 1966.

Laucken, U. *Sozialpsychologie: Geschichte, Hauptströmungen, Tendenzen*. Oldenburg (Germany): BIS, 1998.

Levin, J. S., and L. M. Chatters. "Religion, Health, and Psychological Well-Being in Older Adults: Findings from Three National Surveys." *Journal of Aging and Health* 10 (1998): 504–31.

Levin, J. S., and R. J. Taylor. "Panel Analysis of Religious Involvement and Well-Being in African Americans: Contemporaneous vs. Longitudinal Effects." *Journal for the Scientific Study of Religion* 37 (1998): 695–709.

Loewenthal, K. M., A. K. MacLeod, V. Goldblatt, G. Lubitsh, and J. D. Valentine. "Comfort and Joy? Religion, Cognition, and Mood in Protestants and Jews Under Stress." *Cognition and Emotion* 14 (2000): 355–74.

MacNeill, W. H. *America, Britain and Russia: Their Co-Operation and Conflict 1941–1946*. London: Oxford University Press, 1953.

Manlowe, J. L. *Faith Born of Seduction: Sexual Trauma, Body Image and Religion*. New York/London: New York University Press, 1995.

McCutcheon, R. T. *Manufacturing Religion: The Discourse on Sui Generis Religion and the Politics of Nostalgia*. New York: Oxford University Press, 2003.

Meissner, W. W. *Ignatius of Loyola: The Psychology of a Saint*. New Haven, Conn.: Yale University Press, 1992.

———. "The Pathology of Beliefs and the Beliefs of Pathology," in *Religion and the Clinical Practice of Psychology*. Edited by E. Shanfransky. Washington, D.C.: American Psychological Association, 1995.

———. *Vincent's Religion: The Search for Meaning*. New York: Lang, 1997.

Meng, W. *Narzißmus und christliche Religion: Selbstliebe Nächstenliebe Gottesliebe*. Zürich: Theologischer Verlag, 1997.

Mitchell, S. *Relational Concepts in Psychoanalysis*. Cambridge, Mass.: Harvard University Press, 1988.

Moosbrugger, H. "Religionspsychologischer Standort Deutschland: Eine Betrachtung aus dem Blickwinkel der wissenschaftlichen Psychologie." Pp. 159–80 in *Religion und Religiosität zwischen Theologie und Psychologie*. Edited by C. Henning and E. Nestler. Frankfurt: Lang, 1998.

Much, N. "Cultural Psychology." Pp. 97–121 in *Rethinking psychology*. Edited by J. A. Smith, R. Harré, and L. van Langenhove. London: SAGE, 1995.

Nestler, E. *Pneuma: Außeralltägliche religiöse Erlebnisse und ihre biographische Kontexte*. Konstanz, Germ.: Universitätsverlag Konstanz, 1998.

Neumann, J. K., and D. S. Chi. "Relationship of Church Giving to Immunological and TxPA Stress Response." *Journal of Psychology and Theology* 27 (1999): 43–51.

North, D. C. *Structure and Change in Economic History*. New York: Norton, 1981.

O'Neill, S. A. "Living with Obsessive-Compulsive Disorder: A Case Study of a Woman's Construction of Self." *Counselling Psychology Quarterly* 12 (1999): 73–86.

Paranjpe, A. C. *Self and Identity in Modern Psychology and Indian Thought*. New York: Plenum Press, 1998.

Pargament, K. I. *The Psychology of Religion and Coping: Theory, Research, Practice*. New York/London: Guilford Press, 1997.

———. *Spiritually Integrated Psychotherapy: Understanding and Addressing the Sacred*. New York: Guilford Press, 2007.

Pargament, K. I., K. I. Maton, and R. E. Hess, eds. *Religion and Prevention in Mental Health: Research, Vision, and Action*. New York: Haworth Press, 1992.

Pargament, K. I., N. Tarakeshwar, C. G. Ellison, and K. M. Wulff. "Religious Coping among the Religious: The Relationships between Religious Coping and Well-Being in a National Sample of Presbyterian Clergy, Elders and Members." *Journal for the Scientific Study of Religion* 40 (2001): 497–513.

Parsons, W. B. *The Enigma of the Oceanic Feeling: Revisioning the Psychoanalytic Theory of Mysticism*. New York/Oxford: Oxford University Press, 1999.

Pfeifer, S., and U. Waelty. "Anxiety, Depression, and Religiosity: A Controlled Clinical Study." *Mental Health, Religion and Culture* 2 (1999): 35–45.

Pfister, O. *Die Frömmigkeit des Grafen Ludwig von Zinzendorf: Ein psychoanalytischer Beitrag zur Kenntnis der religiösen Sublimierungsprozesse und zur Erklärung des Pietismus*. Leipzig: Deuticke, 1910.

———. *Die Legende Sundar Singhs: Eine auf Enthüllungen protestantischer Augenzeugen in Indien gegründete religionspsychologische Untersuchung*. Bern: Haupt, 1926.

———. *Christianity and Fear: A Study in History and in the Psychology and Hygiene of Religion*. London: Allen & Unwin, 1944.

Prager, E. "Observations of Personal Meaning in Sources for Israeli Age Cohorts." *Aging and Mental Health* 2 (1998): 128–36.

Pruyser, P. W. *The Play of Imagination: Toward a Psychoanalysis of Culture*. New York: International Universities Press, 1983.

Popp-Baier, U. *Das Heilige im Profanen: Religiöse Orientierungen im Alltag. Eine qualitative Studie zu religiösen Orientierungen von Frauen aus der charismatisch-evangelischen Bewegung*. Amsterdam: Rodopi, 1998.

Razali, S. M., C. I. Hasanah, K. Aminah, and M. Subramaniam. "Religious-Sociocultural Psychotherapy in Patients with Anxiety and Depression." *Australian and New Zealand Journal of Psychiatry* 32 (1998): 867–72.

Ricoeur, P. *Freud and Philosophy: An Essay on Interpretation*. New Haven, Conn.: Yale University Press, 1965.

Rizzuto, A.-M. *The Birth of the Living God: A Psychoanalytic Study*. Chicago: University of Chicago Press, 1979.

———. *Why Did Freud Reject God: A Psychodynamic Interpretation*. New Haven/London: Yale University Press, 1998.

Sandler, J., C. Dare, and A. Holder. *The Patient and the Analyst*. London: Hogarth Press, 1992.

Schnittker, J. "When Is Faith Enough? The Effects of Religious Involvement on Depression." *Journal for the Scientific Study of Religion* 40 (2001): 393–411.

Schultz, W. T. *Handbook of Psychobiography*. Oxford/New York: Oxford University Press, 2005.

Shaddock, A. J., M. Hill, and C. A. H. van Limbeek. "Factors Associated with Burnout in Workers in Residential Facilities for People with an Intellectual Disability." *Journal for Intellectual and Developmental Disability* 23 (1998): 309–18.

Sharpe, E. J. *Comparative Religion. A History*. Illinois: Open Court, 1986.

Sil, N. P. *Ramakrsna Paramahamsa: A Psychological Profile*. Leiden: Bril, 1991.

Smith, D. *The Rise of Historical Sociology*. Cambridge: Polity, 1991.

Stählin, W. Experimentelle Untersuchungen über Sprachpsychologie und Religionspsychologie. *Archiv für Religionspsychologie* 1 (1914): 117–94.

Stone, L. "History and the Social Sciences in the Twentieth Century." Pp. 3–43 in *The Future of History*. Edited by Ch. Delzell. Nashville: Vanderbilt University Press, 1977.

Sundén, H. *Die Religion und die Rollen: Eine psychologische Untersuchung*. Berlin: Töpelmann, 1959.

Szaluta, J. *Psychohistory: Theory and Practice*. New York: Lang, 1999.

Tek, C., and B. Ulug. "Religiosity and Religious Obsessions in Obsessive-Compulsive Disorder." *Psychiatry Research* 104 (2001): 99–108.

Tigert, L. M. "The Power of Shame: Lesbian Battering as a Manifestation of Homophobia." *Women and Therapy* 23 (2001): 73–85.

Treurniet, N. "Wat is psychoanalyse nu [What is Psychoanalysis Now]?" *Tijdschrift voor Psychotherapie* [Journal of Psychotherapy] 19 (1993): 65–84.

Utsch, M. *Religionspsychologie: Voraussetzungen, Grundlagen, Forschungsüberblick*. Stuttgart: Kohlhammer, 1998.

Valsiner, J. "The Saarbrücken Tradition in Cultural Psychology, and Its Legacy." *Culture & Psychology* 3 (1997): 243–45.

Valsiner, J. and A. Rosa, eds. *Cambridge Handbook of Sociocultural Psychology*. New York: Cambridge University Press, 2007.

Vergote, A. *Guilt and Desire: Religious Attitudes and Their Pathological Derivatives* (trans. M. H. Wood). New Haven, Conn.: Yale University Press, 1978/1988.

———. *Religion, Belief and Unbelief: Psychological Study*. Amsterdam/Leuven: Rodopi/ Leuven University Press, 1983.

———. "Psychoanalyse in contact met religie [Psychoanalysis in Contact with Religion]." Pp. 281–98 in *Psychoanalyse: De mens en zijn lotgevallen* [Psychoanalysis: Man and His Vicissitudes]. Edited by A. Vergote and P. Moyaert. Kapellen, Belgium: De Nederlandsche Boekhandel/Pelckmans, 1988.

———. "What the Psychology of Religion Is and What It Is Not." *The International Journal for the Psychology of Religion* 3 (1993): 73–86.

———. *De sublimatie: Een uitweg uit Freuds impasses* [Sublimation: A Way Out of Freud's Impasses]. Amsterdam: SUN, 1997.

Wit, H. F. de. *De verborgen bloei: over de psychologische achtergronden van spiritualiteit* [The Hidden Flowering: On the Psychological Backgrounds of Spirituality]. Kampen (the Netherlands): Kok, 1993.

Wulff, D. M. *Psychology of Religion: Classic and Contemporary*. 2nd edition. New York: Wiley, 1997.

Young, J. S., C. S. Cashwell, and J. Shcherbakova. "The Moderating Relationship of Spirituality on Negative Life Events and Psychological Adjustement." *Counseling and Values* 45 (2000): 49–57.

Zeegers, W. *Andere tijden, andere mensen: De sociale representatie van identiteit* [Other Times, Other People: The Social Representation of Identity]. Amsterdam: Bert Bakker, 1988.

CHAPTER TWO

When Throne and Altar Are in Danger: Freud, Mourning, and Religion in Modernity

Diane Jonte-Pace

Psychoanalysis and Religion: Asking Questions about Life, Theory, and Culture

What can be said about the complex relationship between psychoanalysis and religion?[1] I've found it useful to address this question from three perspectives: life, theory, and culture. These are inevitably intertwined, but can be separated, at least heuristically. The "life" perspective focuses on the founder of psychoanalysis, examining Freud's Jewish background, the significance of his Catholic nanny, the meaning of his beloved collection of antiquities (the gods and goddesses of the past), the impact of Viennese anti-Semitism, and the sources of his personal rejection of religious belief.

The "theory" perspective leads to the texts of psychoanalysis—into Freud's psychoanalytic writings on religion and the writings of his followers. The best known of Freud's are *The Future of an Illusion*, *Civilization and Its Discontents*, *Moses and Monotheism*, and *Totem and Taboo*, but there are many other shorter and lesser known texts on religion, myth, ritual, and belief. Focusing on these leads toward an inquiry into Freud's career-long fascination with the interpretation and critique of religion, into contemporary applications of psychoanalytic theory to religious phenomena, and into questions about whether newer variants of psychoanalytic theory can offer productive readings of religious phenomena and experience.

The "culture" perspective leads toward other sorts of questions. Here we encounter inquiries into whether, for example, a psychoanalytic or "therapeutic" worldview has replaced an earlier "religious" worldview; questions about the impact of modernization on religion and on the emergence of psychological ideas; questions about the adoption of psychoanalytic methods in religious contexts like pastoral care and counseling; questions about the evaluation (and reevaluation) of religious experience in the Diagnostic and Statistical Manual (DSM); and questions about the ways both religious and psychological practices can support human transformation and healing.

Intense debates have marked the scholarship in each of these three areas. Let me mention just a few of these controversies. Interpreters of the "life" have variously acclaimed or denounced Freud as Christian, as Jewish, as religious, and as anti-religious. Oscar Pfister famously said "a better Christian there never was."[2] Yerushalmi, Klein, Rice, and Bakan find Jewish themes, issues, and moral teachings embedded in every part of his work.[3] Ana-Maria Rizzuto explores and critiques the psychodynamics of his atheism in *Why Did Freud Reject God?*, finding his anti-religious stance deeply neurotic or problematic.[4] Yet Freud, calling himself a "godless Jew," presented his atheism as a sign of psychological health.

Among scholars of the theory as well, opinions are diverse and debates are heated. Some argue that Freud is best seen as a critic of religion who mounted an enlightenment-based attack on religious illusion.[5] Others, such as Ricoeur and Kung, suggest that psychoanalysis can purify religion of infantile or authoritarian elements.[6] Some see the theory as contributing to immorality; others find Freud an exemplary moralist.[7] Some suggest that the antagonism between psychoanalysis and religion is a thing of the past;[8] others still seek reconciliation between religion and psychoanalysis by focusing on developments in object relations theory and self-psychology.[9]

Scholars interested in cultural perspectives exhibit a similarly broad range of views: Peter Gay argues that "we all speak Freud today," and Peter Homans suggests that psychoanalysis is the dominant discourse of modernity.[10] Philip Rieff critiques the "triumph of the therapeutic" in contemporary culture.[11] For Frederick Crews Freud is insignificant, "dead," or dangerous.[12] For James Dittes, Freud's psychological teachings are spiritual, wise, deeply religious; for Paul Vitz, psychoanalysis encourages narcissistic self-absorption and contributes to dangerous anti-religious ideologies.[13] In relation to feminism we find similar debates: for some feminist theorists psychoanalysis is irredeemably sexist; for others it provides an insightful analysis of cultural misogyny.[14]

How can we make sense of these polarized and often vituperative debates? One way to trace a path through the labyrinth of diverse interpretations of life, theory, and culture is to acknowledge that Freud is a complex and often ambivalent thinker. There are "many Freuds," and there are good reasons for the debates over whether Freud is religious or not, Jewish or not, moral or not, and "dead" or not. More significantly, however, these polarized positions can be understood from a larger perspective. It is my position that the relation between psychoanalysis and religion is best viewed in interpretive terms. Psychoanalysis can be seen as an analysis of the way that individuals and cultures mourn the losses associated with religion that modernization brings. It is a discourse that, at times, critiques religion, and at other times, defends religion. At its best, however, it steps back to interpret the impact of the loss of religion through a profound inquiry into the mourning and melancholia produced by the loss of religious foundations and communities.

Masterplot and Counterthesis: Many Freuds

I have argued that Freud develops a dominant argument that is critical of religion at the same time that he develops a thesis that subverts, interrupts, or interprets his dominant argument.[15] I call these positions "masterplot" and "counterthesis." Sometimes the masterplot constructs an anti-religious argument while the counterthesis constructs a religious or quasi-religious argument. This tension between masterplot and counterthesis is not simply a manifestation of an internal contradiction or an anticipation of the polarized debates that would later erupt. Rather, in its most developed form it points toward insightful reflections on or analyses of what it means for a culture to lose its religious foundations. In some texts the counterthesis interrupts the masterplot as if Freud were not fully aware of where the ideas were taking him; in other texts Freud explicitly acknowledges the limitations of the masterplot and hesitantly or playfully develops alternate analyses. At times these alternatives are not fully developed: pointing in provocative new directions, they remain incompletely articulated.

The book containing Freud's most dramatic critique of religion, *The Future of an Illusion*, for example, also contains the counterthesis in the form of a religious subtext. Freud develops, in a sense, a grand religious vision in his often quoted appeal to "Our God Logos." He defines this God as Reason or Rationality, a good translation of the Greek "Logos." I have no doubt that Freud knew that the early Christians described Christ as Logos, Divine Reason, or the "Word" of God. His text thus offers a post-Christian replacement for a Logos theology centered on Christ as Word of God. Here, what I've called the counterthesis is quite consciously developed. In other texts it is more tentatively suggested but not fully investigated. Framing the paradoxes in Freud's work on religion as masterplot and counterthesis provides a way to articulate and tolerate the contradictions and ambiguity we encounter. There is no need to join the battle over whether psychoanalysis is friendly or unfriendly toward religion. It is both. And more significantly, it often moves beyond the toleration of ambiguity, beyond a stance that holds the contradictions in creative tension, and toward interpretation and analysis.

As I've pointed out elsewhere, the interpretive counterthesis is especially visible in three clusters of themes in Freud's work.[16] One cluster involves maternity, mortality, and immortality; another involves Judaism and anti-Semitism; the third involves mourning and melancholia. These clusters are often associated with what Freud called the "uncanny," and with death and loss. The counterthesis frequently exposes the presence of the maternal body in fears and fantasies about loss, death, and the afterlife. *The Future of an Illusion*, for example, describes religious ideas about life after death as a "home in the uncanny" (a "*Heim*" in the "*unheimlich*") at the same time that it describes male anxiety about women's genitals as a fear of an "uncanny home": an "*unheimlich Heim*." In this text maternity and the fantasy of immortality are intertwined; loss, death, and the mother are inseparable.

In this chapter I'll pursue this tension between masterplot and counterthesis in Freud's work as a way of asking what can be said about our primary question, the relation between psychoanalysis and religion. In this process I'll attempt to integrate the three perspectives differentiated above—life, theory, and culture. My thesis is that Freud can best be understood as a theorist who analyzes the loss of religion in cultures and individuals by exploring the dynamics of mourning and melancholia. I'll draw from some of Freud's well-known texts on religion and from some that are rarely brought into conversation with religion. And I'll pursue some trajectories in the work of contemporary psychoanalytic thinkers, Peter Homans, Julia Kristeva, and Judith Butler.

Freud and the Loss of Religion: Defensive Panic, Mourning, and Melancholia

In the 1927 essay called "Fetishism," Freud addressed one of his favorite themes: the denial of the male child in his first encounter with sexual difference. He speculated that the child sees the nude body of his mother but refuses to acknowledge that she does not "possess a penis." This child imagines, in Freud's reconstruction, "This cannot be true . . . if a woman had been castrated then his own possession of a penis was in danger." Speculating further Freud proposed, "in later life a grown man may perhaps experience a similar panic when the cry goes up that Throne and Altar are in danger."[17]

These are typical Freudian speculations. They integrate almost all the classic psychoanalytic themes: a focus on the male child and his incestuous interest in his mother, a focus on the penis and on castration anxiety, and an extension of this body-based anxiety into the cultural arena. If the changes associated with modernity involve challenges to thrones and altars, as they surely do, then Freud's speculations here make both modernity and its discontents oedipal and phallocentric.

Judith Butler has noted that the problem of loss emerges vividly when established narratives begin to falter. If narrative once functioned as a way of containing loss, she asks, what happens when the religious narrative that has underwritten historical development fails?[18] Freud's words provide one suggestive psychodynamic answer to Butler's question (we shall encounter other answers as well). The endangered "throne and altar" are cultural institutions, political and religious structures, whose instability evokes anxiety. Freud portrayed throne and altar as fragile stand-ins for the phallus, at risk through the mere presence of the one whose phallus is perceived as absent: woman/mother. His analysis emphasized the phallocentrism of politics, law, and religion. Freud's interpretation of the panic that emerges when throne and altar are in danger hints at the way that castration anxiety is intertwined with misogyny in the social arena: men get worried about dangers involving women—especially women's bodies—when social institutions or grand narratives are threatened. In Freud's analysis, unconscious misogyny amplifies or underlies the state of panic over religious and social instability.[19]

In his speculations on thrones and altars Freud might have been reflecting on the effects of his own work in promoting religious and social instability and the castration anxiety, misogyny, and anti-Semitism that might follow: he had started writing his most famous critique of religious belief and morality, *The Future of an Illusion*, just a few months prior to writing these words about thrones and altars in the essay on "Fetishism." And he finished *Future* just a few weeks afterwards.[20]

"Fetishism" and *Future* function as paired texts. Freud's treatise on the fragility of faith is closely linked to his interest in the fragility marked by the fetish. The link is theoretical, chronological, and cultural: it includes Freud's religious and cultural context—his Jewishness, his ambivalence about his Jewishness, the Roman Catholic anti-Semitism of Vienna where he lived and worked, the process of secularization that he considered inevitable, and the critique of Christian belief he had mounted in *The Future of an Illusion* and other writings. He knew his work was likely to be criticized, rejected, and dismissed as the work of a "godless Jew." He knew that one of the responses to the social, cultural, and religious changes that made up the process of modernization was a kind of defensive panic and that it was likely to be associated with misogyny and xenophobia. Clearly Freud was not simply critiquing religion by celebrating the dangers to altars associated with modernity, secularism, or assimilationism. Rather, he was interpreting psychological and social reactions to such dangers.

This is not Freud's only foray into this territory. I'll turn to another set of responses to loss and change, and to another set of paired Freudian texts. These texts address a different response to dangers to "thrones" and "altars" in a modernizing world: rather than defensive panic, these texts explore mourning and melancholia. I see these texts as Freudian reflections on the tension between masterplot and counterthesis.

In 1915, Freud wrote several essays on death, loss, and mourning. Among these are "Mourning and Melancholia" and "On Transience." These are intertwined texts: "Mourning" was the more theoretical analysis of loss intended for an audience of fellow psychoanalysts and scientists; "On Transience" focused on the same themes but addressed a more general set of broadly humanistic readers.

In "Mourning and Melancholia" Freud looked at the similarities and differences between the process of grieving or mourning, and its more intense, painful, and pathological variant, known to the medical community of his era as melancholia. Both, he argued, originate with the loss of a loved object or ideal: they are "reactions to the loss of a loved person or to the loss of some abstraction which has taken the place of one: one's country, liberty, an ideal, and so on."[21] His definition was broad: it included cultural losses, losses of ideals like freedom and equality, losses of landed identities associated with emigration, and religious losses.

Melancholia, he argued, differs from mourning in several ways. First, it involves a deeper ambivalence in the relationship to the loved object. The lost object is both loved and hated.[22] Second, this ambivalence is internalized in a struggle resulting in a dual or conflicted sense of self and a loss of "self-regard."[23] Third, while mourning is mainly conscious, melancholia can be primarily unconscious.[24] Fourth, while mourning is typically a reaction to a specific loss, melancholia may be a result of a more general sense of loss, including a feeling of fragmentation from having been "slighted, neglected, or disappointed" many times.[25] Fifth, hinting at the notion of the death instinct he would develop more clearly a few years later, Freud argued that melancholia "overcomes the instinct that compels every living thing to cling to life," although at the same time, it involves an intense fear of death.[26] Finally, he stated, the pain associated with mourning comes to an end, but the pain of melancholia is extended endlessly. Melancholia can be said to be a more extreme, protracted, ambivalent, difficult, painful form of mourning. For the most part, Freud seemed to suggest, mourning, a progressive disinvestment from a lost object, is healthier and in some sense preferable. But there's an ambivalence in his stance. I'll come back to this point.

Let us turn to "On Transience," a short essay composed at the request of the Goethe Society in Berlin for a commemorative volume issued in 1916. The volume was called *Das Land Goethes* (*Goethe's Country*). It contained contributions from well-known artists, writers, and poets. In his essay, Freud discussed, less systematically but more poetically and dramatically, the same material presented in "Mourning and Melancholia." He framed an analysis of two distinct reactions to loss within a personal narrative and an account of a cultural tragedy. He referred even more directly to the cultural context hinted at in "Mourning and Melancholia," by alluding explicitly to the tensions between assimilationism and traditionalism for Jews in Germanic culture. He elaborated on the melancholic reaction to loss by introducing the themes of the refusal to mourn and the demand for immortality. Here he seemed (and I emphasize *seemed)* to privilege mourning over melancholia by critiquing the melancholic response. But as we shall see, the thread of ambivalence appears here too.

Freud began the essay for *Goethe's Country* with an idyllic memory of a lovely stroll through the countryside: "Not long ago, I went on a summer walk through a smiling countryside in the company of a taciturn friend and of a young but already famous poet."[27] This peaceful walk was quickly disturbed: Freud's friends found themselves unable to feel pleasure in the beauty of the landscape. The poet "admired the beauty of the scene" but "felt no joy in it." Disturbed "by the thought that all this beauty was fated to extinction . . . all that he would otherwise have loved and admired seemed to him to be shorn of its worth by the transience which was its doom."[28]

Freud offered an interpretation of his companions' dark attitude: "the idea that all this beauty was transient was giving these sensitive minds a foretaste of mourning over its decease." He described the reaction of his friends as a "revolt . . . against mourning"[29] and a "demand for immortality."[30] He added, "since the mind instinctively recoils from anything that is painful, they felt their enjoyment of beauty interfered with by thoughts of its transience."[31] Transience and mourning are thus posed as oppositional to immortality and stability or stasis. This description of the rejection of transience and change, the demand for immortality and the revolt against mourning remains consistent with "Mourning and Melancholia," but it extends the analysis Freud had written a few months earlier: the troubled friends experience a withdrawal of libido from the object (the countryside), a premature, anticipatory grief, and an insistence on the immortality of the object.

Then he shifted the narrative from his friends' melancholic revolt against mourning. He offered what seems to be a superior alternative, an example of good mourning: he argued that we must accept "the transience of all things." He disputed the poet's view that the "transience of what is beautiful involves any loss in its worth." The impermanence of beauty, and of life itself, should neither diminish the beauty nor obstruct our experience of pleasure: the inevitability of death and loss increases the value of the objects we love. To experience this is to be able to mourn; the ability to mourn makes possible the ability to love, to feel pleasure, to enjoy beauty.

Freud situated his account of the walk with the poet and his theory of transience in the context of the war occurring in Europe as he wrote the essay. In 1915, he wrote: "my conversation with the poet took place in the summer before the war. A year later war broke out. . . . It destroyed not only the beauty of the countryside through which it passed . . . but it also shattered our pride in the achievements of our civilization . . . and our hopes of a final triumph over the differences between nations and races."[32] The war led, in other words, to a dramatic encounter with the transience of valued objects and ideals. While deeply saddened by the loss of much that he valued, Freud remained hopeful. Grieving over the loss of what had perished, he noted that the period of mourning would eventually end. He looked forward to the cessation of mourning and the subsequent creation of new achievements, structures, and ideals: "when once the mourning is over . . . we shall build up again all that war has destroyed, and perhaps on firmer ground and more lastingly than before."[33]

In his remarks on the dashed hopes of a final triumph over "differences between nations and races" there may be hints of the hope for an end to tensions associated with anti-Semitism. Writing to the broad audience of readers of the Goethe Society's volume, Freud may have been expressing an assimilationist desire to maintain an enlightened or rational sense of Jewish identity while, at the same time, unreservedly accepting the valuable parts of Germanic culture.[34] His analysis of the tensions between his own position and the reactions of his hiking companions can be read as an account of the tensions between German and Jew, between anti-assimilationism and assimilationism among Jews, or even as an account of conflicting internal desires.

This text reflects Freud's careful observations of his own conscious and unconscious processes during a period of anticipated and actual loss. This text and its companion text were intricately overdetermined. Both were written as Freud approached his sixtieth year—he believed (erroneously, of course) that he had only a year or two to live. They were written shortly after his infamous break with Jung, an experience of disillusionment and loss nearly equivalent to the death of a beloved friend. They were written during a war when he feared for the survival of his two conscripted sons as well as for the survival of psychoanalysis itself. In addition, these texts were written during the period that has been called a "modern crisis of culture" when codes of gender identity and religious identity in Vienna had undergone dramatic shifts. These texts represent both a documentation of a period of grief and loss and a profound meditation on that process of loss.[35] To borrow Freud's own vocabulary of 1927, they represent analyses of dangers to "Throne and Altar."

This short essay expresses a nearly Buddhist acknowledgment of the impermanence of all things. And it provides a cultural and personal framework for Freud's reflections on loss. By situating his speculations in the context of the walk with his friends, the war, and the shattering of pride in the achievements of civilization, Freud gave specificity to the remarks he made in the companion text about mourning as a reaction to "the loss of a loved person or to the loss of some abstraction which has taken the place of one." The text also articulates a deep ambivalence—by giving his companions—the taciturn friend and the poet—the melancholic role, and giving himself the mourning role, he explored the two positions with depth, empathy, and insight.

Explicitly he identified himself as the progressive, optimistic mourner, rather than the resistant melancholic. But his friends may represent, in a sense, not only his actual hiking companions (Rainer Maria Rilke and Lou Andreas Salome, according to Von Unwerth[36]), but also his own melancholic self. As I hinted earlier, an ambivalence appeared in "Mourning and Melancholia," as he alternately privileged one stance, then the other. There he stated that melancholics have remarkable abilities to understand the self, the other, and the world. The melancholic is "like Hamlet." The melancholic has a "keener eye for the truth than other people" and "has come pretty near to understanding himself."[37] Reflecting a widespread trope in the Western literary and philosophical tradition of the melancholy but insightful, poetic, or artistic soul (Schiessari 1992), Freud pondered, "we only wonder why a man has to be ill before he can be accessible to a truth of this kind."[38] By describing the melancholic in terms of his "keener eye for the truth," Freud, who surely saw himself as one with a keen eye for truth, expresses a partial and subtle identification with the melancholic poet. There's an interesting tension between his descriptions, in both of these texts, of the preferred path of the healthy mourner and the wise, self-knowing, but unhealthy path of the poetic melancholic.

Freud's question about why such truth and self-understanding is particularly accessible to the melancholic is reminiscent of the iconic question he posed to pastor and psychoanalyst Oskar Pfister in 1918: "Why was it that none of all the pious ever discovered psychoanalysis? Why did it have to wait for a completely godless Jew?"[39] Freud's remarks in "Mourning and Melancholia" reflect a notion of the Jew—particularly the secular or assimilating Jew—as one with both a keener eye for truth and a melancholic disposition. In addition, these remarks hint at an association we will examine shortly: the loss of religion and the discovery of psychoanalysis. Creativity and discovery, we'll suggest, emerge out of loss, mourning, and melancholia.[40]

The ambivalence here between mourning and melancholia reflects some of the tension between masterplot and counterthesis: Freud cannot simply be situated as one who celebrates the social changes associated with the loss of religions and religious ideals. Rather he is better viewed as an interpreter of those losses. The ambivalence and the interpretive stance evident in his writings can also be traced in the work of contemporary psychoanalytic thinkers Peter Homans, Judith Butler, and Julia Kristeva who offer thoughtful psychoanalytic commentaries on the psychological and cultural responses to the loss of religion. These commentaries provide a way of linking life, culture, and theory in asking about the relation of psychoanalysis and religion.

Contemporary Psychoananalytic Theories of Loss: Mourning or Melancholia?

Peter Homans has argued that "Psychoanalysis arose as the result of a long historical mourning process . . . for lost symbols and the communal wholeness they organize in the West."[41] His theory, developed in *The Ability to Mourn*, *Jung in Context*, and *Symbolic Loss*, suggests that the rapid and traumatic loss of "common cultures" in the context of modernization leads to social individualism and psychological disorientation. Those who are truly "able to mourn" are capable of a kind of introspection that permits an understanding and articulation of this social and psychological disorientation. Homans calls this "introspective analytic access."

In Homans's view, Freud's psychoanalytic ideas emerged out of the introspection and individuation that followed his loss and mourning of traditional communal and religious structures. He argues that Freud developed a remarkable ability to observe and recount the processes and contents of the unconscious, and that his theory of the mind was based on his introspective investigations of the unconscious, initiated by the processes of loss and mourning. Psychoanalysis introduced a systematic method that, for some, escalated this process by further promoting introspection, individuation, and a psychological worldview in the West.

Homans thus finds Freud's psychoanalytic formulations emerging directly from the loss of religion in the context of modernization, from his loss of a sense of a common culture, from his remarkable "ability to mourn," and from his introspective probes into his own mourning psyche. Other theorists and historians have developed related arguments. Le Rider, for example, suggests that while a whole generation of Viennese modernists—Freud, Wittgenstein, Herzl, Schnitzler, and others—lived through the experience of "the fading and loss of traditions," especially religious traditions,[42] Freud was the figure most capable of observing and theorizing the experience of that grief and loss. Schorske argues similarly that Freud functioned as both a culture breaker and a culture maker within the context of European modernity. Homans is thus not alone in making this sort of argument about Freud, loss, religion, and culture. But the Homans thesis is unique in its analytic stance and its linkage of life, culture, and theory. To put this thesis into terminology we borrowed earlier from Freud, we might say that Freud successfully, and without castration anxiety or defensive fetishistic panic, encountered dangers to "Throne and Altar," articulating how we react consciously and unconsciously to those dangers. It was Freud's ability to mourn the losses of symbolic thrones and altars, and to observe and describe that process, that gave rise to the creative ideas constituting psychoanalysis.

In a sense, we might say, extending Homans's thesis, that all moderns (or postmoderns or late moderns) are in mourning. Butler's question about the failure of narratives that contain loss can be answered more broadly: all of us have experienced symbolic loss, which we may or may not be able to mourn successfully. Psychology and individualism are products of the more or less successful mourning of those losses. The shift that gave rise to psychoanalysis can be seen as one piece of a larger (mournful or melancholic) sociohistorical shift that continues to shape us today.[43]

In Homans's view, Freud was a masterful mourner of personal, religious, and social losses, and a masterful observer of the process of mourning. And, most significantly, for Homans, Freud was able to transform his mourning into a culturally significant creative product, psychoanalysis. Freud's question to Pfister mentioned above—"Why was it that none of the pious ever discovered psychoanalysis?"—is relevant in this context. Homans's answer, of course, would be "Precisely! The loss of religion led to mourning, and the mourning to introspective probes which in turn led to the discovery of psychoanalysis." I find Homans's thesis convincing and compelling. Yet there are some threads missing in this tapestry. Let me try to trace these threads, starting with a noticeable gap in Freud's personal ability to mourn. We've seen one of these threads in Freud's ambivalence about whether to privilege melancholia or mourning. Another can be seen in the dramatic contrast between Freud's complex and insightful interpretations of the psychodynamics of loss in the texts of 1915 and his numb response to another loss—the death of his own mother.

Freud's mother lived to age ninety-five. She died in 1930, just nine years before Freud's own death. When she died, Freud wrote to his friend and colleague Ernest Jones. He said "I will not disguise the fact that my reaction to this event has . . . been a curious one . . . there is no saying what effects such an experience may produce in deeper layers, but on the surface I can detect only two things: an increase in personal freedom, since it was always a terrifying thought that she might come to hear of my death;[44] and secondly, the satisfaction that at last she has achieved the deliverance for which she had earned a right after such a long life. No grief otherwise."[45] He reiterated the phrase "no grief" in a letter to another friend a day later: "No pain, no grief, which is probably to be explained by the circumstances, the great age and the end of the pity we had felt at her helplessness."[46]

These statements of his lack of grief were, of course, in letters, not in theoretical texts. But Freud's reiterated description of his reaction—"no grief"—may point toward something deeper. It echoes a very similar remark in *Beyond the Pleasure Principle* (1920), where he described a son's reaction to the death of *another* mother. This is the child who developed the famous game of "*fort*" and "*da*," here and gone, presence and absence, or disappearance and return, involving a spool and a string. He wrote, "When this child was five and three-quarters, his mother died. Now that she was really 'gone' . . . the little boy showed *no signs of grief*."[47] The child was Freud's grandson; the mother his daughter Sophie. Although Freud grieved deeply at his daughter's death, both he and his grandson reacted to the deaths of their own mothers with "no grief."

Grief is the same word translated as "mourning" in "Mourning and Melancholia," *Trauer*. By saying that he experienced no grief, "*kein Trauer*," Freud is saying that he did not mourn. We've seen that among the characteristics of melancholia are the refusal to mourn (a refusal of "*Trauer*"), and a demand for immortality. Is Freud's lack of grief at the death of his mother a sign that his reaction is melancholic rather than mournful? Is this a demand for maternal immortality? I've argued elsewhere that unconscious desires for immortality are closely linked to fears and fantasies of unions with mothers. Freud's description of melancholia in 1915 provides an uncannily accurate portrayal of his reaction many years later to his own mother's death.[48]

Some critics, like Ana-Maria Rizzuto, have found Freud's expression of "*kein Trauer*" pathological, misogynist, indicative of serious problems in his early relationship with his mother, and symptomatic of problems in his theories of psyche and culture.[49] In my view, however, Freud's response to his mother's death, rather than being idiosyncratic, pathological, and misogynist, might represent a widespread experience. Is there a sense in which we're all melancholics in relation to mothers? Melancholia is said to involve many experiences of separation from and temporary losses of the mother, many experiences of having been "slighted, neglected, or disappointed." What maternal relation escapes these separations or disappointments? Other markings of melancholia seem to apply as well: deep ambivalence and anxieties about death and immortality,[50] for example. Is it possible that the difficulty in mourning the mother is virtually ubiquitous, and that it is linked to the "dangers to throne and altar" that Freud outlined in the essay on the fetish?[51]

Freud, Kristeva, and Butler may be able to help us think through this riddle. Their work suggests that we cannot fully mourn our mothers because we must not fully identify with them—and that our melancholic stance toward maternal loss shapes our experience of other losses as well, the religious losses constituting modernity in particular. In Freud's formulation mourning results in the formation of an identification with the lost object. In this process internal psychic structures are created or built up as memorials to lost objects. Identifications are established "with the abandoned object" through the growth of new psychic structures.[52] Freud's rhetoric describing this process is poetic: "the shadow of the object falls upon the ego."[53] These identifications constructed out of shadows and absences lead to the growth of structures within the ego, and to changes in personality. In this process, Freud explained, "an object which was lost is set up again inside the ego . . . an object cathexis is replaced by an identification."[54] The resulting identifications and structures are the basis of what we know as character: "this kind of substitution has a great share in determining the form taken by the ego . . . it makes an essential contribution towards building up (of) 'character.'"[55] Absences become presences, shadows become structures, not unlike the healing that occurs through the creation of scar tissue—wounds become scars, which are the marks or memories of losses. In Freud's analysis the process is complete and closure is attained when the lost other is recreated as character or ego structure through this identificatory process: the ego acts as a memorial or monument or scar covering the wounds that created its structures.[56]

Freud's theory of mourning as identification suggests that to successfully mourn the mother would be to identify with her, to become her. Julia Kristeva argues that we cannot identify with or become the mother because the separation from her is necessary for the birth and continuity of the self.[57] The "abjection" of the maternal, in her terminology, is crucial to the formation of selfhood.[58] For Kristeva the abjection of the mother inevitably involves an abhorrence of the feminine. It sets up an inevitable misogyny or matriphobia that may remain deeply unconscious. In a Kristevan reading, Freud's inability to grieve or mourn the mother is an inability we all share. The melancholic response to the separation from the mother is part of what gives rise to the self.[59] Judith Butler takes Kristeva's point further. She argues that it is "the incorporative logic of melancholia that founds the very possibility of the ego and its psychic topography. Melancholia is the precondition for both the ego and the work of mourning. It creates a realm of traces open to signification."[60] Butler's and Kristeva's formulations lead to a melancholic conclusion: In some arenas we cannot reach the closure or resolution that a "good mourner" reaches. We are all melancholic mourners of lost mothers and lost religions, with a melancholia that resists closure, identification, and stable internal character development, a melancholia that remains ambivalent, conflicted, and unresolved.

Yet this unresolved melancholic ambivalence need not entrap and imprison. Eng and Kazanjian, editors of *Loss*, reflecting on the tension in Freud's thought between mourning and melancholia, defend melancholia.[61] They suggest that in mourning, the past is dead, while in melancholia the past remains alive. They defend melancholia as a continuous and creative engagement with loss and its remains, arguing that a sustained engagement with the remains of loss may be necessary to creative engagement with the future.[62] Like Kristeva, they see modernity as inevitably melancholic, yet they also discover in melancholia a valuable creativity, toleration of ambiguity, and sense of continuity with the past.

Returning to Psychoanalysis and Religion

Let us return to the question with which we began, the question of the relation of psychoanalysis and religion. We've seen that Freud cannot be simply viewed as a critic of religion, nor simply be reconceptualized as a defender of religion. Rather, Freud is better envisioned as a thinker with a deep ambivalence about religion and its loss, an ambivalence that is both personal and theoretical. His ambivalence is expressed in conflicting statements and formulations: he constructs a masterplot critical of religion and a counterthesis that defends religion. More importantly, however, the counterthesis tolerates the ambiguity and moves on to interpret the loss of religion, generating a theory of how we mourn and fail to mourn in relation to "dangers to altars." Freud's own contradictory positions on religion can best be framed as an analysis of how individuals and cultures respond to the loss of religion: Freud's readings of dangers to thrones and altars, and his analysis of transience, mourning, and melancholia, articulate interpretations of the psychological and cultural effects of religious loss and change, interpretations that are carried forward by contemporary psychoanalytic thinkers like Homans, Kristeva, and Butler.

Homans finds Freud a successful mourner and a successful guide through the unconscious terrain of loss, grief, and creativity recovery. He sees psychoanalysis as a theory of and from mourning, i.e., a theory that interprets the experience of mourning, and a theory that emerged out of the experience of loss and mourning. Kristeva's perspective focuses more on melancholia. She shows that Freud was sometimes unable to mourn. Her work suggests that he may have been a better mourner of losses in the social and religious arena of modernity than he was of mothers. In a Kristevan reading, Freud himself is melancholic, and psychoanalysis becomes a theory of and from melancholia.

A focus on life, theory, and culture attentive to paired texts like "Fetishism" and *Future*, or "Transience" and "Mourning," thus allows us to see the relation of psychoanalysis and religion not as a story of polarized debates but as a story of loss and the interpretation of that loss. Entrapment in polarized debates over the value or danger of psychoanalysis, entrapment in controversies over whether psychoanalysis is a critique of religion or a defense of religion is, in a sense, a symptom of the defensive panic that "a grown man may experience" in Freud's essay on fetishism. And this defensive panic in the face of dangers to "throne and altar" is, in essence, the inability to mourn religion. The capacity to tolerate ambiguity, on the other hand, is a capacity on the cusp between mourning and melancholia, both of which, in my view, are adaptive and non-pathological. Psychoanalysis is best understood not as a cultural product that challenges, competes with, or destroys cultural products like religion, but as a method, a practice, a process that articulates how we mourn or how we are melancholic, a process that aids us in tolerating the ambiguity associated with loss and change, a process that carries us toward the creativity and insight that can be the product of successful engagement with loss, whether mournful or melancholic.

This reading of psychoanalysis is echoed by Roy Schafer in a now classic essay, "The Psychoanalytic Vision of Reality."[63] Schafer describes psychoanalysis as the integration of a tragic and an ironic vision. The vision is tragic in seeing human experience pervaded by ambiguities, unanswerable questions, inescapable conflicts. In this vision the past cannot be undone, wishes and desires remain unfulfilled. Yet, at the same time, psychoanalysis is ironic in bringing a sense of detachment from the tragic, a capacity for reflective adaptation and deliberative acceptance. Schafer's description of the psychoanalytic tragic vision and its ironic amelioration, in my view, embodies both the mournful and the melancholic positions. The tragic vision is melancholic; the ironic echoes Freud's analysis of mourning. And both positions are expressed in turn in one of Freud's final essays, "Analysis: Terminable or Interminable."[64] The interminable is the tragic/melancholic position; the terminable is the ironic/mournful position. The ambiguity between the two—terminable and interminable, tragic and ironic—leaves us on the cusp between mourning and melancholia. Thus psychoanalysis not only maps the process of mourning and melancholia, offering a theory of how we respond to loss, but it also embodies those processes in its vision of reality: mourning becomes psychoanalysis.

Mourning and melancholia both permeate our culture in powerful ways today. Attempts to give voice to a deep sense of the losses that have shaped our culture in the past century are evident not only in the work of the psychoanalysts but also in the work of architects, filmmakers, novelists, and artists. It is my view that these culture-makers, to use a term of Peter Homans,[65] are asking the kinds of questions that Freud posed in his remarks on dangers to thrones and altars. Nichanian states it clearly: "there is no art without mourning."[66] The work of these artists and culture-makers provides a deeper answer to Butler's query about the absence of narratives that "contain" loss.

Containing Loss in Narrative

A recent film, Pedro Almodovar's *Talk to Her*, illustrates well this cultural meditation on losses, mourners, and melancholics by offering a narrative that "contains loss." In this film two men mourn the women they love. Both women are comatose as a result of traumatic injuries: both are in the uncanny realm between the living and the dead. Both men, we learn, are also mourners of earlier losses. Benigno mourns his mother; Marco mourns a woman he loved and lost: he cries whenever he sees or hears beautiful art or music, because he cannot share it with her.

The story is complex and nuanced. The mourner and the melancholic slide into one another. But Benigno is primarily a melancholic and Marco a mourner. Benigno's melancholia leads him to try to merge with his beloved—through sex, through fantasies, and through death.[67] Marco is able to live, to leave behind both of the lost women he mourns, and to love someone new. He is finally able to experience cultural forms of beauty without tears. And he takes on the identity of Benigno: mourning merges into melancholia. The film is self-reflexive: it asks how culture, art, film, and silent/unconscious women function as narratives that "contain loss" and to transform melancholia and mourning into new creations.

In many ways Almodovar's film reflects the themes we've addressed here: His alternating differentiation and merging of mourning and melancholia echoes Freud's own speculations. His questions about the role of cultural loss—and of cultural creativity as response to loss—echo Peter Homans's questions. His location of the source of Benigno's melancholia in the loss of the mother echoes Kristeva's insights. Much of Almodovar's work is about how we find meaning in the midst of the losses that characterize modernity. Many of his earlier films, like *Dark Habits* (1983) and *Matador* (1986), were explicitly anti-religious and politically/sexually subversive. His later work, *Live Flesh* (1997), *All About My Mother* (1999), and *Talk to Her* (2002) turned toward religious and existential themes—life and death, resurrection and forgiveness, love, meaning, and morality. Without explicitly using the vocabulary of psychoanalysis, his filmic questions represent a contemporary meditation on how we respond to "thrones and altars in danger."[68]

Notes

1. This chapter extends ideas originally published in my *Speaking the Unspeakable: Misogyny, Religion, and the Uncanny Mother in Freud's Cultural Texts* (Berkeley: University of California Press, 2001). I am grateful to the University of California Press for permission to develop these ideas here.

2. Heinrich Meng and Ernst Freud, eds. *Psychoanalysis and Faith: The Letters of Sigmund Freud and Oskar Pfister*. Trans. Eric Mosbacher (New York: Basic Books, 1963).

3. Yosef Yerushalmi, *Freud's Moses: Judaism Terminable and Interminable* (New Haven, Conn.: Yale University Press, 1991); Dennis Klein, *Jewish Origins of the Psychoanalytic Movement* (Chicago: University of Chicago Press, 1985); Emmanuel Rice, *Freud and Moses: The Long Journey Home* (Albany: State University of New York Press, 1990); David Bakan, *Sigmund Freud and the Jewish Mystical Tradition* (Boston: Beacon, 1958).

4. Ana-Maria Rizzuto, *The Birth of the Living God: A Psychoanalytic Study* (Chicago: University of Chicago Press, 1979).

5. Peter Gay, *Godless Jew: Freud, Atheism, and the Meaning of Psychoanalysis* (New Haven, Conn.: Yale University Press, 1987).

6. Paul Ricoeur, *Freud and Philosophy* (New Haven, Conn.: Yale University Press, 1970); Hans Kung, *Freud and the Problem of God* (New Haven, Conn.: Yale University Press, 1990).

7. Paul Vitz, *Psychoanalysis as Religion: The Cult of Self-Worship* (Grand Rapids, Mich.: Eerdmans, 1994); Philip Rieff, *Triumph of the Therapeutic* (New York: Harpers, 1966).

8. Ernest Wallwork, "Contemporary Perspectives on an Old Antagonism," in *Psychoanalysis and Religion*, ed. Joseph Smith (Baltimore, Md.: Johns Hopkins University Press, 1989).

9. Rizzuto, *Birth of the Living God*; Celia Brickman, *Aboriginal Populations in the Mind* (New York: Columbia University Press, 2003).

10. Peter Gay, "Psychoanalyst Sigmund Freud," *Time* 153, no. 12 (29 March 1999): 64–91; Peter Homans, *The Ability to Mourn: Disillusionment and the Social Origins of Psychoanalysis* (Chicago: University of Chicago Press, 1989).

11. Rieff, *Triumph of the Therapeutic*.

12. Frederick Crews, ed. *Unauthorized Freud: Doubters Confront a Legend* (New York: Penguin, 1998).

13. James Dittes, "Teaching Freud's Teachings," in *Teaching Freud*, ed. Diane Jonte-Pace (New York: Oxford, 2003), 258–70; Vitz, *Psychoanalysis as Religion*.

14. Mari Jo Buhle, *Feminism and Its Discontents: A Century of Struggle with Psychoanalysis* (Cambridge, Mass.: Harvard University Press, 1998); Juliet Mitchell, *Psychoanalysis and Feminism: Freud, Reich, Laing, and Women* (New York: Random, 1974).

15. Jonte-Pace, *Speaking the Unspeakable*.

16. Jonte-Pace, *Speaking the Unspeakable*.

17. Sigmund Freud, *The Standard Edition (SE) of the Complete Psychological Works of Sigmund Freud*, 24 vols., trans. and ed. by James Strachey (London: Hogarth Press, 1953–1974), 21: 153.

18. Judith Butler, "Afterward: After Loss, What Then?" in *Loss: The Politics of Mourning*, eds. David L. Eng and David Kazanjian (Berkeley: University of California Press, 2003), 467–74: 469.

19. Freud extends this analysis in other texts. In a footnote to a 1909 text he suggested, "the castration complex is the deepest unconscious root of anti-Semitism: even in the nursery boys hear that a Jew has something cut off his penis . . . this gives them a right to despise Jews. And there is no stronger unconscious root for the sense of superiority over women" ("Analysis of a Phobia in a Five Year Old Boy," *SE* 10: 36 n. 1).

20. *The Future of an Illusion* was begun in the spring of 1927, finished by September, and published in November 1927 (*SE* 21: 3); "Fetishism" was finished in August 1927 and published almost immediately (*SE* 21: 149).

21. Freud, *SE* 14: 243.

22. Freud, *SE* 14: 256.

23. Freud, *SE* 14: 246.
24. Freud, *SE* 14: 245.
25. Freud, *SE* 14: 251.
26. Freud, *SE* 14: 246.
27. Freud, *SE* 14: 305.
28. Freud, *SE* 14: 305.
29. Freud, *SE* 14: 306.
30. Freud, *SE* 14: 305.
31. Freud, *SE* 14: 305–6.
32. Freud, *SE* 14: 307.
33. Freud, *SE* 14: 307.
34. See Jacques Le Rider, *Modernity and Crises of Identity: Culture and Society in Fin de Siècle Vienna*, trans. Rosemary Morris (New York: Continuum, 1993), 205.
35. Peter Homans, "We (Not-So) Happy Few: Symbolic Loss and Mourning in Freud's Psychoanalytic Movement and the History of Psychoanalysis," *Psychoanalysis and History* 1 (1998): 69–86; Peter Homans, ed. *Symbolic Loss: The Ambiguity of Mourning at Century's End* (Charlottesville: University of Virginia Press, 2000).
36. Matthew Von Unwerth, *Freud's Requiem: Mourning, Memory, and the Invisible History of a Summer Walk*. New York: Penguin, 2005.
37. Freud, *SE* 14: 246.
38. Freud, *SE* 14: 246.
39. Meng and Freud, *Psychoanalysis and Faith*, 63.
40. A melancholic position may be evident in other sites in the correspondence with Pfister as well, especially if we focus on the denial of transience/impermanence and the insistence on immortality as key markers of melancholia. Freud's words to Pfister: "My creation will live forever" (Meng and Freud 1963) and his desire, expressed in "The Question of Lay Analysis," to create a social state for a secular cure of souls (Freud, *SE* 20), hint at this aspect of melancholia. I am indebted to Bill Parsons for this observation.
41. Homans, *The Ability to Mourn*, 4, 13.
42. Le Rider, *Modernity and Crises of Identity*, 294.
43. Eric Santner, in an analysis of the "crisis of investiture" (by which he means disruptions in social roles and status), from which both the Nazi "final solution" and the paranoid and messianic fantasies of Judge Daniel Paul Schreber (Schreber 1903) emerged, suggests that Freud's psychoanalytic theory represented an alternate reconstruction of this crisis: Freud was particularly sensitive to the crises and disruptions of modernity (Santner 1996: 17). Not unlike Homans, Santner sees fascism and psychoanalysis as opposite responses to the crises invoked by modernity.
44. The "terror" over the thought that his mother "might come to hear of (his) death" was shared by other members of Freud's family. According to letters between Freud and his nephew Samuel in 1925, Amalie Freud could not tolerate hearing about any death in the family. Through a familial conspiracy of silence she was

protected from the knowledge of several deaths over many years. Family members explained: "We made a secret of all the losses in the family" (Clark 1980: 481).

45. Ernest Jones, *Sigmund Freud, Life and Work.* 3 vols. (London: Hogarth, 1953–1957), 162. Poor health prevented his attendance at the funeral. His daughter Anna had become his emissary to public events and ceremonies.

46. Jones, *Sigmund Freud* (1957), 162.

47. Freud, *SE* 18: 16.

48. Donald Capps suggests that C. G. Jung and Erik Erikson (along with psychologist William James and phenomenologist Rudolf Otto) experienced traumatic separations from their mothers which led to lifelong struggles with melancholia (Capps 1997). This melancholic disposition, in Capps's view, directed these men inexorably toward a psychological, introspective, and highly individualized encounter with religious ideas. Extending Capps's thesis, one might expect to find a similar relationship with the mother in Freud's case, since Freud clearly shared this approach to religion with these four thinkers. Freud's response to his mother's death would seem to confirm this application of Capps's thesis to Freud's case. Capps's provocative analysis might be expanded further into an analysis of cultural change in modernity: we might ask what sorts of social changes in the late nineteenth and early twentieth centuries influenced these men and these mothers, leading to the emergence of these introspective individualized theories of religion.

49. Rizzuto, *Birth of the Living God.*

50. Freud, *SE* 14: 251.

51. Freud's discussion of the misogynist panic experienced by "grown men" in the encounter with dangers to throne and altar would seem to suggest that misogyny is a male reaction to cultural instability. Others have pursued the same line of thought: Margarete Mitscherlich (1985) has argued that the sources of xenophobia and anti-Semitism lie specifically in castration anxiety and that men are therefore primarily responsible for prejudice and racism of all types. There may be some truth to this in a world where power is phallic and men are the keepers of that power. But Freud's speculations on melancholia challenge this formulation. His discussions in "Mourning and Melancholia" and "On Transience" suggest that another response to loss lies deeper than castration anxiety; that this response is common to both women and men; and that this response involves a memory of necessary but traumatic separations or "abjections" from a mother who cannot be fully mourned. If melancholia in response to a lost mother is virtually universal, and if melancholia and misogyny are closely related, then misogyny is not simply a male failure, because mourning the mother is a problem for all of us. Misogyny may be deeply embedded in our psyches as well as our cultures. Transformation will be impossible unless we can begin to acknowledge our complicity in these patterns.

52. Freud, *SE* 14: 249.

53. Freud, *SE* 14: 249.

54. Freud, "Ego and the Id," *SE* 19: 28.

55. Freud, *SE* 19: 28–29.

56. This can happen culturally as well as psychologically. Maya Lin's design for the Vietnam Veterans Memorial in Washington D.C. becomes an elaborate scar over the wound of the losses associated with Vietnam: "The character of the [community] contains the history of those [lost] object choices," as Freud put it ("Ego and the Id," *SE* 19: 29, my brackets). We become, psychologically and culturally, what we have lost; the shadow of the lost object becomes the content and structure of the ego (see Homans and Jonte-Pace 2006).

57. Julia Kristeva, *Powers of Horror: An Essay on Abjection*, trans. Leon S. Roudiez (New York: Columbia University Press, 1982).

58. Diane Jonte-Pace, "Julia Kristeva and the Psychoanalytic Study of Religion: Rethinking Freud's Cultural Texts," in *Religion, Society, and Psychoanalysis: Readings in Contemporary Theory*, ed. Janet Liebman Jacobs and Donald Capps (Boulder: Westview, 1997), 240–68; Diane Jonte-Pace, "'Legitimation of Hatred or Inversion into Love': Religion in Kristeva's Re-Reading of Freud," *Journal of Research in the Social Scientific Study of Religion* 10 (1999): 17–35.

59. My own mother suffers from Alzheimer's disease. There's a sense in which this lack of closure is very personal for me: she's here but not here; she's present but absent; she's both *fort* and *da*, to use Freud's vocabulary.

60. Butler, Judith, cited in *Loss: The Politics of Mourning*, eds. David L. Eng and David Kazanjian (Berkeley: University of California Press, 2003), 4.

61. Eng and Kazanjian, *Loss*, 4.

62. Eng and Kazanjian, *Loss*, 4.

63. Roy Schafer, "The Psychoanalytic Vision of Reality," *International Journal of Psychoanalysis* 51 (1970): 279–97.

64. Freud, *SE* 23.

65. Homans, *Ability to Mourn*.

66. Marc Nichanian, "Catastrophic Mourning," in *Loss: The Politics of Mourning*, ed. David L. Eng and David Kazanjian (Berkeley: University of California Press, 2003), 99–124: 99.

67. Alice, Benigno's beloved, comes back to life as a result of her pregnancy and childbirth. Although her child dies, she is reborn: she gives birth to herself, in a rebirth conceived through Benigno's melancholia. I am indebted to Amy Pace for this observation.

68. Does the art resolve the grief? Does it cover the loss? Some have suggested that art has replaced religion in the twentieth and twenty-first centuries as a source of meaning and community. Butler postulates that in the contemporary era "community does not overcome loss . . . community cannot overcome the loss without losing the very sense of itself as community" (Butler 2003: 468). Perhaps belonging now takes place in and through a common sense of loss, and by its memorialization in structures, art works, and films. In this sense, loss may become the condition and necessity for a certain sense of community.

References

Bakan, David. *Sigmund Freud and the Jewish Mystical Tradition*. Boston: Beacon, 1958.

Brickman, Celia. *Aboriginal Populations in the Mind*. New York: Columbia University Press, 2003.

Buhle, Mari Jo. *Feminism and Its Discontents: A Century of Struggle with Psychoanalysis*. Cambridge, Mass.: Harvard University Press, 1998.

Butler, Judith. "Afterward: After Loss, What Then?" Pp. 467–74 in *Loss: The Politics of Mourning*. Edited by David L. Eng and David Kazanjian. Berkeley: University of California Press, 2003.

Capps, Donald. *Men, Religion, and Melancholia: James, Otto, Jung, and Erikson*. New Haven, Conn.: Yale University Press, 1997.

Clark, R. W. *Freud, The Man and the Cause: A Biography*. New York: Random House, 1980.

Crews, Frederick, ed. *Unauthorized Freud: Doubters Confront a Legend*. New York: Penguin, 1998.

Dittes, James. "Teaching Freud's Teachings." Pp. 258–70 in *Teaching Freud*. Edited by Diane Jonte-Pace. New York: Oxford, 2003.

Eng, David L., and David Kazanjian. "Introduction: Mourning Remains." Pp. 1–25 in *Loss: The Politics of Mourning*. Edited by David L. Eng and David Kazanjian. Berkeley: University of California Press, 2003.

Freud, Ernst, ed. *Letters of Sigmund Freud, 1873–1939*. Translated by Tania Stern and James Stern. New York: Dover, 1992.

Freud, Ernst, and Lucie Freud, eds. *Sigmund Freud Briefe, 1873–1938*. Frankfurt am Main: S. Fischer Verlag, 1960.

Freud, Sigmund. *Gesammelte Schriften (GS)*. Wien: Internationaler Psychoanalytischer Verlag, 1924–1928.

———. *Die Zukunft Einer Illusion*. *GS* 11 (1928): 411–66.

———. "Ein religiöses Erlebnis." *GS* 11 (1928): 467–70.

———. *Gesammelte Werke (GW)*, Zweiter und Dritter Band. Frankfurt am Main: S. Fischer Verlag, 1942.

———. *Collected Papers (CP)*. Vol. 4. Translated and edited by Joan Riviere. London: Hogarth Press, 1946.

———. *The Interpretation of Dreams*. *SE* 4–5 (1953): 1–722.

———. *The Standard Edition (SE) of the Complete Psychological Works of Sigmund Freud*. 24 vols. Translated and edited by James Strachey. London: Hogarth Press, 1953–1974.

———. "Three Essays on Sexuality." *SE* 7 (1953): 125–248.

———. "Analysis of a Phobia in a Five Year Old Boy." *SE* 10 (1955): 5–153.

———. "Beyond the Pleasure Principle." *SE* 18 (1955): 3–143.

———. *Totem and Taboo*. *SE* 13 (1955): 1–163.

———. "Two Encyclopedia Articles." *SE* 18 (1955): 235–59.

———. "The Uncanny." *SE* 17 (1955): 217–52.

———. "Mourning and Melancholia." *SE* 14 (1957): 239–57.

———. "On the History of the Psychoanalytic Movement." *SE* 14 (1957): 3–66.

———. "On Transience." *SE* 14 (1957): 303–7.

———. "Thoughts for the Times on War and Death." *SE* 14 (1957): 275–301

———. "The Unconscious (Papers on Metapsychology)." *SE* 14 (1957): 159–206.

———. "Psychoanalytic Notes on an Autobiographical Account of a Case of Paranoia." *SE* 12 (1958): 1–80.

———. "Theme of the Three Caskets." *SE* 12 (1958): 291–301.

———. "Inhibitions, Symptoms, and Anxiety." *SE* 20 (1959): 77–174.

———. "Analysis, Terminable or Interminable." *SE* 23 (1961): 209–53.

———. *Civilization and its Discontents*. *SE* 21 (1961): 64–148.

———. "Economic Problem of Masochism." *SE* 19 (1961): 157–70.

———. "Ego and the Id." *SE* 19 (1961): 3–66.

———. "The Future of an Illusion." *SE* 21 (1961): 5–58.

———. "Female Sexuality." *SE* 21 (1961): 223–45.

———. "Fetishism." *SE* 21 (1961): 151–57.

———. "On Negation." *SE* 19 (1961): 235–40.

———. "The Question of Lay Analysis." *SE* 20 (1961): 179–250.

———. "Religious Experience, A." *SE* 21 (1961): 167–72.

———. *Introductory Lectures on Psychoanalysis*. *SE* 15 (1963): 1–239.

———. "Comment on Antisemitism, A." *SE* 23 (1964): 287–93.

———. *Moses and Monotheism*. *SE* 23 (1964): 1–138.

———. *New Introductory Lectures*. *SE* 22 (1964): 3–183.

Gay, Peter. *A Godless Jew: Freud, Atheism, and the Meaning of Psychoanalysis*. New Haven, Conn.: Yale University Press, 1987.

———. "Psychoanalyst Sigmund Freud." *Time* 153, no. 12 (29 March 1999): 64–69.

Homans, Peter. *Theology after Freud*. Indianapolis: Bobbs-Merrill, 1970.

———. *The Ability to Mourn: Disillusionment and the Social Origins of Psychoanalysis*. Chicago: University of Chicago Press, 1989.

———. *Jung in Context*. 2nd edition. Chicago: University of Chicago Press, 1995 (1979).

———. "We (Not-So) Happy Few: Symbolic Loss and Mourning in Freud's Psychoanalytic Movement and the History of Psychoanalysis." *Psychoanalysis and History* 1 (1998): 69–86.

Homans, Peter, ed. *Symbolic Loss: The Ambiguity of Mourning at Century's End*. Charlottesville: University of Virginia Press, 2000.

Homans, Peter, and Diane Jonte-Pace. "Tracking the Emotions in the Stone: An Essay in Psychoanalysis and Architecture." *The Annual of Psychoanalysis* 33 (2006): 261–84.

Jones, Ernest. *Sigmund Freud, Life and Work*. 3 vols. London: Hogarth, 1953–1957.

Jonte-Pace, Diane. "Julia Kristeva and the Psychoanalytic Study of Religion: Rethinking Freud's Cultural Texts." Pp. 240–68 in *Religion, Society, and Psychoanalysis: Readings in Contemporary Theory*. Edited by Janet Liebman Jacobs and Donald Capps. Boulder: Westview, 1997.

———. "'Legitimation of Hatred or Inversion into Love': Religion in Kristeva's Re-Reading of Freud." *Journal of Research in the Social Scientific Study of Religion* 10 (1999): 17–35.

———. *Speaking the Unspeakable: Religion, Misogyny, and the Uncanny Mother in Freud's Cultural Texts.* Berkeley: University of California Press, 2001.

Kakar, Sudhir. *The Inner World.* New York: Oxford University Press, 1981.

Klein, Dennis. *Jewish Origins of the Psychoanalytic Movement.* Chicago: University of Chicago Press, 1985.

Kristeva, Julia. *Powers of Horror: An Essay on Abjection.* Translated by Leon S. Roudiez. New York: Columbia University Press, 1982.

———. *In the Beginning was Love: Psychoanalysis and Faith.* Translated by Arthur Goldhammer. New York: Columbia University Press, 1987.

———. *Black Sun: Depression and Melancholia.* Translated by Leon S. Roudiez. New York: Columbia University Press, 1989.

———. *Strangers to Ourselves.* Translated by Leon S. Roudiez. New York: Columbia University Press, 1991.

Kung, Hans. *Freud and the Problem of God.* New Haven, Conn.: Yale University Press, 1990.

Le Rider, Jacques. *Modernity and Crises of Identity: Culture and Society in Fin de Siècle Vienna.* Translated by Rosemary Morris. New York: Continuum, 1993.

Meng, Heinrich, and Ernst Freud, eds. *Psychoanalysis and Faith: The Letters of Sigmund Freud and Oskar Pfister.* Translated by Eric Mosbacher. New York: Basic Books, 1963.

Mitchell, Juliet. *Psychoanalysis and Feminism: Freud, Reich, Laing, and Women.* New York: Random, 1974.

Mitscherlich, Alexander, and Margarete Mitscherlich. *The Inability to Mourn: Principles of Collective Behavior.* New York: Grove Press, 1976.

Mitscherlich, Margarete. *Die Friedfertige Frau: Ein Psychoanalytische Untersuchung zur Aggression der Geschlechter.* Frankfurt: S. Fischer Verlag, 1985.

Nichanian, Marc. "Catastrophic Mourning." Pp. 99–124 in *Loss: The Politics of Mourning.* Edited by David L. Eng and David Kazanjian. Berkeley: University of California Press, 2003.

Pfister, Oscar. *Psychoanalysis and Faith: The Letters of Sigmund Freud and Oskar Pfister.* Edited by Heinrich Meng and Ernst L. Freud. Translated by Eric Mosbacher. New York: Basic Books, 1963.

Rice, Emmanuel. *Freud and Moses: The Long Journey Home.* Albany: State University of New York Press, 1990.

Ricoeur, Paul. *Freud and Philosophy.* New Haven, Conn.: Yale University Press, 1970.

Rieff, Philip. *Triumph of the Therapeutic.* New York: Harpers, 1966.

———. *Freud: The Mind of the Moralist.* Chicago: University of Chicago Press, 1979.

Rizzuto, Ana-Maria. *The Birth of the Living God: A Psychoanalytic Study.* Chicago: University of Chicago Press, 1979.

———. *Why Did Freud Reject God? A Psychodynamic Interpretation*. New Haven, Conn.: Yale University Press, 1998.

Santner, Eric. *Stranded Objects: Mourning, Memory, and Film in Postwar Germany*. Ithaca, NY: Cornell University Press, 1990.

———. *My Own Private Germany: Daniel Paul Schreber's Secret History of Modernity*. Princeton, NJ: Princeton University Press, 1996.

Schafer, Roy. "The Psychoanalytic Vision of Reality." *International Journal of Psychoanalysis* 51 (1970): 279–97.

Schiessari, Juliana. *The Gendering of Melancholia: Feminism, Psychoanalysis, and the Symbolics of Loss in Renaissance Literature*. Ithaca, NY: Cornell University Press, 1992.

Schorske, Carl. "Politics and Patricide in Freud's Interpretation of Dreams." *American Historical Review* 78 (1973): 328–47.

Schreber, Daniel Paul. *Memoirs of My Nervous Illness*. New York: New York Review of Books Press, 1903; 2000.

Von Unwerth, Matthew. *Freud's Requiem: Mourning, Memory, and the Invisible History of a Summer Walk*. New York: Penguin, 2005.

Vitz, Paul. *Psychoanalysis as Religion: The Cult of Self-Worship*. Grand Rapids, Mich.: Eerdmans, 1994.

Wallwork, Ernest. "Contemporary Perspectives on an Old Antagonism" in *Psychoanalysis and Religion*. Edited by Joseph Smith. Baltimore, Md.: Johns Hopkins University Press, 1989.

Yerushalmi, Yosef. *Freud's Moses: Judaism Terminable and Interminable*. New Haven, Conn.: Yale University Press, 1991.

PART TWO

PERSPECTIVES FROM THE NATURAL AND SOCIAL SCIENCES

CHAPTER THREE

Love the Mother, Hate the Father: Understanding Sociology's Vehement Rejection of Freud on Religion

Michael P. Carroll

For quite some time now, it has seemed obvious to me that Catholicism—popular Catholicism in particular—is a religion especially well-suited to psychoanalytic investigation. For example, imagine a dream in which you saw a heart that had been ripped from a man's body, wrapped tightly with thorns, and then placed on the man's chest and imagine as well that you associated the imagery in this dream with a vague need to make "reparation" for some misdeed. In such a case, I doubt that anyone would challenge the suggestion that psychoanalytic reasoning might possibly be useful in uncovering the underlying associations that gave rise to a dream like this. And yet precisely this imagery and this emphasis on reparation are the defining elements of devotion to the Sacred Heart of Jesus, a Catholic cult that soared in popularity during the late nineteenth century. Or imagine confronting someone who feels compelled to walk around a loose pile of stones exactly seven times and always in a clockwise direction, and then compelled to repeat this process over and over again with other stone piles nearby. Here again, I suggest, few would challenge the suggestion that psychoanalysis might prove useful in determining the cause of such behavior. And yet "rounding rituals" of exactly this sort were central to the holy well cults which soared in popularity among Irish Catholics in the early 1600s.

In fact, what I have found, both in these two cases and a range of others, is that psychoanalytic reasoning generally—and Freud's theory of religion in particular—can help us make sense out of patterns associated with the practice of Catholicism that are otherwise difficult to understand. Furthermore, though my own special concern has been with the Catholic tradition, other scholars—many of whom have chapters in this book—have found psychoanalysis (and Freud) useful in studying religious beliefs and behaviors found in a range of Western and non-Western contexts. Unfortunately for me, very few of these other scholars have been sociologists.

The simple fact is that most sociologists of religion in the United States have never regarded psychoanalysis as a particularly useful theoretical perspective. This is evident, for example, in the fact that none of the essays in Michele Dillon's recent *Handbook of the Sociology of Religion*,[1] the vast majority of which were written by American sociologists, makes mention of psychoanalysis. Similarly, Beckford and Demerath's *The SAGE Handbook of the Sociology of Religion*[2] devotes two paragraphs to Freud's *The Future of an Illusion* (mainly to argue that Freud's prediction regarding the decline of religion was wrong) and then ignores psychoanalysis in the remainder of its 700-plus pages.

This is not to deny, of course, that the occasional article drawing on psychoanalysis does appear in the two American journals devoted to the sociology of religion, namely, the *Journal for the Scientific Study of Religion* (hereafter JSSR) and the *Sociology of Religion* (hereafter SR). Such articles, however, are infrequent and do not usually draw on Freud's original work. Furthermore, when the rare article that does draw directly on Freud happens to make an appearance in these journals, well, all hell breaks loose.

For example, in the reviewing the history of the JSSR (which began publication in 1960), Ralph Hood, himself a former JSSR editor, identifies only one article that provoked any degree of controversy.[3] That was my own 1987 article on the anal-erotic origins of the Catholic rosary.[4] The rosary, as you might recall, is a form of prayer in honor of the Virgin Mary characterized by the excessive repetition of particular prayers in a particular order. My article did two things: it linked this excessive repetition and orderliness to Freud's arguments on the anal personality, and then used this argument to explain certain historical patterns (in particular, why the rosary first became a popular devotion in the German-speaking areas of Catholic Europe and why an earlier version of the rosary, associated with God the Father, not the Virgin Mary, had failed to become a popular devotion). Hood goes on to explain that in the face of much negative reaction to Carroll's piece, Donald Capps (who was the editor at the time) took the unprecedented step of devoting a portion of JSSR to an interview with Carroll. What Hood does not mention is that a campaign was organized to remove Capps as editor (which, thankfully, failed). The intense negative reaction that article, I might add, nowhere took the form of a reasoned rebuttal to the argument; the argument was simply rejected as offensive and implausible, and Capps was castigated for publishing it.

Freud's arguments on anal eroticism of course have always provoked an especially strong and negative reaction—something that Freud himself noted.[5] Still, remember that in this case the negative reaction came not from the general public but from scholars supposedly committed to the scientific study of religion. In any event, Hood concludes by noting that Capps went on to be the president of JSSR, surviving the controversy over publishing Carroll's piece. Implicit here is the suggestion that the outcry over the publication of that one article is something that might have impeded the professional career of any editor crazy enough to publish it!

What I want to do in this chapter is to offer some thoughts on *why* sociologists of religion in the United States have rejected Freud's work on religion. What I hope to demonstrate is that some of the more obvious and commonly encountered explanations do not hold up under scrutiny and that viewing this (often) vehement rejection of Freud through a psychoanalytic lens brings to light some cultural biases that have shaped, and continue to shape, the way in which American sociologists study religion.

Some Common Objections to Freud

Outsiders, I suspect, might easily attribute sociology's rejection of Freud to the fact that Freud's work is so much at variance with the unbridled positivism—with its emphasis on testing hypotheses using large data sets and elaborate statistical procedures—that seems to dominate the field. And yet, that cannot be right. Sociology is in fact a very diverse discipline which encompasses a number of research traditions (including symbolic interactionism and ethnomethodology) that privilege the study of subjective experience using non-quantitative methodologies—and sociologists studying religion, in particular, have often been drawn to these nonquantitative traditions. Indeed, some commentators have suggested that the sociology of religion has taken an ethnographic turn in recent years that is transforming the field.[6] Positivism, then, is not the culprit.

Another commonly encountered explanation for sociology's rejection of Freud—and certainly one that I hear often from colleagues and students—is that Freud's theory of religion is too psychological. What this seems to mean, when the people making this argument are pressed for details, is that Freud's theory of religion focuses too much on the individual and so ignores those macrosciological processes—having to do with class, social change, and so on—that shape all belief systems. But here too the argument does not stand up to scrutiny, if only because it is not at all difficult for Freud's theory of religion to take such macrosociological processes into account. Let me demonstrate that (again) using examples from my own work.

The Mary cult has long been one of the defining features of the Catholic tradition, just as a rejection of the Mary cult has been a defining feature of Protestantism. One of the most interesting historical patterns associated with the Mary cult, however, is that it emerged only in the fifth century, i.e., there is no evidence of any popular devotion to Mary during the first four centuries of the Christian era. What accounts for this historical patterning? In an earlier work[7] I pointed out that the sudden emergence of the Mary cult was preceded by the social transformation of the Christian Church. During the first three centuries of the Christian era, the membership of the Church was drawn disproportionately from the urban middle class. This changed dramatically over the course of the fourth century as Christianity increasingly became the only legal religion in the Roman Empire. One consequence of this was that the class composition of the Christian Church underwent a dramatic change. Basically, what happened is that the Church was flooded by new members coming from the poorest stratum of the Empire, and indeed the Roman poor likely became a majority within the Church for the first time during this period. Moreover, there are theoretical and historical reasons for believing that the poor who were flooding into the Church would have been associated with a distinctive form of family organization, what I and others have called the father-ineffective family. This is important because there is a theoretical basis (reviewed in that earlier work) for believing that individuals raised in a father-ineffective family would have found a supernatural being like Mary (who was simultaneously Mother and Virgin) to be especially appealing. The final argument, then, is that the Mary cult emerged in response to the changing class composition of the early Church and was an attempt to cater to the religious predictions of individuals raised in father-ineffective families.

The emergence of the Mary cult, in other words, was likely caused in the first instance by precisely the sort of macrosociologial process (the changing class composition of the Church) favored by sociologists. What psychoanalysis adds to the analysis however is an understanding of why the cult took the form it did. Nor is this an isolated instance. On the contrary, in other work I have traced the rise of the Sacred Heart cult (mentioned at the beginning of this chapter) to the attacks on papal authority during the late nineteenth century;[8] the rise of holy well cults in Ireland to the conflicts between an imported Tridentine emphasis on hierarchical authority and the communal emphasis that was part of local Irish cultures;[9] the rise of the Penitentes (a lay confraternity which emerged in northern New Mexico in the early 1800s and whose members engaged in extreme penitential practices) to the effect of the Bourbon economic reforms on local patterns of land tenure;[10] and so on. In each case, psychoanalytic reasoning is valuable precisely because it provides a basis for understanding how and why these macrosociological changes functioned to produce the new religious forms that undeniably emerged in their wake.

So if the standard answers do not work, the question remains: why the near-complete rejection of Freud's work on religion by sociologists studying religion? Part of the answer here, I suggest, is to be found by looking carefully at those (few) psychoanalytic arguments that have been relatively *well*-received in the sociology of religion.

Love the Mother, Hate the Father

In recent years one of the most visible psychoanalytic arguments to be found in books and articles addressed to sociologists of religion has been the argument that Janet Liebman Jacobs has developed in connection with her study of crypto-Judaism.[11] The empirical core of Jacobs's work is a number of interviews she conducted in the American West and Southwest with Hispanics claiming a crypto-Jewish identity, that is, who claimed to be the descendants of crypto-Jews who settled in areas under Spanish control during colonial period. Jacobs uses self-in-relation theory to interpret her data, and she describes this theory in this way:

> Originating in the object relations school of psychoanalysis, self-in-relation theory emphasizes the role of female caregivers, especially mothers, in fostering empathic attachment in girls. As perhaps the most widely adopted feminist perspective on personality development, the self-in-relation paradigm has been applied to the study of moral behavior, adolescent social relations, family violence and early childhood experience.[12]

Self-in-relation theory, in other words, is a variant of the well-known argument developed some time ago by theorists like Nancy Chodorow and Carol Gilligan—and indeed commentators like Mary Jo Nietz have singled out Jacobs's work as demonstrating the value of the Chodorow/Gilligan theory in the sociology of religion.[13] What makes the appeal of Jacobs's argument in the sociology of religion especially puzzling is that it is likely built upon a false premise.

Crypto-Jewish communities did exist in various parts of the Spanish empire well into the seventeenth century, and there is no denying that since the 1970s an increasing number of Spanish-speaking residents of the American Southwest have been claiming a crypto-Jewish identity. Nevertheless, there is now a substantial body of literature suggesting that these recent claims of crypto-Judaism cannot be taken at face value. The folklorist Judith Neulander, in particular, has pointed out that evidence of crypto-Judaism is usually obtained by following a simple formula: find a similarity between some particular Hispano practice and some particular Jewish practice, ignore any differences that might exist between the two practices, and then take the former (the Hispano practice) as evidence of an imagined crypto-Jewish past. In other cases, Neulander points out, the practices taken as evidence of crypto-Judaism are indeed the remnants of a hidden religious tradition but that the tradition involved was Protestant (not Jewish) and arose in the recent (not the colonial) past. Here she builds upon the work of Raphael Patai, who had investigated an Indian community in Mexico in the 1940s and 1960s. Although the members of this community claimed to be the descendants of Spanish crypto-Jews, Patai's research established that in fact their Judaism had originated with the Iglesia de Dios (an organizational offshoot of Seventh Day Adventism) that had missionized the area in the early twentieth century. Like many Adventist groups, the Iglesia de Dios had promoted a number of quasi-Judaic practices (i.e., they kept the Sabbath; refrained from eating pork; etc.) and these practices, Patai argued, became the basis for claiming a crypto-Jewish identity. Neulander suggests that many of the practices that lead Jacobs to take serious her informants' claims of a crypto-Jewish heritage originated from the same missionizing activities. Moreover, both Patai and Neulander provide a basis for understanding these claims to a Jewish ancestry: in the strongly racialized culture of New Mexico and Mexico, claiming a Spanish ancestry, even Spanish-Jewish ancestry, conveys status.[14]

In this case then, we have a psychoanalytic argument wrapped around empirical claims that are shaky at best, if not actually falsified by existing research—and yet, as I have said, Jacob's work has been well-received in sociology and the work by Neulander and Patai generally ignored. Why? One obvious possibility is that the particular psychoanalytic argument she develops has an appeal that is independent of the evidence.

At one level, such a suggestion is not new. Many feminist scholars have suggested that the immense popularity of the Chodorow/Gilligan theory derives in part from the fact that one of the central contentions of the theory (namely, that males and females follow different developmental paths by virtue of being raised by a female caretaker) reinforces the sort of essentialist thinking about gender that pervades our culture.[15] In connection with the sociology of religion, however, I want to suggest that there is another reason for the appeal of arguments (like Jacobs's) that utilize the Chodorow/Gilligan theory: such arguments privilege the pre-Oedipal period and/or the child's relationship with the mother. That these particular emphases are critical in securing a nonhostile reaction from sociological audiences gains plausibility, I suggest, from the fact that most of the other psychoanalytic arguments that occasionally appear in venues addressed to sociologists of religion also—like Jacobs's argument—privilege the pre-Oedipal period and/or the child's relationship with the mother.[16]

Let me be clear: I am not suggesting that these two emphases are problematic in themselves. On the contrary with the rise of the object relations tradition, an increasing emphasis on the pre-Oedipal period and/or the child's relation with the mother have become commonplace within the psychoanalytic tradition generally. Moreover, an increasing number of psychoanalytic investigators—including here William Meissner, Ana-Maria Rizzuto, and others—have used object relations theory, and more specifically D. W. Winnicott's work on transitional objects, to study religion.[17] My point, however, is that in the sociology of religion, unlike what is true of the psychoanalytic tradition itself, arguments which draw on object relations theory are the *only* sort of psychoanalytic arguments that are tolerated. Why? I suggest that these arguments are tolerated because they negate precisely those two emphases (on the Oedipal period and the child's relationship with the father) that are absolutely central to Freud's own work on religion. What I am suggesting, in other words, is that the rejection of psychoanalysis by sociologists studying religion is less a rejection of psychoanalysis in general than a rejection of Freud's specific theory, and—more generally—of Freud himself.

To make such a claim of course is to beg the question of *why* American sociologists might be predisposed to reject Freud personally. Here, I think, it will be useful to look carefully at how one prominent sociologist, who has been especially vociferous in his rejection of Freud over the past several decades, justifies that rejection.

Here I Stand: Rodney Stark and Luther-ian Challenge

The single most important theoretical perspective to emerge in the sociology of religion over the past twenty years is the rational choice perspective, and the one theorist most often cited in connection with rational choice models of religion is Rodney Stark.[18] Stark and a variety of associates have developed what they call a theory of religious economies whose essential features are captured succinctly in the following passage:

> Religious economies are like commercial economies in that they consist of a market made up of a set of current and potential customers and set of firms seeking to serve that market. The fate of these firms will depend upon (1) aspects of their organizational structure, (2) their sales representatives, (3) their product, and (4) their marketing techniques. Translated into more churchly language, the relative success of religious bodies (especially when confronted with an unregulated economy) will depend upon their polity, their clergy, their religious doctrines, and their evangelization techniques.[19]

Stark is relevant to the present discussion because over the years he has regularly contrasted his own theory, which is rational, with what he calls irrational theories of religion (not theories of the irrational, mind you, but irrational theories), and he invariably cites Freud's analysis as epitomizing an irrational theory of religion.[20]

In reviewing Freud's work, Stark recurrently takes Freud's theory of religion to consist primarily of the claim that religion is a form of mental illness. Freud's contention that there are structural similarities between the processes that produce religion and the processes that produce mental illness is a nuance lost entirely on Stark, and Stark pays no detailed attention whatsoever to Freud's contention that religion derives from the experience of infantile helplessness and the desire for paternal protection. Put as gently as I can, Stark seems to have rejected Freud's theory of religion without having come to grips with that theory in any serious way.

Just as revealing, I think, are the examples that Stark holds up as epitomizing Freudian theorizing: in his earlier works[21] the only study he pointed to was my article on the anal erotic origins of the rosary. In later works,[22] he regularly cites *two* articles: my article and an article on Protestant fundamentalism by Mortimer Ostow.[23] My article, as I indicated, is one of the very few articles using Freud's theory to have been published in a mainstream "sociology of religion" journal. The choice of Ostow's article, however, is puzzling given that there is in fact very little "psychoanalysis" in that article. Ostow's main concern is to demonstrate that there is a historical continuity between modern fundamentalist Protestantism and earlier apocalyptic traditions by virtue of a common emphasis on death and rebirth. True, at one point (p. 113) Ostrow does suggest that this emphasis on death and rebirth is a form of regression to the pre-Oedipal period—but this is a point he makes in passing (and in any event is not an argument drawn from Freud). So, why hold up Ostow's article as one of two articles that *epitomize* Freud's approach to religion? The answer, I think, is that even now, after literally decades of rejecting Freud in a very public and explicit way, Stark has little familiarity with the psychoanalytic literature on religion outside of the occasional argument published in sociology journals or outside of material that he has came across in connection with topics (like fundamentalism) that have been of concern to sociologists.

In short, then, there is nothing in Stark's brief allusions to Freudian theory to indicate that he has any deep familiarity either with Freud's original argument or with the (vast) psychoanalytic literature on religion. But if this is so, then what has fueled his very vehement and very public rejection of Freud over the past few decades? A clue to the answer here, I think, is to be found in a passage that Stark published some time ago. Thus, after noting that his professors in graduate school had failed to tempt him into Freudian irrationality, Stark says

> And here I take my stand, for not only do I cling to the notion that humans are primarily rational creatures, but I believe that when they do science correctly humans must respect the rules of logic and evidence that are the hard won fruits of their millennia of rationalism.[24]

This passage is important for two reasons. First, it suggests that Stark sees a rejection of Freud as a necessary precondition of the advancement of knowledge. After all, he seems clearly to be saying that not to reject Freudian irrationality would be to threaten the "hard-won fruits" of rationalism, namely, the triumph of logic and evidence over superstition and irrationality. But even more significant, I suggest, is the phrase "And here I take my stand." It is of course a phrase that evokes the image of Martin Luther at the climactic moment of his appearance before the Diet of Worms in 1521. Thus, after being asked if he would retract his works, Luther replied that councils and popes had been wrong in the past and might be wrong again, and so he would not retract unless proven wrong on the basis of Scripture and Scripture alone. He is then supposed[25] to have said, "I can no other! Here I stand! God Help Me!"

Stark, in short, is quite explicitly drawing a metaphorical parallel—a parallel that would be likely obvious to most educated readers but which would certainly be obvious to sociologists of religion—between *his* vehement rejection of Freud (and Freud's theory of religion) and *Luther's* vehement rejection of papal authority. It might seem strange, especially to an audience familiar with Freud's attitude toward the Catholic Church, to suggest that rejection of Freud is somehow analogous to the Reformation's rejection of Papal authority—nevertheless that is precisely the metaphor that Stark is invoking here.

While it might be tempting to dismiss Stark's use of this metaphor as simple hyperbole, we are better served, I suggest, by trying to uncover the psychological associations that would lead an American sociologist as prominent as Stark to make such an allusion in the first place *and* that would allow this metaphor to make sense to his intended (sociological) audience.

American Exceptionalism and the Protestant Roots of American Sociology

In a number of publications now spanning three decades, Seymour Martin Lipset[26] has argued that there are systematic cultural differences between the United States and Canada and, more generally, between the United States and most other Western nations. In particular, he suggests that American cultural traditions have emphasized disdain for authority, individualism, and egalitarianism while Canadian cultural traditions have emphasized respect for authority, collectivism (e.g., groups are more important than individuals), and elitism.

For Lipset there are two intertwined causes of this American exceptionalism. First, the United States experienced a revolution that gave rise to a cultural tradition marked by a basic distrust of government and a strong emphasis upon individualism. Second, the decades following the Revolution witnessed the emergence of a Protestant sectarian tradition that reinforced precisely these same cultural emphases. In his own words,

> The strong ideological and achievement orientations in the American experience [were] strengthened by its special religious character. . . . Since most of the Protestant sects are congregational, not hierarchical, they have fostered egalitarian, individualistic, and populist values which are anti-elitist. Hence, the political ethos and the religious ethos [have] reinforced each other.[27]

In short, Lipset is suggesting that the individualism and strongly antihierarchal emphasis promoted by Protestant sects reinforced the cultural emphases associated with the rhetoric of the American Revolution. Moreover, in the face of various criticisms of his account of the American Revolution, Lipset has increasingly come to see the dominance of these Protestant sects as the major cause of American exceptualism.

Lipset sees the disdain for hierarchical authority that pervades American culture as explaining a number of sociological patterns, ranging from high crime rates in the United States to the American refusal to adopt the metric system. But it also explains what he calls the "Oedipal" themes in American literature:

> A revolt against tradition and authority, against King and ancestral fatherland is and always must remain at some deep level an Oedipal act. The writings of American authors as various as Nathaniel Hawthorne, Herman Melville, Hart Crane, Booth Tarkington, Mark Twain, Theodore Dreiser, Robert Penn Warren, Eugene O'Neil, J.D. Salinger, and Norman Mailer are identified by critics as reflecting Oedipal themes: a rejection of the father and an emotional relationship with the mother.[28]

What makes this relevant to the present discussion is that the Oedipal themes identified here, namely, a rejection of the father and a concern with an emotional relationship with the mother, are the same themes which emerged from our consideration of those psychoanalytic arguments (like Jacobs) that are received favorably by sociologists of religion. I want to suggest that the same process is operative in both cases. In other words, I suggest that the antihierarchal and individualistic heritage of sectarian Protestantism in the United States, which in Lipset's view has shaped so many aspects of American culture, has *also* shaped the sociological study of religion.

The idea that the discipline of sociology generally has been shaped by sectarian Protestantism is not new. On the contrary, it is commonplace in accounts discussing the rise of sociology in the Unites States to argue that sociology emerged out of the Social Gospel movement which had developed within the American Protestant tradition in the late 1800s. Sometimes the linkage was fairly direct. As Lewis Coser has demonstrated, a great many early sociologists had either trained for the Protestant ministry at some point in their life or had been raised in clerical homes.[29] In other cases, the linkage was less direct. Vidich and Lyman, for example, have documented the influence of the Social Gospel movement even in the case of those sociologists who were not especially religious or who were in fact actively hostile to organized religion.[30]

Robert Orsi has recently added to this discussion (of American sociology's Protestant roots) by pointing out that the academic study of religion in early twentieth century were concerned with demonstrating that religion was necessary for the maintenance of American democracy so long as it was the "right" sort of religion. What they took to be the right sort of religion, Orsi continues, was a denominationally neutral version of Christianity that had been purged of "primitive" elements. By the same token, Orsi argues, these scholars saw religions that had *not* been purged of "primitive" elements to be a threat to American democracy. When Orsi runs through the list of the primitive religions that these scholars saw as a threat to the social order—a list that includes not simply the religious practices of dark-skinned peoples but also Roman Catholicism and Mormonism—it seems clear that the denominationally neutral version of Christianity that these scholars saw as necessary for the maintenance of American democracy was ultimately Protestant.[31]

Most discussions, including Orsi's, imply that the Protestant influence on sociology as a discipline ended some time ago. Darryl Hart, for example, argues that it lasted only into the 1940s.[32] In the specific case of sociology, however, there is evidence that this influence has continued.

This Protestant influence is most evident when American sociologists try to develop a general definition of religion or to develop general measures of religiosity. Thus, to take just two recent examples, Smith et al suggest that one of the most basic ways of assessing subjective religiosity is to ask people of the "importance of faith"[33] whereas in their meta-analysis of studies linking religiosity and mental health, Hackney and Sanders only include studies whose measures of "religiosity" have some relevance to attempts "to acknowledge and maintain some relationship with the transcendent."[34] Despite the supposed generality of the language used, these formulations seem clearly to reflect that emphasis on the overwhelming importance of faith and on "maintaining a relationship with God" that are the hallmarks of the Protestant tradition but which are NOT central to all religious traditions. In a similar vein, Stark and his associates have consistently argued that the most popular sort of religion is (universally) going to be religion that maintains some degree of "tension" with its environment, by which he means an emphasis on distinctiveness, separation, or antagonism in relation to others.[35] Although phrased as a prediction, the underlying imagery here seems to draw heavily upon evangelical Protestantism, which has historically stressed self-denial and the need to confront others who fail to feel the same way.

Protestant influence is also evident, I think, in the many studies that are purportedly concerned with "Christianity" but whose vision of Christianity, upon reflection, turns out to have a decidedly Protestant flavor. For example, Krause and Ellison argue that "forgiveness" is a central theme in the Christian religion (which in itself is not problematic) but then go on to measure the degree to which individual respondents have internalized this theme by asking them if they believe "God has forgiven me for the things I've done wrong" and by asking respondents about the degree to which they have forgiven other people.[36] Lying just beneath such questions, I suggest, are those emphases on individualism and on unmediated access to God which are central elements in the Protestant tradition but not, say, in the Catholic tradition.

Let me be clear: I am not suggesting that most sociologists of religion are practicing Protestants, only that the culture of sectarian Protestantism continues to shape the sociology of religion just as it continues to shape American culture generally.

If we now view Rodney Stark's vehement rejection of Freud against the backdrop of the discussion by Lipset, Orsi, and others, we find emphases very similar to those distinctively "American" emphases that these authors trace to the influence of sectarian Protestantism. Certainly, there would seem to a strong rejection of someone (Freud) who is a father figure not simply by virtue of the fact that he established an "orthodoxy" that was later challenged by his successors but also by virtue of the fact that an emphasis on the father pervades his work (especially his work on religion). Further, if we read Stark in this way, then his explicit claim that Freud's "irrational" theory of religion is a threat to the "hard-won fruits of civilization" seems little more than a updated variant of the claim made by sociologists of religion in the early twentieth century that "primitive" (i.e., hierarchical and non-Protestant) forms of religion were a threat to American democracy.

Rodney Stark is of course only a single individual—a very visible and highly respected individual within the discipline, to be sure, but an individual nonetheless. Even so, I suggest that his Luther-like rejection of Freud is best seen as giving precise form to sentiments that in a more diffuse form pervade the study of religion in American sociology generally. Sociologists of religion in the United States may or may not be religious, but they operate in a culture and in an academic discipline that has been strongly influenced by that disdain for paternalistic authority that is a heritage of the Protestant sectarian tradition. In this context, I suggest, sociologists of religion reject Freud (or rather, the figure of Freud) because, rightly or wrongly, Freud has come to be defined as a symbol of that sort of paternalistic authority whose rejection is so central to the Protestant tradition.

What of the Future?

In light of the analysis and speculation presented to this point, is there anything we can say about the likely relationship between the sociology of religion and psychoanalysis in the future? A few things, maybe. First, if indeed the rejection of Freud is an Oedipal act ultimately rooted in the culture of sectarian Protestantism, it is a rejection that will continue so long as the sociology of religion continues to be shaped by that culture. Further, like the proverbial fish unable to perceive water because it is all around them, I suspect that most sociologists of religion have never thought about the continuing ways in which the uniqueness of the American religious experience may have influence their subdiscipline. Becoming more self-aware of possible influence here, then, would seem a necessary first step in opening up the subdiscipline to theoretical perspectives like Freud's theory of religion, now rejected because of that influence. This would involve a sustained effort to determine the ways in which the problems chosen for study; the conceptual model utilized in studying those problems; the general definition of religion used, etc. do or do not, even now, reflect a distinctively Protestant agenda.[37]

One way, perhaps, to jump start the process of self-reflection would be to invert the question that I have addressed in this essay. Thus, instead of asking why so few sociologists of religion make use of psychoanalysis, American sociologists of religion might ask themselves why so many scholars in other disciplines find psychoanalysis to be a source of much insight. Addressing such a question in a systematic and evenhanded way, I suggest, would likely lead—if not to precisely the same conclusions reached here—at least to something similar.

Notes

1. Michele Dillon, ed., *Handbook of the Sociology of Religion* (Cambridge: Cambridge University Press, 2003).

2. James A. Beckford and N. J. Demerath, eds., *The SAGE Handbook of the Sociology of Religion* (Los Angeles: SAGE Publications, 2007).

3. Ralph Hood, "American Psychology of Religion and the Journal for the Scientific Study of Religion," 39, no. 4 (2000).

4. Michael P. Carroll, "Praying the Rosary: The Anal-Erotic Origins of a Popular Catholic Devotion," *Journal for the Scientific Study of Religion* 26, no. 3 (1987).

5. Sigmund Freud, "Character and Anal Eroticism," in *The Standard Edition of the Complete Psychological Works of Sigmund Freud* (London: Hogarth, 1959).

6. James V. Spickard and J. Shawn Landres, "Introduction: Whither Ethnography? Transforming the Social-Scientific Study of Religion," in *Personal Knowledge and Beyond: Reshaping the Ethnography of Religion*, ed. James V. Spickard, J. Shawn Landry, and Meredith McGuire (New York: New York University Press, 2002).

7. Michael P. Carroll, *The Cult of the Virgin Mary* (Princeton: Princeton University Press, 1986).

8. Michael P. Carroll, *Catholic Cults and Devotions* (Montreal: McGill-Queen's University Press, 1989), 132–53.

9. Michael P. Carroll, *Irish Pilgrimage: Holy Wells and Popular Catholic Devotion* (Baltimore: The Johns Hopkins University Press, 1999).

10. Michael P. Carroll, *The Penitente Brotherhood: Patriarchy and Hispano-Catholicism in New Mexico* (Baltimore: The Johns Hopkins University Press, 2002).

11. Janet Liebman Jacobs, *Hidden Heritage: The Legacy of the Crypto-Jews* (Berkeley: University of California Press, 2002), Janet Liebman Jacobs, "The Spiritual Self-in-Relation: Empathy and the Construction of Spirituality among Modern Descendents of Spanish Crypto-Jews," *Journal for the Scientific Study of Religion* 39, no. 1 (1996).

12. Jacobs, *Hidden Heritage*, 70.

13. Mary Jo Nietz, "Gender and Culture: Challenges to the Sociology of Religion," *Sociology of Religion* 65, no. 4 (2004).

14. See Judith Neulander, "Crypto-Jews of the Southwest: An Imagined Community," *Jewish Folklore and Ethnology Review* 16, no. 1 (1994); Judith Neulander, "The New Mexican Crypto-Jewish Canon: Choosing to Be Chosen in Millennial Tradition," *Jewish Folklore and Ethnology Review* 18, no. 1–2 (1996); Raphael Patai, *On Jewish Folklore* (Detroit: Wayne State University Press, 1983). For a more detailed review of the claims and counter-claims relating to a crypto-Jewish presence in the American Southwest, see Michael P. Carroll, "The Debate over a Crypto-Jewish Presence in New Mexico: The Role of Ethnographic Allegory and Orientalism," *Sociology of Religion* 63, no. 1 (2002).

15. Mary Crawford, "Agreeing to Differ: Feminist Epistemologies and Women's Ways of Knowing," in *Gender and Thought: Psychological Perspectives*, ed. Mary Crawford and Margaret Gentry (New York: Springer-Verlag, 1989); Kathy Davis, "Toward a Feminist Rhetoric: The Gilligan Debate Revisited," *Women's Studies International Forum* 15, no. 2 (1992).

16. See for example Marion S. Goldman, "Alice Miller's Insights into Religious Seekership," in *Religion, Society and Psychoanalysis*, ed. Janet Liebman Jacobs and Donald Capps (Boulder, Colo.: Westview Press, 1997); Lynn Davidman, "Studying Close to Home," *Sociology of Religion* 61, no. 4 (2000).

17. For a review of such work see Samuel J. Liebman and Steven C. Abell, "Reconstructing the Sacred: Evolving Conceptualizations of Religious Faith in Psychoanalytic Theory and Practice," *Journal of Contemporary Psychotherapy* 30, no. 1 (2000).

18. For a review of the rational choice literature, see Michael Hechter and Satoshi Kanazawa, "Sociological Rational Choice Theory," *Annual Review of Sociology* 23 (1997); Frank J. Lechner, "Rational Choice and Religious Economies," in *The SAGE Handbook of the Sociology of Religion*, ed. James A. Beckford and N. J. Demerath (Los Angeles: SAGE Publications, 2007).

19. Roger Finke and Rodney Stark, *The Churching of America, 1776–1990* (New Brunswick, N.J.: Rutgers University Press, 1992), 17.

20. See Rodney Stark, "Response," *Journal for the Scientific Study of Religion* 29, no. 3 (1990); Rodney Stark, "Normal Revelations: A Rational Model of Mystical Experiences," in *Religion and the Social Order*, ed. David Bromley (Greenwich, N.Y.: JAI Press, Inc., 1991); Finke and Stark, *The Churching of America, 1776–1990.*; Rodney Stark, *One True God: Historical Consequences of Monotheism* (Princeton: Princeton University Press, 2001), 4; Rodney Stark and Roger Finke, *Acts of Faith: Explaining the Human Side of Religion* (Berkeley: University of California Press, 2000), 12.

21. Stark, "Response"; Stark, "Normal Revelations: A Rational Model of Mystical Experiences."

22. Stark, *One True God*, 254; Stark and Finke, *Acts of Faith*, 12.

23. Mortimer Ostow, "The Fundamentalist Phenomenon: A Psychological Perspective," in *The Fundamentalist Phenomenon*, ed. Norman J. Cohen (Grand Rapids, Mich.: William B. Eerdmans Publishing, 1990).

24. Stark, "Response," 386.

25. I say "suppose" because historians seem generally agreed that Luther may not have used these precise words.

26. For an overview of Lipset's work, see Seymour Martin Lipset, *Continental Divide: The Values and Institutions of the United States and Canada* (New York: Routledge, 1990); Seymour Martin Lipset, "Steady Work: An Academic Memoir," *Annual Review of Sociology* 22 (1996); Seymour Martin Lipset, "Defining Moments and Recurring Myths: A Reply," *Canadian Review of Sociology and Anthropology* 38, no. 1 (2001).

27. Seymour Martin Lipset, *American Exceptionalism: A Double-Edged Sword* (New York: W.W. Norton, 1996), 60–61.

28. Lipset, *Continental Divide*, 62.

29. Lewis A. Coser, "American Trends," in *A History of Sociological Analysis*, ed. Tom Bottomore and Robert Nisbet (New York: Basic Books, 1978).

30. Arthur Vidich and Stanford Lyman, *American Sociology: Worldly Rejections of Religion and Their Directions* (New Haven: Yale University Press, 1985).

31. Robert A. Orsi, "Is the Study of Lived Religion Irrelevant to the World We Live In?" *Journal for the Scientific Study of Religion* 42, no. 2 (2003): 170.

32. Darryl Hart, "Review of the Churching of America," *Theology Today* 50, no. 3 (1993).

33. Christian Smith et al., "Mapping American Adolescent Subjective Religiosity and Attitudes of Alienation toward Religion: A Research Report," *Sociology of Religion* 64, no. 1 (2003).

34. Charles H. Hackney and Glenn S. Sanders, "Religiosity and Mental Health: A Meta-Analysis of Recent Studies," *Journal for the Scientific Study of Religion* 42, no. 1 (2003): 46.

35. Stark and Finke, *Acts of Faith: Explaining the Human Side of Religion*, 142–46.

36. Neal Krause and Christopher G. Ellison, "Forgiveness by God, Forgiveness by Others, and Psychological Well-Being in Late Life," *Journal for the Scientific Study of Religion* 42, no. 1 (2003).

37. For examples of what might be done here, see Michael P. Carroll, *American Catholics in the Protestant Imagination: Rethinking the Academic Study of Religion* (Baltimore: The Johns Hopkins University Press, 2007).

References

Beckford, James A., and N. J. Demerath, eds. *The SAGE Handbook of the Sociology of Religion*. Los Angeles: SAGE Publications, 2007.

Carroll, Michael P. *The Cult of the Virgin Mary*. Princeton: Princeton University Press, 1986.

———. "Praying the Rosary: The Anal-Erotic Origins of a Popular Catholic Devotion." *Journal for the Scientific Study of Religion* 26, no. 3 (1987): 486–98.

———. *Catholic Cults and Devotions*. Montreal: McGill-Queen's University Press, 1989.

———. *Irish Pilgrimage: Holy Wells and Popular Catholic Devotion*. Baltimore: The Johns Hopkins University Press, 1999.

———. "The Debate over a Crypto-Jewish Presence in New Mexico: The Role of Ethnographic Allegory and Orientalism." *Sociology of Religion* 63, no. 1 (2002): 1–19.

———. *The Penitente Brotherhood: Patriarchy and Hispano-Catholicism in New Mexico*. Baltimore: The Johns Hopkins University Press, 2002.

———. *American Catholics in the Protestant Imagination: Rethinking the Academic Study of Religion*. Baltimore: The Johns Hopkins University Press, 2007.

Coser, Lewis A. "American Trends." Pp. 287–320 in *A History of Sociological Analysis*, edited by Tom Bottomore and Robert Nisbet. New York: Basic Books, 1978.

Crawford, Mary. "Agreeing to Differ: Feminist Epistemologies and Women's Ways of Knowing." Pp. 128–45 in *Gender and Thought: Psychological Perspectives*. Edited by Mary Crawford and Margaret Gentry. New York: Springer-Verlag, 1989.

Davidman, Lynn. "Studying Close to Home." *Sociology of Religion* 61, no. 4 (2000): 425–32.

Davis, Kathy. "Toward a Feminist Rhetoric: The Gilligan Debate Revisited." *Women's Studies International Forum* 15, no. 2 (1992): 219–31.

Dillon, Michele, ed. *Handbook of the Sociology of Religion*. Cambridge: Cambridge University Press, 2003.

Finke, Roger, and Rodney Stark. *The Churching of America, 1776–1990*. New Brunswick, N.J.: Rutgers University Press, 1992.

Freud, Sigmund. "Character and Anal Eroticism." Pp. 167–75 in *The Standard Edition of the Complete Psychological Works of Sigmund Freud*. London: Hogarth, 1959.

Goldman, Marion S. "Alice Miller's Insights into Religious Seekership." Pp. 200–17 in *Religion, Society and Psychoanalysis*. Edited by Janet Liebman Jacobs and Donald Capps. Boulder, Colo.: Westview Press, 1997.

Hackney, Charles H., and Glenn S. Sanders. "Religiosity and Mental Health: A Meta-Analysis of Recent Studies." *Journal for the Scientific Study of Religion* 42, no. 1 (2003): 43–55.

Hart, Darryl. "Review of the Churching of America." *Theology Today* 50, no. 3 (1993): 497–99.

Hechter, Michael, and Satoshi Kanazawa. "Sociological Rational Choice Theory." *Annual Review of Sociology* 23 (1997): 191–214.

Hood, Ralph. "American Psychology of Religion and the Journal for the Scientific Study of Religion." 39, no. 4 (2000): 531–43.

Jacobs, Janet Liebman. "The Spiritual Self-in-Relation: Empathy and the Construction of Spirituality among Modern Descendents of Spanish Crypto-Jews." *Journal for the Scientific Study of Religion* 39, no. 1 (1996): 53–63.

———. *Hidden Heritage: The Legacy of the Crypto-Jews*. Berkeley: University of California Press, 2002.

Krause, Neal, and Christopher G. Ellison. "Forgiveness by God, Forgiveness by Others, and Psychological Well-Being in Late Life." *Journal for the Scientific Study of Religion* 42, no. 1 (2003): 77–93.

Lechner, Frank J. "Rational Choice and Religious Economies." Pp. 81–97 in *The SAGE Handbook of the Sociology of Religion*. Edited by James A. Beckford and N. J. Demerath. Los Angeles: SAGE Publications, 2007.

Liebman, Samuel J., and Steven C. Abell. "Reconstructing the Sacred: Evolving Conceptualizations of Religious Faith in Psychoanalytic Theory and Practice." *Journal of Contemporary Psychotherapy* 30, no. 1 (2000): 7–23.

Lipset, Seymour Martin. *Continental Divide: The Values and Institutions of the United States and Canada*. New York: Routledge, 1990.

———. "Steady Work: An Academic Memoir." *Annual Review of Sociology* 22 (1996): 1–27.

———. *American Exceptionalism: A Double-Edged Sword*. New York: W.W. Norton, 1996.

———. "Defining Moments and Recurring Myths: A Reply." *Canadian Review of Sociology and Anthropology* 38, no. 1 (2001): 97–100.

Neulander, Judith. "Crypto-Jews of the Southwest: An Imagined Community." *Jewish Folklore and Ethnology Review* 16, no. 1 (1994): 64–68.

———. "The New Mexican Crypto-Jewish Canon: Choosing to Be Chosen in Millennial Tradition." *Jewish Folklore and Ethnology Review* 18, no. 1–2 (1996): 19–58.

Nietz, Mary Jo. "Gender and Culture: Challenges to the Sociology of Religion." *Sociology of Religion* 65, no. 4 (2004): 391–402.

Orsi, Robert A. "Is the Study of Lived Religion Irrelevant to the World We Live In?" *Journal for the Scientific Study of Religion* 42, no. 2 (2003): 169–74.

Ostow, Mortimer. "The Fundamentalist Phenomenon: A Psychological Perspective." In *The Fundamentalist Phenomenon*. Edited by Norman J. Cohen. Grand Rapids, Mich.: William B. Eerdmans Publishing, 1990.

Patai, Raphael. *On Jewish Folklore*. Detroit: Wayne State University Press, 1983.

Smith, Christian, Robert Faris, Melinda Lundquist Denton, and Mark Regnerus. "Mapping American Adolescent Subjective Religiosity and Attitudes of Alienation toward Religion: A Research Report." *Sociology of Religion* 64, no. 1 (2003): 111–33.

Spickard, James V., and J. Shawn Landres. "Introduction: Whither Ethnography? Transforming the Social-Scientific Study of Religion." Pp. 1–14 in *Personal Knowledge and Beyond: Reshaping the Ethnography of Religion*. Edited by James V. Spickard, J. Shawn Landry, and Meredith McGuire. New York: New York University Press, 2002.

Stark, Rodney. "Normal Revelations: A Rational Model of Mystical Experiences." Pp. 239–51 in *Religion and the Social Order*. Edited by David Bromley. Greenwich, N.Y.: JAI Press, Inc., 1991.

———. *One True God: Historical Consequences of Monotheism*. Princeton: Princeton University Press, 2001.

———. "Response." *Journal for the Scientific Study of Religion* 29, no. 3 (1990): 361–62.

Stark, Rodney, and Roger Finke. *Acts of Faith: Explaining the Human Side of Religion*. Berkeley: University of California Press, 2000.

Vidich, Arthur, and Stanford Lyman. *American Sociology: Worldly Rejections of Religion and Their Directions*. New Haven: Yale University Press, 1985.

CHAPTER FOUR

Of Chariots, Navels, and Winged Steeds: The Dialogue between Psychoanalysis and Buddhism

William B. Parsons

It is now a truism to say that Freud did not accord to culture a place of primacy in his theory. This negation of culture is manifestly evident in his classic work *Totem and Taboo* where, in an attempt to extend the hegemony of psychoanalysis relative to other social sciences, undercut the ontological basis of religion and ward off the budding psycho-religious theory of Jung, Freud theorized Oedipus to the extent that it became the phylogenetic basis for all individual fantasies as well as societal and religious expressions. Oedipus was the only and original archetype, and Freud's structural theory of the mind and the dynamics between its components as they were expressed in dreams, parapraxes, and neurotic symptoms became his seminal contribution. Most importantly, psychoanalysis was seen as universal. It, and it alone, was the key to unlocking the origins and historical trajectories of human beings and their cultural expressions.

Certainly psychoanalysis has been in need of the kindness of its social scientific partners to illuminate its own illusions. Fortunately a stellar array of anthropologists and sociologists have found Freud and his heirs to be both problematic yet worthy of dialogue. They have, for example, in seeking a corrective to the tendency to universalize, framed Freud as a psychologically gifted enthnographer and psychoanalysis as an ethnopsychological system, emphasized the relativity of developmental lines and the need for a psychoanalytic ethnography of thick-descriptive activity, and shown the multiple ways in which culture has entered into the supposed objective and value-neutral formulations of psychoanalytic theory. Cultural revisioning of foundational psychoanalytic postulates can be extended to include the findings of related scholarly interpreters: gender and feminist theory, which has been at pains to expose psychoanalytic essentialism and patriarchy, and race theorists, who have unearthed the hidden connection between psychoanalysis, class, race, and colonialism.

It has been further well catalogued that when Freud extended his analysis of religion in *The Future of an Illusion* a series of critical response came to fruition in the works of several noted philosophers and theologians. This is understandable given Freud's entry into the sizable debates that have raged over how to define religion. For him the only deserving definition was the common man's understanding of religion: an understanding which was Western, assumed institutionalized patriarchal forms of sociocultural power, and whose normative expression was centered in the monotheistic "mighty personality" of an exalted Father-God. Indeed, in *The Future of an Illusion* he defiantly chastised those "philosophers" who tried to "stretch the meaning of words" to the point that words like "God" and "religious" ceased to bear any resemblance to the Being worshipped by the common man. It is hardly a surprise that by the mid-twentieth century the central feature of the psychoanalytic study of religion became the dialogue between Christian theologians and various psychoanalytic schools.

In looking to other traditions, this essay seeks to illumine a poorly understood dimension of the psychoanalytic study of religion: its engagement with Buddhism. In general, the approach championed is that psychoanalysis, in order to promote an evolving bona fide dialogue with Buddhism, must engage in interdisciplinary conversation with the resources of religious studies and its fellow social sciences. Indeed, the present chapter can be viewed as but one illustration of how such an approach can be fruitfully employed. Indeed, our presentation will be facilitated if we think of both psychoanalysis and Buddhism as ethnopsychological systems whose origins are born of a distinct social context, their subsequent development as influenced by the changing conditions of history and culture, and attempts at mutual dialogue as necessitating engagement with current issues and debates within religious studies.

On "the More": Opening Remarks

At first glance psychoanalysis and Buddhism appear to be alternate, if not radically different, healing enterprises. One aspires to assuage suffering, strengthen the self, and facilitate adaptation to the world: *Wo Es war, soll Ich werden*, as Freud's "psychoanalytic motto" would have it; the other, reminding us of the inadequacy of characterizing it as but a *psychological* system, holds to the aims avowed by religious soteriology in proclaiming there is an end to all suffering while insisting on the illusion of an eternal, ontological self. Initially, there seems to be both a religious and cultural divide that threatens any attempt at a bona fide dialogue. On the other hand, it is good to keep in mind that psychoanalysis and Indian religions have more historical and cultural continuities than is usually acknowledged. For example Freud, relying on Plato's *Phaedrus*, was fond of likening his structural model of the mind in works like *The Ego and the Id* to a chariot: the rider (*das Ich*) was always at pains to control the noble (*das Uber-Ich*) and ignoble (*das Es*) horses. And Plato undoubtedly derived this image from Indian sources: *his* steeds had wings. Then again Freud, the beneficiary of what Raymond Schwab referred to as the "oriental renaissance" and well aware of the Western debates over the meaning of "nirvana" sweeping the Academy (including his own University of Vienna) during the late nineteenth century, was willing to admit (if one is to believe Bruno Goetz) that the Indian poets had, unlike the "second attempt" of Schiller's brave diver, arrived at the depths of the "ocean-womb" of consciousness, there to gain "an all surpassing, superhuman insight."[1] Even if one were to conclude that Goetz "misremembered," Freud was to use the same Schiller poem a quarter-century later to characterize mystical trances and ecstasies to his friend Romain Rolland, one of the first Western biographers of Ramakrishna and Vivekananda. Indeed, the psychoanalytic motto (*wo Es war, soll Ich werden*) set in a paragraph referencing oceans, rivers, and mystical practices, is itself a response to Rolland and his mystic friends.[2] Indeed, did not Freud expressly state in his *Interpretation of Dreams* that there existed a bottomless "navel" to the self? Yet such observations would be misused if used in the service of putting a happy face on Freud's limited engagement with Buddhism. What little Freud had to say about Buddhism was generally reductionistic, and he was uninterested in pursuing a meaningful dialogue with its representatives. What one can say is that a progressive dialogue between Buddhism and psychoanalysis can center on the metaphor "of chariots, navels, and winged steeds."

While a comprehensive, detailed, and, most importantly, accurate history of psychoanalytic encounters with Buddhism has yet to be written, one can point to some important historical markers.[3] Freud was writing during the birth of the "psychology and religion movement."[4] The latter, during the course of the last century, has incorporated a variety of different psychological models ranging from depth-psychological, existential, humanistic, and transpersonal approaches to those emphasizing physiology, empirical testing, evolutionary biology, and the neurocognitive. So too has this "movement" been quite interdisciplinary, drawing from studies in the hard and social sciences as well as from the wide spectrum of disciplines within the humanities. Freud, Jung, and James are usually cited as the major figures of the originative period of this movement, which many see as stretching from the 1880s to approximately the Second World War.[5] Of course the most well known of the specifically psychoanalytic forays into religion is Feud's reductionistic *Future of an Illusion*. Psychoanalytic studies of Buddhism in this "first" period tended to mirror Freud's pejorative interpretation of Western religion. While Freud said little about Buddhism in particular, his general view of mysticism as consisting of "oceanic feelings" alongside prominent psychoanalytic studies of this period, notably those of Ferdinand Morel (in his 1918 work *Essai sur l'introversion mystique*) and Franz Alexander (in his 1931 essay "Buddhistic Training as an Artificial Catatonia"), both of which interpreted the Buddhist nirvana as a regression to the womb, helped form the enduring perception that psychoanalysis views Buddhism as regressive, lacking in reality testing and possibly pathological.

In the "second period" of the psychology and religion movement (the postwar period to 1970) one finds the emergence of a much more positive psychoanalytic view of religion in general and Buddhism in particular. Freud, Alexander, and Morel had been armchair anthropologists relying on secondhand sources, incomplete translations, Western-based studies of Buddhism, and little if any direct contact with Buddhist practitioners. The "dialogue" was marred by orientalism, colonialism, and eurocentrism. The more positive engagement with Buddhism of this "second" period was due to several interrelated factors: the emergence of more religion-friendly theories (e.g., ego-psychology, object-relations theory, the neo-Freudians); a cultural hunger for nondogmatic, experience-based religious practices (as found especially in Zen and exemplified in the rise of entheogens); and the convergence of Western psychologists (notably Karen Horney, Erich Fromm, and Harold Kelman) with Asian psychologists sympathetic to Buddhism (e.g., Akihisa Kondo; Koji Sato) and Buddhist practitioners capable of framing Buddhism in psychological terminology (e.g., D. T. Suzuki, Shin'ichi Hisamatsu). Generally speaking, the Western psychologists saw Buddhist practice as a healing enterprise which was on a par with psychoanalytic practice—"Eastern" psychoanalysis, as it were. To be sure, Buddhism employed different terminology, but properly "translated" and seen in light of advances in psychoanalytic theory, bona fide dialogue could take place. Thus it is that Karen Horney could see in Zen reflections of her notions of the Real Self and "wholeheartedness," Erich Fromm reflections of his notions of the "full recovery" of the unconscious and "total experience of the total man," and Herbert Fingarette could conclude that the Zen notion of "no-self" was not nilhistic but in actuality the "loss" of the "transference self."[6]

The last few decades, falling under the most recent and "third phase" of development within the psychology and religion movement, have seen yet another series of advances. With respect to psychoanalysis one finds, in addition to the classic, Neo-Freudian, and ego-psychological models of the previous two periods, a more liberal use of object-relations theory, Self psychology, intersubjectivity, and post-structural perspectives. Many of the scholars/clinicians instrumental to furthering the psychoanalytic dialogue with Buddhism in this period (e.g., Michael Eigen, Jack Engler, Paul Cooper, Judith Blackstone, Mark Epstein, John Suler, Jeffrey Rubin) reflect a baby-boomer generation socialized into the liminal, pluralistic, and experimental decades of the sixties. They became attracted to Eastern religions and have integrated meditational practices into their own therapeutic work. Many espouse multiple professional identities: they are practicing psychoanalysts (who have been analysands) and teachers of Buddhist meditation (who have been students of an assortment of Buddhist masters/gurus). One distinguishing mark of this period is the attempt to integrate the insights of psychoanalysis with a realm of introspective discourse that is understood to map dimensions of experience and subjectivity that go beyond existing psychoanalytic theory. From this perspective Buddhist practice is not simply therapeutic but soteriological. These authors do acknowledge that Buddhist traditions contain ideation and practices that contain elements reflecting pathological dimensions and adaptive benefits. But they also claim that Buddhism presents us with forms of deep subjectivity and wisdom that go beyond existing psychoanalytic formulations. This presents a problem: how should we conceive of what William James refers to as this "More," and what kind of bridges need to be built to bring it into proper relation with existing psychoanalytic theory? Indeed, are their discernable limits to any psychoanalytic attempt to build bridges to the Buddhist More?

On Psychoanalysis, Mysticism, and Spirituality

Starting with the generation after Freud the psychoanalytic study of religion has seen fit to go beyond Oedipus in the attempt to provide interpretative models for those religious experiences and states which consist of more than the kind of projections and regressive fixations Freud found in the religion of the "common man." Within psychoanalysis proper the names of, among others, Erik Erikson, W. W. Meissner, and Ana-Maria Rizzuto come to mind, as do those of Paul Tillich, James Fowler, and Don Browning in that enterprise known as the "psychology-theology dialogue" (or "practical theology").[7] Recent psychoanalytic studies of Buddhism have also attempted to expand psychoanalytic theorizing of the More. Indeed, they are specifically dialogical projects in that they receive their understanding of the More from a particular religio-cultural strand from within Buddhism, then attempt to build bridges between them and sympathetic concepts drawn from various "schools" within psychoanalysis. Insofar as they emphasize meditation, altered states, and the attainment of nirvana, one could say that they engage the "mystical" or "spiritual" element in religion. While this is hardly incorrect, it is less than precise. This is in part because the terms "mysticism" and "spirituality," as is now well known in religious studies, are somewhat problematic.

The term "mysticism" is of Western origin. More specifically, it is derived from the Greek verb *muo* (to close) which, in its original usage, lacked any direct reference to God. The latter became the case when the Greek "mystikos" was appropriated by the early Christian Church Fathers. There "mysticism" was used in its adjectival form (mystical theology, mystical theology) and was defined, as Louis Boyer notes, with respect to participation in a total religious matrix.[8] From this perspective, what we know as "mystical experiences" could be accessed only through the auspices of the Christian church and its various accoutrements. That is, one could not properly say that mystical experiences pointed to an innate, generic religious dimension of consciousness. On the contrary, such experiences were gifts of grace and, further, signified the presence of a specifically Christian objective reality above and beyond the wholly subjective. This is important for in the vast academic study of "mysticism" one finds theologians who are engaged in the task of articulating what has been called "mystical theology," an enterprise in which subjective religious "experience" is acknowledged but one "element" within a total religious matrix. Mysticism is, then, fully embedded in, and in some sense secondary with respect to scripture, ritual, liturgy, theological reflection, and church tradition. There is no "raw" or basic, innate, or generic form of "experience" that exists "apart from," "beneath," or "before" its complicity in a total religious matrix. From this perspective, one cannot gain access to a bona fide "Christian" mystical experience without entry into the Church and its accoutrements. With respect to this enterprise, then, it is better to speak of "mysticisms" (Christian, Jewish, Buddhist, Hindu, etc.) as over against "mysticism."

Moving on, Michel DeCerteau has noted that it was not until the sixteenth and seventeenth centuries that one finds the emergence of mysticism as a substantive, the delineation of the topic in terms of a subjective "experience" divorced from church and tradition and, subsequently, the investigation and interpretation of such experiences from a psychological perspective, notably in the early psychologists of religion like Charcot, Morel, and Flournoy.[9] The view of the divine as "God" was replaced by the generic term "the Absolute," now framed "as an obscure, universal dimension of man, perceived or experienced as a reality [un réel] hidden beneath a diversity of institutions, religions, and doctrines."[10] Mystical experiences, now conceived of as an innate part of human equipment, became associated with a laundry list of generic terms (e.g., peak experiences, joy, bliss, transcendence of space and time, heightened empathy and morality, sense of immortality). Paradigmatic in this regard is the work of William James who, in his *Varieties of Religious Experience*, articulated five characteristics (passivity, noesis, ineffability, transiency, and unity) as being essential to the fiber of things mystical.[11] Tradition and its accoutrements, by which James meant theology, philosophy, liturgy, ritual, and the various aspects of church organizations, all crucial for access to the Presence of God for the Church Fathers, were understood by James as secondary phenomena, derived from the primary experiential matrix as located in the individual, and thus unessential for access to the divine. There is, then, an evident sea change in the meaning of the term "mysticism" from the Church Fathers to the researches of James.

The term "spirituality" (from the Latin term *spiritualitas*), which is often allied with and indistinguishable from "mysticism," has followed a similar historical trajectory. At first the Pauline pneuma (rendered as *spiritus* in the Latin translation of his letters) characterized a person guided by the spirit of God (as over against the carnal man who turned toward materiality). In the early Christian use of the term what was emphasized was growth in the spirit (i.e., the development of virtues, dispositions, and ideals in the striving towards Christian perfection). It is true that one can discern through the centuries deviations in meaning (for example, at one point spirituality came to denote ecclesiastical property and persons who exercised ecclesiastical jurisdiction), but in the main spirituality held fast to its moral, psychological, and religious meanings.[12] Adhering to its biblical roots, much of current spirituality in theological literature refers to religious growth within a particular tradition (e.g., the "spirituality" of St. Teresa of Avila). In this way "classic spirituality" (as some refer to it) and what we referred to above as the project of articulating a "mystical theology" are commensurate: they both refer to growth and mystical experiences within a total religious matrix.

What is important for our purposes is that alongside this "classical spirituality" one can also find a form of "modern" spirituality which, like the "modern" mysticism as defined by James and his followers, is nontraditional, noninstitutional, and hence, if one were to target its specifically Western and Christian roots, "unchurched."[13] While both modern and classic forms of spirituality emphasize mystical experience and even the "development" of the self, only classic forms are defined with respect to allegiance to a particular religious tradition. Indeed, modern spirituality often portrays institutional religion as the enemy. In line with Freud's "hermeneutics of suspicion," modern spirituality often portrays institutional religion as the home of authoritarianism, mendacity, and dogmatism. The adherents of modern spirituality are notably eclectic, adopting a supermarket approach to religious traditions and practices. It is the norm to find them constructing a highly individualized private spirituality which is decidedly psychological and holds to a conception of the Divine as innate and within: a "deeper me." Robert Fuller sees an affinity to those multiple practices designated by the term the New Age, further locating it as part of a long unchurched religious tradition with roots in the Western past (e.g., Unitarianism, Theosophy, Spiritualism, Mesmerism, Transcendentalism, New Thought, Swedenborgianism, Humanistic-Transpersonal psychology).[14] In sum, what we have here is an unchurched mysticism and spirituality divorced from religious institutions and their accoutrements (as the saying goes: "I'm spiritual, but not religious") which is highly individualized, very psychological, and predictably capitalistic in its stress on human potential and techniques for growth. One can readily see, then, see how "modern" mysticism and "modern" spirituality have become interchangeable terms (mystical experiences are seen as part of, indeed the denouement of, the spiritual path).

Historically speaking, where does psychoanalysis fit in these various construals and debates? The *locus classicus* of the psychoanalytic interpretation of mysticism lies in Freud's interpretation of the "oceanic feeling." Romain Rolland, the man responsible for introducing Freud to the term, posited that it was essentially unchurched: it was prior to yet was responsible for the variety of the world's religious traditions and their accoutrements. He also suggested to Freud that they work together to develop and implement an unchurched, noninstitutional "mystical psychoanalysis" and universal "science-religion." In other words, he was operating firmly in the modern, psychological Jamesian understanding of mysticism. Significantly, while de Certeau has nothing to say about the figures, characteristics, and subsequent career of unchurched mysticism during the course of the twentieth century he does make note of what he refers to as "a significant debate," namely, that between Sigmund Freud and Romain Rolland. De Certeau finds in Rolland's reflections on the oceanic feeling evidence of one aspect of the historical trend he attempts to delineate: the shift away from defining mysticism solely with respect to a particular religious matrix.

The psychoanalytic studies of Buddhism under consideration here also partake of this trend. Their collective efforts amount to a "translation project" of sorts, and what remains of traditional forms of Buddhism needs to be closely examined. This is not to assume a "pure" form of Buddhism; Buddhism changes depending on place and time. The issue is how it changes when "translated" by sympathetic psychoanalysts born of American soil. While this task is beyond the parameters of this essay, a few important observations can be made. It is clear, for example, that multiple stands of Buddhism are now meeting, for the first time, in a cultural soil that resolves many of their differences by valorizing the technological and psychological over the ritualistic, ideological, and scriptural. These studies, as is true of psychoanalysis as a whole, are clinically oriented and focus on "experience."[15] At times one wonders what remains of traditional Buddhist cosmology and its various ideological tenets. Most evident is the absence of Buddhist explanations of why it is that change or development occurs—or not. This is, of course, one of the major issues within any psychotherapeutic system. That one can change, and what enables one to change, are the focal points of psychoanalysis. Buddhism has its multiple views on this, but most central is the notion of karma. Put baldly, *no traditional (i.e., pre-psychoanalytic and non-American) form of Buddhism would ever think to describe the "developmental" path to enlightenment without recourse to the twin, related concepts of karma and reincarnation.* Such concepts are as central to Buddhism as, for example, God-given "grace" is to Christianity. Indeed, a traditional Buddhist conception of "development" would speak of the "lives-cycle." But as a strictly developmental concept there is no place for this in psychoanalytic theory. One could only include it if treated as a transitional form of experiencing relevant to the ideological over-belief of a particular individual (an over-belief, one might add, which is by no means universal to those "unchurched" who may incorporate meditation as part of their spiritual regimen). In other words, the psychoanalytic studies of Buddhism advocate a technologized, therapeutized, growth-centered form of Buddhism. While some may call these studies one form of "American Buddhism," and there is certainly some truth to this assertion, the observations here suggest it is admissible to refer their project as instances of the "psychology-comparativist dialogue" which partake of those forces that ushered in "modern" construals of mysticism and spirituality.[16] Their "translation" project is one born of that cultural soil seeded by the rise of this noninstitutional, unchurched spirituality.

Calvin, Freud, and the Buddha

To take this a step further, one can ask about the nature of the forces responsible for the turn to "modern" forms of mysticism and spirituality. In other words, what is the sociology behind the rise of the psychology-comparativist projects of which we speak?

Certainly the eddies of cultural change are complex to the point of escaping the conceptual grasp of any one theoretical framework. Nevertheless, without any pretense to completeness, a compelling (if sweeping) narrative can be woven adducing studies which have followed a specifically Weberian plotline in order to indicate how the mutual interplay of religion, psychoanalysis, and culture have furthered the establishment of an unchurched spirituality.

As is well known, in his classic work *The Protestant Ethic and the Spirit of Capitalism* Weber cast the world Catholicism built as magical and enchanted, populated by a host of saintly intermediaries to God. The latter, alongside the church and confessional, gave the believer a psychological release from guilt and anxiety over salvation. The emergence of the Protestant tradition and its attendant social type, the inner-worldly ascetic, sheared the world of such magical releases. Faced with the twin theological doctrines of predestination and salvation, with only scripture and conscience as conduits to God, the Protestant, more anxious and guilty relative to his fellow Catholic, was particularly ripe for psychoanalytic therapy. The success and widespread appeal of Freud was in part due to the ability of his psychology, whose theory and practice focused on the *uber-ich*, guilt and anxiety, to address the psychological world of the inner-worldly ascetic. As Rieff has noted, classic Freudian psychoanalysis fits hand-in-glove with inner-worldly asceticism.[17] In this regard it is relevant to note that while Catholics and those believers in other religious traditions, as well as their scholarly representatives (e.g., Hans Kung, Mircea Eliade), took to dialogue with psychoanalysis, the most creative, popular, and powerful form of the dialogue between depth-psychology and religion during the mid-twentieth century was that between psychoanalysis and Protestant theology, the predominant issues being the nature of sin, determinism, freedom, guilt, and the "heteronomous" God.[18] Indeed, it is no accident that the creation of pastoral psychology was a mid-twentieth century enterprise and that, as a "response" to Freud, it was predominantly the result of the efforts of Protestant Christians.

Psychoanalysis, born of disenchantment, contributed to the further undermining of institutionalized religion. This is so because the psychological representative of the latter in one's inner world is the cultural super-ego. Classic Freudian psychoanalytic therapy operates by taking the individual into a socially liminal space: the "double-doors" of the therapeutic encounter, where the depths of the cultural super-ego are uncovered and undermined, resulting in a more unique sense of self and a more suspicious relation to cultural forms. In Rieff's terminology, the shift is from a "positive community," defined as cultures dominated by a religious symbolic, the hegemony of the religiously based cultural super-ego, the valorization of the community over the individual, an idealized "language of faith," and an ethic which promotes repression and guilt, to a "negative community" inhabited by "psychological man," which promotes the analytic attitude, sociological "deconversion," the tolerance of unconscious discontents, and the valorization of the individual over the community.[19]

Peter Homans, while applauding Rieff's efforts, argues that some depth-psychologies have a more integral relationship with the religions of the Western past than allowed for by Rieff. The paradigmatic case in this regard is Carl Jung. Using a psychosocial variant of Weber's ideal types, Homans shows how Jung, disillusioned with his native Protestantism, rejected certain elements of his religious past only to reserve a space for the reintegration of religion in the form of a generic religious dimension to the unconscious.[20] In effect Jung, like Rolland, in following the trend of "modern" spirituality, deconstructed institutional religion in favor of an unchurched one that saw us all as "congregations of one," as housing in our unconscious a veritable storehouse of the collective wisdom of religion. The psychoanalytic correlate to this would be that group of innovative clinicians who Kakar has referred to as the "mystics of psychoanalysis."[21] The formulations of the latter include Erikson's reference to the "unborn core of creation" (*ein lauter Nichts*)—a phrase indebted to Silesius and elaborated in Erikson's later works in terms of the "numinosity" of the "I"; the British analyst Wilfred Bion, who speaks of "O," the actualization of which is the ideal aim of the therapeutic encounter, in explicitly mystical terms as "the absolute truth, the godhead, the infinite, the thing-in-itself . . . it can 'become,' but it cannot be known"; and Lacan's conception of "the Real."[22] Lacan was heavily influenced by Plotinus and Teresa and objected to reducing mysticism to sex. He thought his own work should be regarded as essentially "of the same order" as mysticism. Finally, one could point to Heinz Kohut's concept of "cosmic narcissism," a concept which clearly captures the religio-ethical goal of his psychology, which is framed as a developmentally mature attainment indicative of ethical and existential achievement beyond the results of a successful analysis, and understood as "a shift of the narcissistic cathexis from the self to a concept of participation in a supraindividual and timeless existence."[23] Cosmic narcissism "transcends the bounds of the individual," and one lives "sub specie aeternitas" without elation or anxiety, bathed in a continual communion with a contentless, supraordinate Self, participating in "supraindividual ideals and the world with which one identifies."[24] It is further interesting to note that to this ideal Kohut conjoins a cultural agenda. In his essay "On Leadership" Kohut suggests the need for a new, unchurched rational religion, "an as yet uncreated system of mystical rationality which could take the place of the religions of the past."[25] He then points to "instances of heroic men of constructive political action who have achieved a transformation of their narcissism into a contentless, inspiring personal religion," further commenting that humanity will have to produce such types in greater numbers in order to survive.[26] As to who might embody such an achievement, Kohut points to Dag Hammarskjöld, the former secretary-general of the United Nations: "Dag Hammarskjöld . . . an example of this type, describes his contentless mysticism in the following words: "Faith is a state of mind and of the soul . . . the language of religion is (only) a set of formulas which register a basic religious experience."[27]

These formulations have in common the attempt to legitimate the More of mysticism in generic, psychological terms. Indeed, their formulations lead one to conclude that psychoanalysis has come full circle, only this time back to Jung, not Freud. They belong with the psychoanalytic encounter with Buddhism in that both can be said to address the More of mysticism and both have been influenced by the cultural soil of unchurched spirituality. In this sense both are forms of psychoanalytic spirituality. On the other hand, the project of the psychoanalytic mystics is not explicitly dialogical or "in the service" of Buddhism. Insofar as the psychoanalytic encounter with Buddhism is a specifically dialogical project and aims at cultural translation, it also has affinities with the psychology-theology dialogue.

Returning to the sociology of spirituality and psychoanalysis, our contribution to this line of argument lies in suggesting that the social counterpart to the emergence of the popularity of depth-psychological probes into the More of spirituality is not that of the inner-worldly ascetic but that of what Weber called the inner-worldly mystic. Elaborated further by Roland Robertson, the inner-worldly mystic is described as a modern form of adaptation to a culture characterized by the rise of capitalism, individualism, pluralism, and various introspective techniques, many of which influenced the babyboomer generation (some now practicing analysts) in the essentially "liminal" decade of the 1960s. Viewed in the context of the capitalistic ethos, inner-worldly mysticism expresses the need to work "in the world" while striving for wholeness and the actualization of the "self." Therapy, yoga, meditation, dietary and exercise programs, and the individualistic, eclectic supermarket approach to religion are part and parcel of inner-worldly mysticism.[28] As Fuller notes, empirical studies estimate that up to 21 percent of the current population have chosen to express their religious sentiments in this unchurched, spiritual manner.[29]

With respect to Buddhism, contemporary psychoanalytic literature suggests that spirituality has crept into multiple aspects of the practice of analysts and of the therapeutic expectations of analysands. To cite but a few examples, the British psychoanalyst Nina Coltart, referring to matters of technique, speaks of "bare attention," a Buddhist meditative term, and how the practice of it has helped her to empathize with her analysands. The training analyst Michael Eigen, particularly influenced by Jewish mysticism and Zen refers to psychoanalytic therapy as "a pyschospiritual journey," further arguing that meditative practices and psychoanalysis are not separate but part of an allied process of growth.[30] The training analyst Paul Cooper thinks that spiritual practices have influenced multiple dimensions of psychoanalytic therapy (e.g., theory, technique, training, and supervision) and draws attention to the important empirical fact that many of his analysands understand psychoanalytic therapy as part of their spiritual growth. There is, thinks Cooper, an undeniable cultural drift in this direction.[31] These observations indicate that psychoanalytic therapy is engaging a new social base, and that the latter is at least in part responsible for analysts and analysands with spiritual concerns. The psychology-comparativist dialogue, of which specifically psychoanalytic encounters with Buddhism form a part, is thus analogous to the pastoral psychology movement of the mid-twentieth century. Just as the rise of the inner-worldly ascetic was in part responsible for pastoral psychology, so too is the rise of the inner-worldly mystic responsible for the rise of that form of psychoanalytic spirituality bent on engaging Buddhism.

The Variety of Mystical Navels

Moving forward from the sociology of the emergence of a psychoanalytic spirituality, it behooves us to delve deeper into the content of the psychoanalytic studies of Buddhism under consideration. That is, what specifically do they prescribe when speaking of the Buddhist More? This is important, for these studies, lacking coordination with religious studies and the wider psychology and religion movement, often implicitly take positions on issues which have been hotly debated for some time. At the very least, an indication of how this may be the case provides the function of a cautionary tale.

To begin we can inquire as to the status within these studies of mystical "experience." In the discourse created by the academic study of religion, the above historical narrative of mysticism and spirituality has given life to a series of theoretical projects, the most distinct of which during the twentieth century being that of perennialism. While perennialism has evolved, becoming more sophisticated and nuanced, it will suffice to remain simple by defining it as the postulation of a universal "common-core" to mysticism. Over time perennialism was supplemented by typologies of various kinds, and both became problematic by virtue of not simply variations found in mystical texts and the epistemological difficulties encountered in the search for a common-core but also, in the attempt to articulate that elusive common-core, unexamined normative, orientalist, and colonialist tendencies. A new "school," present but buried during the earlier part of the century, emerged with force in the later 1970s. Argued most forcefully by Steven Katz, the "constructivist" school argues that all mystical experiences are mediated; that the notion of there being a basic universal "raw experience" which can be siphoned out from the text, and which underlies the various cultural and religious "interpretations" of it, is demonstrably (read: textually) wrong and epistemologically (and here the constructivists follow Kant) impossible to prove. Most (but not all) constructivists are not arguing that there is no transcendent dimension to mysticism. Rather, they are arguing that it is impossible to locate a common core: mystical experiences and states are multiple and varied, some different in degree and perhaps others in kind, and all must be contextualized in the religious tradition in which they arise. From this perspective it is better to speak of "mysticisms" than of "mysticism" and the plea is that for the recognition of differences and the need to include context.[32] As such, their project is much closer to the project (that of "mystical theology") championed by those intellectuals representing particular religious traditions.

As mentioned above, the *locus classicus* of the psychoanalytic interpretation of mysticism lies in Freud's interpretation of the "oceanic feeling," understood as the perennial core of mysticism (with its focus on oneness and unity) and interpreted with respect to preoedipal ideation. Romain Rolland, the man responsible for introducing Freud to the "oceanic feeling," not only tended toward modern "spirituality" and construed "mysticism" in the Jamesian sense, but also declared an unsophisticated form of perennialism by positing that there existed a perennial "raw core" to mysticism which lay outside of, and yet was responsible for, the variety of the world's religious traditions. Historically speaking, then, psychoanalysis fits quite neatly into the modern construal of mysticism and spirituality with an attendant focus on perennialism.

Psychoanalytic perennialism, so to speak, is problematic for reasons germane to this chapter. First, many (but not all) contemporary psychoanalysts still equate the oceanic feeling with mysticism everywhere. Indeed, some analysts involved in recent psychoanalytic dialogues with Buddhism use the term "the oceanic feeling" rather loosely, finding easy analogs in the Buddhist tradition. But the oceanic feeling reflects primarily the mysticism of one man, Romain Rolland. And Rolland's own comparativist conclusions, that is to say his avowal of perennialism, which played no small role in the adoption of perennialism by psychoanalysis, was based on his own mystical experiences. Indeed for Rolland it was the latter that became the norm and "common-core" of mysticism everywhere. Such an assertion, which Rolland never backed up with sophisticated textual and epistemological arguments, is akin to the claim that, for example, the phenomenology, dynamics, and etiology of obsessional neurosis can be universalized to apply to any psychological illness. That oceanic feelings *may* be present in some mystical texts of a religious, philosophical, or literary nature is beyond dispute. To render all mysticism, which may be varied in degree and kind and in need of multiple models of explanation, as reducible to a common-core of oceanic feelings is demonstrably false.

Second, Freud's views on the oceanic feeling and mysticism continue to be misunderstood and misrepresented. As the "received view" would have it, Freud understood the oceanic feeling as an instance of a transient mystical experience and interpreted it as a regression to primary narcissism. But when one looks through Rolland's journals, letters, autobiographical reflections, novels, and religious writings, one is able to reconstruct details of Rolland's mysticism—details which allow us to make deeper sense of the continued correspondence between the two men (wholly ignored by those who are content to regurgitate the "received view") over the nature of mysticism. While this analysis can be found in full elsewhere[33] we can summarize the conclusions briefly as follows: (1) Rolland's mysticism was idiosyncratic, unchurched, psychologically nuanced (all characteristics of DeCerteau's and James's "modern mysticism") and close to what R. C. Zaehner dubs "nature mysticism." That is, his autobiographical mystical "texts" all describe felt mergings with his natural surroundings; (2) Rolland distinguished between episodic, unitive nature mystical experiences which engaged the working of a faculty commensurate with but above reason he called "intuition" and that enduring, constant mystical state, which was a later, more mature mystical phenomenon, he referred to as the "oceanic feeling." Strictly speaking, then, the latter is not commensurate with episodic mystical experiences, being far closer (without drawing an exact equivalence) to other statelike mystical states in religious traditions (notably Sri Ramana Maharshi's *sahaja samedhi*); (3) mystical experiences and the oceanic feeling were existentially related: transient mystical experience contained the teleological injunction to introspect and purify one's internal world (one of the reasons he was so attracted to Freud). This process eventuated in the deeper, more mature and permanent oceanic feeling; (4) Freud as well understood the oceanic feeling as an enduring state (he refers to it as something Rolland was "never without"—a fact which accounts for why it caused Freud, who was clearly well acquainted with mystical experience proper, so much perplexity) and interpreted it as the *preservation of* (not momentary *regression* to) the all-embracing feeling of primary narcissism (as it continued to be felt alongside the more clearly demarked ego of adulthood); and (5) Freud initiated a different hermeneutical strategy for the interpretation of mystical experiences proper by noting that mystical practices and the "intuitions" they unearthed approximated the efforts of psychoanalytic techniques: both methods "upset" the "normal" relations between the ego and id, so that the ego might glean the deeper dimension of unconscious content. Freud suggested that episodic mystical experiences could be a defensive maneuver but also held out the possibility that it contained valuable psychological knowledge and, properly integrated, could be the source of adaptive behavior.

The above argues not only for the reinstatement of an accurate understanding of Rolland's oceanic feeling and Freud's understanding and interpretation of it but also, in eschewing a misleading perennialism based on the oceanic feeling, a much more precise, careful, and contextualized series of analyses when dealing with any mystical phenomena. This conclusion, albeit after a rather extended sojourn into the land of debates in religious studies, brings us back to the most recent period in the psychoanalytic encounter with Buddhism. In the case of the latter, the "constructivist" Robert Gimello begins to make the case for us when he attempts to distinguish between types of Buddhist meditative experiences. Gimello laments that the word "mysticism" carries with it echoes of the Western mystical past, further complaining "it is difficult to apply any of the widely accepted definitions or descriptions of mysticism to Buddhist praxis without the most serious reservations."[34] Gimello notes that the usual notion that mystical experience is constituted by oneness or unity of some kind is certainly true in some sense for Buddhist meditative practices that emphasize concentration (e.g., *jnana*) and produce states of absorption and *samedhi*, but not for the insight into the nature of conditioned origination and *anatta* reserved in Theravada

Buddhism for *vipassana*. The term "mysticism" can only be used for the latter if qualified with respect to the specific Buddhist tradition and meditative case—or, rather, "cases"—under scrutiny.

Gimello's cautionary series of observations are directly relevant to recent psychoanalytic encounters with Buddhism. A case in point is one prominent study, revolving around *vipassana* meditation, which belongs to Jack Engler. Reflecting on years of experience as a professor (in holding a doctorate from the University of Chicago), as Buddhist *vipassana* meditation teacher *and* as a psychoanalytic clinician, Engler became convinced that those psychoanalytically minded interpreters of the Buddhist *anatta* before him had only understood but a part of the Buddhist meditational process. Buddhism was not, as with the early effort of Franz Alexander, simply a regression to early development and the womb or, as with the mid-century efforts of Karen Horney and Erich Fromm, simply an Eastern form of psychoanalysis. Engler agreed that, depending on the individual, one could find Buddhist practices linked to pathology or, alternately, evincing adaptive and healing effects. However, in engaging the Jamesian More, Engler thought that the deepest forms of Buddhist insight "went beyond" existing psychoanalytic conceptions of the Self. And so it is that he articulated the first compelling thesis of the third period of the psychoanalytic engagement with Buddhism which, as Engler summarily put, is as follows: "one has to be somebody before one can be nobody."[35]

In stating his case so plainly, Engler had overlooked Erik Erikson's correction of Freud's view of the monastery. For Freud the latter became a socially sanctioned institution for the neurotic and also, one could surmise, those with other than heterosexual aims. Erikson, in his analysis of Luther and his early life in an Augustinian monastery, not only referred to monastic activity as a moratorium, thereby giving it adaptive value, but more, in thinking explicitly of German mystics (of whom he was well acquainted) like Angelus Silesius, as reflecting those who had the prerequisite strong enough and cohesive enough selves to see into the bottomless pit of the Godhead. But whereas Erikson's Silesius and Engler's meditator agree that deep insight into the navel of the Self may require a cohesive Self, they differ on what one may find therein. Engler's focus is on Theravada Buddhism and its central practice, *vipassana* meditation. His "More," in other words, is a specifically Theravadin one. Here is how Engler describes the insight of *anatta*:

> Discovering that there is no ontological core to consciousness or self that is independent and enduring and no stable "objects" of perception . . . no "I" or "thing" enduring across the gap between one construction and arising of the

> next—this is a profound shock. It is experienced as a free fall into a looking-glass world where, as the Mad Hatter tells Alice, "Things are not as they seem!" It so turns our normal sense of self and reality on its head that, as Niels Bohr once remarked about quantum physics . . . if you don't get dizzy thinking about it, you haven't understood it.[36]

For Engler psychoanalysis and Theravada Buddhist employ different techniques for different aims. Free association, dream interpretation, transference etc., are all fruitful ways of heightening introspection and deepening the awareness of the discontents of repressed thoughts and feelings. But *vipassana* is designed to heighten attention to the extent that one is able to retrace the representational process whereby a sense of self, world, and other come to exist. In its most profound sense the practice of *vipassana* leads to the above description of *anatta*: the insight into the absence of an enduring self. If the therapeutic task can be conceived along the lines of mourning, the psychoanalytic encounter with Buddhism now reveals that the latter engages an even deeper level of mourning and working through: that of the existence of a continuous, stable, enduring self. The consequences of this perspective for psychoanalytic understandings of self and healing are dramatic. Engler proposes the radical claim that the construction of a separate, enduring, continuous self is "a compromise formation with defensive aims."[37] In other words, we repress the fact of an unconstructed core to existence. Indeed, Engler is quick to point out that the insight into *anatta* is not necessarily a discovery. From the Theravadin Buddhist perspective, the common-sense understanding that an enduring self exists is an illusion. There never was a self to begin with.

Of course Engler's is not the only attempt to account for the More of Buddhism. One could, for example, note the work of Paul Cooper who, banking off Ignacio Matte-Blanco's revisionist formulations of the unconscious, argues that Koan activity unearths the deepest dimensions of the unconscious, characterized as the "indivisible mode" where total symmetry prevails, or Judith Blackstone who, in engaging formulations of non-self states and their relation to conceptions of self-other found in intersubjective theory, argues that the former "goes beyond" the latter in the claim, central to Mahayana and Vajrayana strands of Buddhism, that there exists a Buddha nature within: a nonorganized self-existing nondual ground.[38] These conceptions of the "not-self" differ, and it is important to note that while Engler is allied with Theravada Buddhism, Cooper is a practitioner of Zen and Blackstone hails from lineages within Tibetan Buddhism. Indeed, Blackstone explicitly takes on Jack Engler and Mark Epstein, both of whom she thinks represent what the Tibetan Buddhist Rinpoche Tsultrim Gyamtso refers to as the Rangtong understanding of Self. In the Rangtong view, says Blackstone, the "eye" of the observing self cannot find a way to "turn around" and "know" itself. In the Rangtong view, all that one can "see" are fragments of emotions, sensations, thoughts, and volitional urges. This is the view, proclaims Blackstone, which is found in Mark Epstein's proclamation of "thoughts without a Thinker" and in Engler's description of *anatta*. In the Shentong view, on the other hand, the "eye" can see itself. The Shentong view is expressed by the Tibetan notion of the "clear light" of consciousness: a "knowing" that is completely unimaginable and nonconceptual, luminous and blissful, self-knowing and self-aware, naturally shining forth as conceptual and emotional obstructions are dissolved.[39]

The conclusions reached by the above studies reveal that there exists a disjunction between their primarily clinical focus and the kinds of debates and issues that animate the study of mysticism in the Academy. That is to say, here the Clinic and the Academy can and should work in tandem. For example, with regard to the perennialist/constructivist debate, it is clear that the studies by Engler, Cooper, and Blackstone fail to engage the broad range of issues this debate has engendered. And one would expect, if the authors of these primarily clinical studies had intentionally sought to bring these debates into their respective analyses and conclusions, that a more nuanced position with respect to the twin poles of the debate would result. However, as it stands, and one could argue perhaps unwittingly and unintentionally, the studies under consideration do tend to champion a position closer to that of perennialism. An illustration of this is when Engler, in the midst of being quizzed by the eminent psychoanalyst Steven Mitchell over the constructed nature of the insight into *anatta* (and here Mitchell, although unaware of the debate within religious studies, is clearly advocating a "constructivist" claim), responds by indicating that while the common, everyday view of *anatta* as a conceptual ideology may well be used in a way that speaks to it being constructed, the actual experience of or insight into no-self is not constructed.[40] This is in part due to the fact that Engler thinks that the attentive tracing of the emergence of self-representations as demanded by *vipassana* involves that cognitive process Arthur Deikman, following ego-psychology, called "de-automatization."[41] It is not accidental and relevant to our discussion that many recent attempts in perennialism aimed at promoting a nonconstructed mystical event also depend on de-automatization to buttress their claims. And it should be admitted that this might be not only descriptive of such forms of meditation, but also the experiential outcome of those who practice a technique of *vipassana* for long periods of time. But as it stands, the formulation that there never was a self to begin with which also can be "experienced" as a nonconstructed event is a claim that can be read as tending toward a perennialist position. If there is and never was at bottom a self, then the deepest common-core of any and all mystical traditions would be found by privileging those texts (as with Buddhism) which explicitly posit *anatta* or (with respect to other religious traditions) come close to it by positing a nondual, endless, bottomless navel to what "conventionally" appears to be a self (e.g., Eckhart's "godhead" or the Jewish "ayin"). Again Blackstone, who clearly has a different understanding of the deepest recesses of the not-self and who cautions of making universalistic ontological claims, nevertheless goes on to espouse a soft perennialism. Thus it is that she is willing to argue that "the universality of nondual consciousness can be inferred from the broad, cross-cultural consensus of descriptions of nondual experience," offering a mix of mystical texts from "Shendong" Tibetan Buddhism, Vedanta, and Kashmir Shaivism that she thinks convey the same essence.[42] But the constructivist claim would beg to differ. Nondual states are beyond ordinary conceptual modes of knowing (a deep epistemological problem in and of itself) and are never self-evident but, rather, always communicated within language, the medium of the sensible world and within a total religious matrix. By definition they will differ. One only need contrast Theravadin/Rangtong and Tibetean/Shendong views on the nondual. Comparatively speaking, one could also ask about those religious traditions that do not valorize the nondual and yet are "mystical" and harbor claims to ultimacy (e.g., St. Paul's ascent to the third heaven and Paradise [emerging as it did from Jewish Merkabah mysticism] and Mohammed's "Mi'raj" or night journey). It is hard to find some compelling argument that would convincingly demonstrate that there is one type of insight or experience that is deserving of ontological superiority. Indeed, any postulation of a common-core is bound to be reductive and, as important, normative.

These observations are hardly meant to undermine the efforts of those psychoanalytically inclined to build bridges to Buddhism. It is, however, to note that with respect to not only the psychoanalytic encounter with Buddhism, but also the wider psychoanalytic entry into the comparative study of mysticism and spirituality, there is at the very least a lack of engagement with the perennialist/constructivist debate as well as a *tendency* toward perennialism. To avoid such difficulties, one can translate such observations into a series of suggestions for psychoanalytic forays into Buddhism and the More in general. To wit: (1) psychoanalysis can work well with that form of constructivism which agrees that there is a More, but that it is always mediated, making difficult to isolate a common-core, much less legitimate a particular ontology or valorize one view of the core over another. In other words, psychoanalysis should proceed with a postmodern mentality when it comes to analyzing the More; (2) the psychoanalytic interpretation of Buddhism (and of the More in general) is best advised to proceed on a tradition-by-tradition and case-by-case basis. Mystical experiences and states are related in a family sense, but different in degree and, in certain instances, perhaps even in kind; and (3) given that multiple and different mystical experiences and states require multiple, different models, and in order that the mystical phenomenon is accurately understood and presented, any analysis would be helped by enlisting the efforts of clinicians, those in the social sciences, and specialists within religious studies.

A Myriad of (not) Selves: The Ambiguity of Development

Many of the clinicians of this "third" period of psychoanalytic encounters with Buddhism do not stop with "experience" or insight. They go on to develop full-fledged theories about the nature of psycho-spiritual "development." In this, of course, they are following a path well-trodden in mystical literature, from the "stations and stages" of the Sufi's to the familiar purgation/illumination/union progression found most notably in the Christian Spanish mystics (and made famous by Evelyn Underhill) to the Zen ox-herding pictures. But these developmental schemes, which may share general, underlying themes apparent in any transformative healing enterprise (e.g., models of the mind, introspective techniques, markers and aims of development, the establishment of virtues, etc.) also display different and at times incommensurate variations as to how such themes are defined and elaborated. So here as well, in mirroring the difficulties encountered concerning the essentialism linked with mystical experience, one encounters a series of problematic issues.

Of course generally speaking psychoanalytic theorizing about development has, as is well known from the perspective of the other social sciences and within religious studies, come under no dearth of criticism. As noted earlier, Freud was notoriously prone to essentialism, gender-bias, colonialism, and orientalism. For example, feeling under attack from Jung, Freud universalized and (in borrowing a religious term) "ontologized" Oedipus in *Totem and Taboo* so that it became the phylogenetic basis for all individual fantasies as well as societal and religious expressions. Oedipus was the original archetype. And it was but one small step from this to the application of his theories to, for example, explain (away) Buddhism as a simple regression to the womb, women as lacking in a sense of justice (and hence exempted from service in the social realm of Law), or to equate one's "negro" patients with primitives and an innate tendency to regression and fixation (as did, unfortunately, the early analysts).[43] It was only through the initial efforts of anthropologists and psychoanalysts who listened to them that we can now safely say that Freud is best framed as a psychologically gifted enthnographer of his culture and Oedipus as a universal possibility (but, taking into account place and time, not a universal actuality).

What is of further interest is how personal experience, in psychological developmental therories of all stripes, becomes the basis for normative theorizing about development. For example, one could point to Freud's cocaine inspired dreams and confession to Fleiss of finding Oedipus within as being instrumental to his emerging libido theory. Or, with respect to "mysticism" one could cite William James's experiments with nitrous oxide in his formulations on the varieties of religious experience and R. C. Bucke's sudden and life-altering experience of cosmic consciousness. But the paradigmatic example may well be that of Carl Jung. In chapter six of his *Memories, Dreams, Reflections*, Jung relates how, during the period following his divorce from Freud, he was seized by a period of personal disintegration and numerous visions which he describes as that "confrontation with the unconscious" that gave him "the *prima materia* for a lifetime's work."[44] Jung begins his account of his entry into the unconscious labyrinth by stating how the "Christian myth" no longer possessed him: "In what myth does man live nowadays? In the Christian myth, the answer might be. 'Do *you* live in it?' I asked myself. To be honest, the answer was no. 'Then do we no longer have any myth?' No, evidently we no longer have any myth."[45] The existential issue facing Jung was thus how to find (or create) his own "personal myth." The latter was slowly formed through Jung's encounter with fantasy figures like Salome, Philemon/Elijah and, most importantly, the spontaneous emergence of mandala figures and the wholeness of the Self archetype. Later, as articulated most clearly in what is now known as his *Two Essays on Analytical Psychology* he lent theoretical sophistication to his introspective probes: the process of individuation, the notion of the collective unconscious and delineation of its archetypes, the objectivity of the psyche, active imagination, and so on. Private experience had become the basis for public theory. And this theory rendered religion, its myths and symbols, as nothing more than "cultural containers" for the eruptions of the collective unconscious. His psychology was not only a psychology *of* religion; it had become a psychology *as* religion. That is, it has become, in essence, an integral part of the emerging "tradition" of unchurched spirituality which has come to fruition in the past decade.

All this is hardly to discount the importance, properly qualified and monitored, of personal experience in theory building or, for that matter, the value of theorizing about development. It is, however, to draw attention to the problems associated with the easy tendency to universalize. Normative elements abound, and one must remember that "experience" might well be culturally constituted and, while germane to a certain group of people in a particular historical-cultural locale, not necessarily universally actualized or acknowledged. When Jung took exception to some of Shin'ichi Hisamatsu's comments concerning Zen notions of the self and the attainment of nirvana, it was because Jung assumed that his theory was universal in scope. One could say that the "experiences" of Jung, which led to his psychological developmental scheme, were not those of Hisamatsu. Indeed, one gets the impression that Hisamatsu, with his notion of the "true self," is speaking of an insight—accessible through Rinzai Koans but not through Jung's analytic therapy—that lay entirely outside Jung's introspective probes. Certainly Hisamatsu made this claim.[46]

These preliminary observations bring us back to the "third" period of the psychoanalytic encounter with Buddhism for, as stated above, many of these theorists, privy to both clinically-based psychoanalytic encounters and the insights gained through meditational retreats, have endeavored to turn their own personal experience into developmental theories. Engler, for example, puts the matter quite plainly. In his dialogue with the eminent psychoanalyst Steven Mitchell over the meaning and nature of the insight into the absence of an enduring self, it is both striking and expected that Engler would inject a personal element. He admits that his entire theory is built on "experience"—that of the insight into *anatta.* It was this deep insight into the More, alongside his own introspective and clinical acquaintance with subjective structures theorized by psychoanalysis, that led Engler to turn the episodic insight of *anatta* (his "mystical experience") into a psycho-mystical developmental theory (his "mystical process").

In his initial formulations, Engler depicts psychoanalysis and Buddhism as mapping discrete states of a single developmental sequence.[47] Psychoanalysis describes the lower stages of "conventional" development and Buddhism the subtler, spiritual stages of "contemplative" development. In speaking to how these stages relate, Engler claims that psychoanalytic therapies (and here he is speaking mainly of object-relational theories), in accordance with Western understandings of health and adaptation to reality, seek to help "grow" a self. However, once a cohesive enough self has developed, one can then engage in a new form of introspection: *vipassana* meditation. This form of mental exercise is designed to gain insight into the reality that there is no enduring self. While it takes a strong cohesive self to properly integrate such deep insight, it is the case that such an understanding of Self and Reality, while commensurate with a Buddhist worldview, is not wholly commensurate with traditional Western orientations and therapeutic aims. Psychoanalysis, to the extent that it is imbued with Western values of individualism, and Buddhism are seen by Engler as having different aims: psychoanalysis aims to grow a cohesive self, Buddhism to realize there is no self. But again to repeat: the insight that there is no self is seen as the deeper one for in the end there never *was* a self. As noted earlier, for Engler the self is seen to be but a "compromise formation"—one with "defensive aims."

Evidence from Rorschach tests, case histories, reports of abuse within Buddhist communities as well as anecdotal evidence concerning the seemingly bizarre, defensive, and even pathological behavior of supposed Buddhist masters and gurus have called into question Engler's initial notion of discrete, hierarchically ordered stages of development. As a result, in his "later" work, he has taken these criticisms to heart, noting that the relation between the conventional and contemplative lines of development is complex and perhaps not as linear as his initial formulations suggest. So too does he agree with the notion that while anchored to the material body and existing in society one must operate with what can be called a "conventional" self. But Engler does not shy away from the claim that at bottom there is no enduring self. It is the episodic insight into the lack of an enduring Self which, in accord with the volitional and emotional changes it demands, can eventually lead to a process of extinguishing desire altogether—a state which Buddhists describe as being that of absolute freedom from suffering but which, as Engler notes, Freud held to be nothing but an "ideal fiction." Surely we have here two very different understandings of Self, World, and Other.

Engler's thesis has spurred not only criticism but also the creation of alternate developmental trajectories from those engaged in the recent psychoanalytic dialogue with Buddhism. A paradigmatic case is that of Jeff Rubin, who thinks the "early" Engler's efforts amount to a "pseudo-complimentary" approach in which "the complexity and multidimensionality of human experience and development is obscured by linear, hierarchical, developmental models."[48] Rubin argues that the relation between psychoanalysis and Buddhism "is more complex than the existing accounts suggest, forming not a singular pattern of influence but rather resembling a heterogeneous mosaic composed of elements that are—depending on the specific topic—antithetical, complementary and synergistic."[49] By "synergy" Rubin means that psychoanalysis can help Buddhism investigate unconscious determinants, idealizing transferences, life-cycle difficulties and the like, while Buddhism can help psychoanalysis with non-self centered subjective states and meditational techniques. And for Rubin "non-self centered subjective states" (and here he differs from Engler, giving as examples not only *anatta* but being in love, art, flow states, meditative absorption) are defined as being "open to the moment without a sense of time, unselfconsciousness but acutely aware, highly focused and engaged yet related without fear. . . . characterized by heightened attentiveness, focus and clarity, attunement to the other as well as the self, non-self preoccupied exercise of agency, a sense of unity."[50] These states are neither pathological nor archaic states of non-differentiation. The view of personhood of psychoanalysis and Buddhism respectively are not better than one another. Rather, they can be mutually enriching: they are "alternating positions of being rather than hierarchically ordered stages."[51] The melding together of psychoanalysis and Buddhism can lead to "a bifocal conception of subjectivity." Rubin sees a "new" self emerging—a "species-self . . . for whom both individuation and non-self centricity are seen as two interpenetrating facets of what it means to be a human being."[52] This new self, thinks Rubin, demands a certain obligation to be socially engaged (the latter being seen as missing from most of the history of Buddhism). In effect, Rubin is taking bits and pieces from both psychoanalysis and Buddhism in creating an adaptive vision that is both conditioned and demanded by a twenty-first century spirituality.

Judith Blackstone, for her part, offers yet another concept of development: one that reaches into Tantric conceptions of spirituality and chakra development: the More of the Body.[53] In her attempt to bring together Tantra and intersubjective theory, Blackstone relativizes psychoanalytic views of healing to "fit" into the larger, soteriological emphasis endemic to religious healing enterprises. Her premise is, as she says, that "as human development progresses, psychological and spiritual maturity become inseparable."[54] This mix of intersubjectivity and Asian nondual thought becomes the basis for her articulation of a therapeutic process she terms the "realization process." Blackstone prefers intersubjective theory because: (1) it is a psychoanalytic postmodern movement that seeks to undermine any final sense of "authority" with respect to the analyst or to any preconceived notion of Reality; and (2) it valorizes the notion that the therapeutic project is always mutual, involving the interface of reciprocal interacting subjectivities with the aim of gaining a more flexible and functional organization of personality. On the other hand, she aims at providing a corrective to intersubjective theory on two basic grounds: (1) the fact that it does not take into account the somatic component of the healing process; and (2) the fact that its guiding assumption is that all experience is constructed and organized—an assumption which brings it into alignment with postmodern constructivist thought.

In providing this "corrective," Blackstone relies on Vajrayana Buddhism as framed by Dzog-Chen and Mahamudra. While Blackstone opines that intersubjectivity has "fixed" many of the problems of classic, ego, object-relational, and Self psychological "schools" of psychoanalysis, she also thinks it needs to take into account the views of Asian nondual thought. In its stress on the constructed nature of the Self, intersubjectivity denies that there exits a deeper level of unmodified Being. All experience is modified and organized with respect to relations with others. Asian nondual thought, on the other hand, proclaims that there is an innate "nonorganized, self-existing (unconstructed) basis of subjectivity."[55] It is nondual, underlying, and pervading both subject and object. Nondual "realization," the goal of nondual Asian thought, is the nonconceptual awareness of this base. Nondual consciousness is "one's subjectivity free of conceptual representations, constrictions and fragmentations. It is one's own personal self, unbound."[56] As Blackstone puts it: "In the language of intersubjective theory, we can say that the realization of nondual consciousness is a direct encounter with the one who is doing the organizing of experience."[57]

The nonorganized self-existing nondual ground which is the basis of all subjectivities can be experienced in meditation. It is the experience not of the contents of consciousness but of consciousness itself: an unmodified dimension of subjectivity beyond the self-representations addressed by psychoanalysis. This deep field of nondual consciousness slowly becomes more apparent as we deconstruct the obstacles which keep it from manifesting itself. Psychoanalysis helps this process along, for it deconstructs unconsciously held patterns of behavior and helps us develop more flexible organizations of self. As we do this, the more essential nondual field of consciousness begins to naturally emerge. So while the intersubjective goal of an "expanded repertoire of organizing principles" is not enough, being "far from the spontaneity, openness, and directedness of experience that occurs with nondual realizations," psychoanalysis can be "reconfigured" to aid in the task of deconstructing the "obscurations" that impede the manifestation of nondual consciousness.[58]

In articulating this unmodified core Blackstone allies herself with the Tibetan Buddhist "Shentong" view which posits nothing less than the fact that the "eye" of the "observing self" can "turn around," so to speak, and "see" itself. What it "sees" is the Tibetan notion of the "clear light" of consciousness: it is luminous and blissful, self-knowing and self-aware. It "knows" this in a way that is completely unimaginable and nonconceptual. But more,

Blackstone posits that this core, is "alive" and "energetic," and has a "heart" (hence, one assumes, the centrality of the term "empathic" in the title of her book). It is as if Blackstone has negated the Freudian body and its energies in favor of a Divine ground whose fundamental energetic core is empathic and compassionate (which in turn is a more particularized religious form of Erikson's attempt to correct Freud by postulating an "instinctual" basis for "generativity" and care). Intentionally drawing on the Tantric concepts of the kundalini/*sushumma* energetic flow, the chakra system, and the Tibetan Buddhist "rainbow body," Blackstone then argues for the inclusion of the somatic, understood as being pervaded with this subtle, empathic, energetic ground, as an integral part of the healing enterprise. Thus she notes how archaic, affect-laden emotions and structures can become lodged in the tissues of our body. Her form of therapy involves multiple exercises (e.g., the "core breath" exercise) to help get one into contact with somatic holding patterns and the movement and constriction of the kundalini. For Blackstone "the subtle core is our entranceway into nondual awareness."[59] Through cultivating the subtle core one can let go of the somatically based emotions and concepts that impede nondual awareness. Similarly the therapist, banking off an empathy rooted in (and here she goes well beyond Kohut) nondual awareness and based on a "transpersonal dimension of our senses," has the ability to actually perceive another person's emotions within the internal space of that person's body:

> We can conceive of levels of consciousness as levels of subtlety in our attunement to ourselves. Although we do not yet know what this causal or imprinted level of consciousness is, we can experience it. In realization process I call this level the moveable mind because it seems to be a link between our specific mental patterns and the constrictions in our body. This moveable mind causes static or repetitive configurations in our energy system, which, over time, cause the connective tissue of our body to harden, augmenting the pattern. A sensitive observer can actually see or touch these rigidities in another person's body, and see or feel the quality held there, the bound emotional charge, and the age (or ages) of the person when the holding pattern occurred. We can also find this level in ourselves—we can refine our focus to contact this subtle level of our consciousness within the rigidities in the body. When we do this, the holding patterns can release spontaneously.[60]

The above formulations of Engler, Rubin, and Blackstone have been recounted not only to illustrate various strategies for psychoanalysis in engaging the More of Buddhism but also to evince just how different are the results of that engagement. Certainly the various attempts at translation share the common frame of reinterpreting Buddhism along the lines of a "psychoanalytic spirituality." At the same time, being dialogical projects that engage different strands within Buddhism, they appear to have a *normative* element. This is not in any way to claim that their formulations about development, much of which is based on personal experience, are invalid. Rather, it is merely to point out that such studies often blur the line between value-neutral descriptive activity and the implicit or explicit proscriptive activity which offers value-laden aims and ideals concerning development. As we have noted (repeatedly), their understanding of the More is based on a particular religio-cultural strand of Buddhism, and they attempt to build bridges between Buddhist notions and various concepts drawn from psychoanalysis. Theirs is a translation project that takes bits and pieces from Buddhism in order to extend psychoanalytic theorizing. Even if they repudiate some element of Buddhism by virtue of engaging in the translation project endemic to a psychoanalytic spirituality, they cannot but help evince the assimilation of yet other, value-laden aspects of the Buddhist strand they are analyzing. In order to accentuate this point, one can simply look back into the past of the psychology and religion movement where one finds multiple attempts at bringing together depth psychology and the More of mysticism in a manner that also evinces normativity. Along these lines, it is instructive to revisit two other understandings of "experience" and "developmental process," both essentially Christian and both dealing with mysticism. They are, as opposed to the psychology-comparativist dialogue, instances of the psychology-theology dialogue.

The first involves a now classic work, R. C. Zaehner's *Mysticism Sacred and Profane*. Zaehner was interested in creating a dialogue between Jung's analytic psychology (which several recent psychoanalytic thinkers have virtually equated with object-relations theory and the developmental line of narcissism) and the Christian mystical tradition. His immediate concern lay in the figure of Aldous Huxley who, partaking of a new cultural narrative which valorized the ingestion of entheogens, advocated perennialism and concluded that mescaline was the royal road to a mystical experience that lay at the root of all religion. In theorizing this core, Huxley was eclectic in his approach: he took bits and pieces from a number of different philosophies, from Buddhism and Hinduism, and Henri Bergson's concept of "Mind at Large." But, as Zaehner points out, Mind at Large is heavily psychological. And the psychologist he thinks Huxley comes closest to is none other than Jung. For Zaehner, Mind at Large is but a rudimentary version of Jung's concept of the collective unconscious. For Zaehner, Huxley's postulation of a core to all mysticism lay in his championing of Jung's notion of the Self archetype.

Zaehner, a stanch Catholic, admitted that his outrage is based on his Catholic faith. "The intelligent reader," he states, "should be able to detect this bias (for bias there is bound to be) at an early stage."[61] In responding to Huxley, Zaehner advocated a psycho-mystical developmental stage that engaged Huxley on his own terms. Zaehner wanted to show a type of religious, mystical subjectivity which was qualitatively different from that depicted by Huxley. This subjectivity presupposed and transcended the level of Jungian individuation and could not possibly be reached without the aid of grace. Zaehner thought that Huxley's mescaline induced mystical visions were synonymous with the unitive experience with all of creation—experiences he termed "nature mysticism" (and of which Freud and Romain Rolland's "oceanic feeling" would be an example). Nature mystical experiences signified "inflation," the experience of the Self archetype and the foretaste of the more permanent state the ego is privy to when fully individuated. But Zaehner makes it equally clear that individuation is but the first stage on the theistic mystic's path to his ultimate destination, union with God. Jung and his theories apply only to nature mysticism and its "pan-en-henic" experiences. At this stage, states Zaehner, "religious or theistic mysticism begins."[62] While nature mysticism is unchurched, promotes individuation, and can be interpreted through a Jungian psychological model, theistic Christian mysticism presupposes individuation and is dependent on a transcendent Therapist beyond our control. Thus it is that alongside Zaehner's phenomenological distinctions between nature, monistic, and theistic mysticism lies a psycho-religio stage theory of mysticism which, while incorporating and utilizing Jungian psychology, ultimately reserves an explanation of its highest stages for that conceptual scheme endemic to traditional religious theism. It is in this way that Zaehner reaffirms the Christian message, complete with its focus on ethics, grace, and the need for participation in liturgy and the sacraments in light of the threat posed by a counter-cultural movement which, in the form of Aldous Huxley, was arguing for a normative core. It should come as no surprise that Buddhist "mysticism," in Zaehner's stage theory, was seen as a real but lesser attainment than any mysticism based in theism.

To take a second example, we can look at the mid-century efforts of the psychology-theology dialogue—a time in which the Protestant fascination with various depth psychologies was as new, exciting, and *au courant* as the current psychoanalytic encounter with Buddhism. The work of Paul Tillich is a paradigmatic case in point for Tillich conversed not only with the leading psychologists of his day but also with representatives from Buddhism. Tillich's dialogical project was at least in part rooted in the very intimate and very Protestant "experience" of being justified by faith alone, and while he never promoted an explicit developmental scheme, one can tease out something akin to that in his many writings which endeavored, following his "method of correlation," to use various psychologies of his day to promote a deeper understanding of religious subjectivity—one which amounted to a Protestant understanding of faith development. What he found useful in Freud were the tools to decipher the origins of the "heteronomous" God, understood as the product of projection, Oedipus, and sociological demands for authority. But such a God needed to be transcended philosophically, for it held fast to the subject-object dichotomy, and psychologically, for it was held fast by the emotional bondage of the *uber-ich*. Tillich began this project by noting that Freud misunderstood the distinction between pathological and realistic anxiety. The former, well catalogued by Freud, lay in the seepage of usually repressed unconscious content. The latter, which entirely bypassed Freud, consisted of the structural (read: ontological) anxieties of fate/death, guilt/condemnation, and emptiness/meaninglessness. A successful stage approach to religious subjectivity for Tillich would be to first visit a psychoanalyst, there to investigate pathological anxiety and deconstruct the power of the heteronomous God, then proceed on to the office of the existentialist, who would affirm the reality and ineradicable nature of ontological anxiety. And who was it that best dealt with such anxieties? For Tillich it was the pastoral psychologist, whose cure consisted of mediating the healing power of the notions of providence (fate/death), justification by faith (guilt/condemnation) and the "courage to be" (emptiness/meaninglessness). This form of religious subjectivity combined mystical "participation" in the divine ground of Being in the context of a non-heteronomous, non-idolatrous and fully transparent religious community (i.e., Protestantism, the courage to be "as a part") alongside the full affirmation and uniqueness of the individuating "I" (Tillich's courage to be "as oneself"). The image Tillich used to present this understanding of being fully human was the synoptic gospels portrait of Jesus' anguish cry on the cross: "why has thou forsaken me?" This is a cry that reveals the recognition and power (read: "grasped by faith") of the "God beyond God" who grants one the courage to be in the face of total disintegration. It signifies the acceptance yet transcendence of the basic anxieties and the fullness of the courage to be as oneself. This developmental scheme is bound up with a specific ontology: that of Being eternally faced with and overcoming non-Being. It is this dynamic ontological core that serves as the ground and base for the individual person's process of self-actualization.[63]

The projects undertaken by Zaehner and Tillich reflect just how normative might be any dialogical attempt to engage the More of a religious tradition. These projects can well be incommensurate. Tillich's rejection of Indian mysticism (as lacking in the ability to address the courage to be as oneself, and thus a mitigated response to the meaning of being human) in favor of intense Protestant individuality, his description of Being itself as composed of Being eternally overcoming non-Being, and his utilization of psychoanalysis as part of a vision of what it means to be truly human and truly religious cannot be seen as commensurate with Engler's Theravadin vision of the end of suffering as articulated through the concept of *anatta* as it impacts conventional and contemplative lines of development. We have here two *normative* conceptions of development, based on different "experiences" (of *anatta* and being justified by faith) that reflect *dialogical* projects within the psychology and religion movement.

Given opposed views on mysticism and development, what might one conclude about the psychoanalytic engagement with the More? While much can be said of this issue, we will rest content with emphasizing what was articulated in the first few paragraphs of this section where we recalled past critiques of social science theorizing which have convincingly showed numerous violations (e.g., race and gender bias, ethnocentrism and orientalism) of what is narrated as being scientific "objectivity" at work. Surely many of Freud's initial concepts (e.g., the universality of Oedipus, concepts of femininity and feminine development, defense mechanisms, the structural theory) have been relativized along such lines as have later developmental theories (e.g., Erikson's life-cycle theory). These biases may not be intentional on the part of the theorizer(s), and it often takes those in other disciplines with a less myopic cultural focus (in noting that the psychoanalysts' best friend is the anthropologist) or those whose personal experience is quite different (and here one can only applaud the immense contributions of women from Simone de Beauvoir to Carol Gilligan) to provide the necessary corrective. And while this hardly undermines the attempt to look for universals or to theorize about development, it does ask that such theorizing take place with an eye to hidden assumptions, unconscious personal and cultural determinants, and a willingness to seek out multiple dialogue partners.

To illustrate these arguments in yet another way, we can look at competing theory building within psychoanalysis that seeks to legitimate the More of spirituality. For example, as Celia Brickman has noted in her study of racial bias in Freud's work, William Meissner is no stranger to repeating such mistakes when, in his efforts to tease out a religious vision commensurate with psychoanalysis, he avows that "earlier modalities of individual development correspond to the more primitive polytheisms" while the later stages of development correspond "to a more advanced form of Christian theological monotheism. Psychological maturity is represented . . . by the attainment of specifically Christian belief."[64] In Brickman's view "Freud's antipathy towards religion has been avoided but at the cost of a questionable pairing of psychoanalytic maturity with Christian supersessionism."[65] Similarly one can question the adequacy and universality of Rizzuto's notion of a God representation (which she portrays as sympathetic enough to religion to legitimate even the deepest mystical experiences) as it evolves in the context of the assumed adequacy and universality of the Eriksonian life cycle. Rizzuto is willing to admit that her study cannot admit of universality before clinical studies have been undertaken in other cultures and other religious traditions, but this merely serves to beg the question: what is one to do about Engler's developmental scheme, which is thoroughly Theravadin in that it does not admit the existence of a God and posits *anatta* as an experiential fact? At the very least, the notion of a "God" representation is linguistically awkward and explicitly, if unintentionally, carries with it charges of colonialism and orientalism. One need only to reverse the relation and ask the consequences of positing a Theravadin form of such a representation, namely: the existence of a psychological universal framed as the *Anatta*-representation, set in the context of those scientific studies attempting to legitimate reincarnation and the existence of a lives cycle, whose final aim is nothing less that the erasure of all desire and all representations.

The Aftermath: Toward a Psychoanalytic Spirituality

If the foregoing amounts to a series of observations on the psychoanalytic attempt to engage the More of Buddhism and, indeed, of religious mystical "experience" and "process" in general, then the matter resolves itself into articulating a prescriptive formula for going forward. In general, we can say that the proponents of the various enterprises which make up the world of psychoanalysis and spirituality are united in that they see, contra Freud (yet so akin to Jung) religious traditions as storehouses of insight, wisdom, and the development of mental and moral techniques aimed at actualizing a variety of experiences and states of consciousness. These theoreticians are also united in the slow appropriation of this wisdom into psychoanalytic jargon. At times this enterprise may not sit entirely well with those within traditional religious communities. This is so for those who are bona fide representatives of religious traditions, harboring as they do deep ontological commitments, and no matter how sympathetic they may appear to be to psychoanalysis, must ultimately reject the advocacy of those nontraditional, noninstituional and "unchurched" elements of spirituality present in some forms of psychoanalytic theorizing. Given the emotional force behind such commitments, it may well be that any reasonable attempt to argue to the contrary will prove to be futile. More optimistically, if change occurs generationally, and if the species is increasingly being socialized into a global, pluralistic socio-cultural surround, and if a psychologically informed inner-worldly mysticism is on the rise, then perhaps the future widespread influence of a nontraditional yet dialogical psychoanalytic spirituality is near at hand.

In any event, the question is how such a project can move forward under the present conditions. Surely one can debate alternate avenues for psychoanalysis as it engages the More of religion. This chapter has suggested, with respect to psychoanalysis, that commensurate with the cultural soil of spirituality is the adoption of a constructivist stance toward mystical experience per se and the adoption of a postmodern antidote with respect to the tendency to reify experience and what are clearly normative "mystical" developmental schemes. Here "constructivism" means acknowledging what Kant taught us centuries ago: we are not the kinds of beings that have the mental capacity to fully know the noumenon. The latter is in some sense beyond comprehension and thus in its totality unknowable. If one *had* to "go metaphysical" it is helpful to keep in mind James's view that in relation to the More we are surely like cats and dogs in their owner's library, hearing but not grasping the full meaning and import of the messages of their alien masters.[66] Indeed, might it be the case, as James goes on to say, that the universe is *not* a monistic block-whole akin to a vast Kingdom but an "unfinished" pluralistic multiverse fashioned after a federal republic.[67] In any event, what is clear is that many religions treat the More as if they and they alone had the inside story on its deepest nature and essence. For some a psychoanalytic spirituality is an advance in that it can admit such "over-beliefs" only as a form of Winnicottian transitional experiencing. Such a view is compatible with constructivism, and it allows for difference and a postmodern perspective on development. At the same time, it has the advantage of avoiding the pitfalls of dogmatic intransigence and, further, cannot be utilized in the service of promoting the kinds of socio-cultural power abuse that has been historically linked to ontological difference. Again, if one had to straddle the ontological line, and if one had to posit a "metaphysical horizon" of transitional forms of mystical experiencing, then the latter is commensurate with James's notion of a pluralistic universe. Conversely, the most palatable psychoanalytic infrastructure of James's "multiverse" lies in Winnicott's notion of transitional objects.[68] Contra Freud, Winnicott's notion of reality as an *x* "out-there" is ever receding and never fully discerned. Any worldview or proclaimed *ontos*, if qualified psychoanalytically as transitional, can be allowed in its normativity and adaptive value without proclaiming finality, and can further be held as participating in a More that could well be not singular but plural. A dialogical, constructivist, postmodern psychoanalytic spirituality metaphysically situated by James and psychologically nuanced by Winnicott: this is a formula that can provide guidance going forward and, in "debating-it-through," produce the fruits of change.

Notes

1. See W. B. Parsons, *The Enigma of the Oceanic Feeling* (New York: Oxford University Press, 1999); R. Schwab, *The Oriental Renaissance: Europe's Rediscovery of India and the East, 1680–1880*, trans. Gene Patterson-Black and Victor Reinking (New York: Columbia University Press, 1984).

2. Parsons, *The Enigma of the Oceanic Feeling*, p. 79–80.

3. I have attempted a beginning of such an overview in my "Psychoanalysis Meets Buddhism: The Development of a Dialogue," in *Changing the Scientific Study of Religion: Beyond Freud?* ed. J. Belzen (New York: Springer, 2009), 179–209.

4. I am indebted to Peter Homans for his use and definition of this term. See P. Homans, "The Psychology and Religion Movement," in *The Encyclopedia of Religion*, ed. M. Eliade (New York: Macmillan, 1987), 12: 66–74.

5. See W. B. Parsons "Psychology of Religion,"in *The Encyclopedia of Religion*, 2nd edition, ed. L. Jones (New York: MacMilllan, 2005), 7473–81; David Wulff, *Psychology of Religion: Classic and Contemporary* (New York: Wiley and Sons, 1997).

6. See Herbert Fingarette, *The Self in Transformation* (New York: Harper and Row, 1965); Erich Fromm, D. T. Suzuki, and R. de Martino, eds., *Psychoanalysis and Zen Buddhism* (New York: Harper, 1960); Karen Horney, "Free Associations and the Use of the Couch," in *The Couch and the Tree*, ed. Anthony Molino (New York: North Point Press, 1998), 35–36.

7. See for example Erik Erikson, *Young Man Luther* (New York: W.W. Norton, 1962); W. W. Meissner, *Psychoanalysis and Religious Experience* (New Haven: Yale, 1984); A. Rizzuto, *The Birth of the Living God* (Chicago: University of Chicago Press, 1981); D. Browning, *Religious Thought and the Modern Psychologies* (Philadelphia: Fortress, 1987); J. Fowler, *Stages of Faith* (San Francisco: Harper and Row, 1981).

8. L. Bouyer, "Mysticism: An Essay on the History of the Word," in *Understanding Mysticism*, ed. Richard Woods (Garden City, N.J.: Image, 1980), 42–56. In this section and in the following one I follow the socio-historical narrative I laid down in two previous essays: "Psychologia Perennis and the Academic Study of Mysticism"(in *Mourning Religion*, ed. W. B. Parsons, D. Jonte-Pace, and S. Henking (Charlottesville and London: University of Virginia Press, 2008), 97–124; "Psychoanalytic Spirituality" (in *Spirituality and Religion: Psychoanalytic Perspectives*, ed. J. Winer and J. Anderson. Catskill N.Y.: Mental Health Resources, 2007), 83–97.

9. M. de Certeau, "Mysticism," *Diacritics* 22, 1992: 11–25.

10. Certeau, "Mysticism," 14.

11. Technically speaking it is true that James listed only passivity, noesis, ineffability, and transiency as the "marks"of mysticism. I add the mark of "unity" in that I think James, who comes around to it later in his lecture on mysticism, all but says that it too is a mark of mysticism.

12. Wulff, *Psychology of Religion*; W. Principe, "Toward Defining Spirituality," *Studies in Religion* 12 (1983): 127–41.

13. M. MacDonald, "Spirituality," in *The Encyclopedia of Religion*, 2nd ed., ed. Lindsey Jones (New York: Macmillan, 2005): 8718–21.

14. R. Fuller, *Spiritual but not Religious* (New York: Oxford University Press), 2001.

15. On the role of D. T. Suzuki in mediating to the Western world a form of Buddhism centered on experience, see R. Sharf, "The Zen of Nationalism,"in *Curators of the Buddha: The Study of Buddhism under Colonialism*, ed. D. Lopez (Chicago: The University of Chicago Press, 1995), 107–61. One central point Sharf makes is that Buddhism, as a result of Western influence, changed from a heavily scriptural and ritualistic system to one based on the value of immediate experience. It was this trend that Suzuki was socialized into and then took back to the West—a fact that accounts in no small way for his popularity and success. And psychoanalysis, through the efforts of Karen Horney and Erich Fromm, was complicit in this endeavor.

16. I am using the term "the psychology-comparativist dialogue" in the sense defined in *Religion and Psychology: Mapping the Terrain*, ed. D. Jonte-Pace and W. B. Parsons (New York: Routledge, 2001).

17. P. Rieff, *The Feeling Intellect* (Chicago: The University of Chicago Press, 1990).

18. See Jonte-Pace and Parsons, *Religion and Psychology*.

19. P. Rieff, *Triumph of the Therapeutic* (New York: Harper, 1966).

20. P. Homans, *Jung in Context* (Chicago: The University of Chicago Press, 1995).

21. S. Kakar, *The Analyst and the Mystic* (Chicago: The University of Chicago Press, 1991).

22. See E. Erikson, *Young Man Luther* (New York: W.W. Norton 1962); E. Erikson "The Galilean Sayings and the Sense of 'I,'" *Yale Review* 70 (1981): 321–62; W. Bion, *Attention and Interpretation* (New York: Jason Aronson, 1983), 26; J. Lacan, "God and the Jouissance of Women" in *Feminine Sexuality*, ed. J. Mitchell and J. Rose (New York: W.W. Norton, 1982).

23. H. Kohut, *The Search for the Self: Selected Writings of Heinz Kohut, 1950–1978*, ed. Paul Ornstein (New York: International Universities Press, 1978), 456.

24. Kohut, *The Search for the Self*, 455–56.

25. H. Kohut, *Self Psychology and the Humanities* (New York: W.W. Norton, 1985), 70.

26. Kohut, *Self Psychology*.

27. Kohut, *Self Pscyhology*, p. 71. I have made a similar point in my essay "Psychoanalytic Spirituality."

28. R. Robertson, *Meaning and Change* (New York: New York University Press, 1978).
29. Fuller, *Spiritual but not Religious*.
30. See A. Molino, *The Couch and the Tree*, 225.
31. Molino, *The Couch and the Tree*.
32. See S. Katz, ed., *Mysticism and Philosophical Analysis* (New York: Oxford University Press, 1979).
33. See Parsons, *Enigma*.
34. See R. Gimello, "Mysticism and Meditation," in *Mysticism and Philosophical Analysis*, ed. S. Katz (New York: Oxford University Press, 1979, p. 173).
35. See Ken Wilber, Jack Engler, and Daniel Brown, eds., *Transformations of Consciousness* (Boston: Shambhala, 1986), 24.
36. See Jack Engler, "Can We Say What the Self 'Really' Is?" in *Psychoanalysis and Buddhism*, ed. J. Safran (Boston: Wisdom Publications, 2003), 92–93.
37. Engler, "Can We Say," 87.
38. See P. Cooper "Unconscious Processes: Zen and Psychoanalytic Versions," *The Journal of Religion and Health* 39, no. 1 (2000): 61; J. Blackstone, *The Empathic Ground* (Albany, N.Y.: State University of New York Press, 2007).
39. Blackstone, *Empathic Ground*, 25, 49, 54.
40. See J. Engler, "Can We Say What the Self "Really"Is?" 86–95.
41. See A. Deikman, "Deautomatization and the Mystic Experience," *Understanding Mysticism*, 240–60.
42. See J. Blackstone, *The Empathic Ground*, 8.
43. See, for example, C. Brickman, *Aboriginal Populations in the Mind* (New York: Columbia, 2003).
44. C. Jung, *Memories, Dreams, Reflections* (New York: Vintage, 1961), 199.
45. Jung, *Memories, Dreams*, 171.
46. See D. Meckel and R. Moore, eds., *Self and Liberation* (New York: Paulist, 1992).
47. See Wilber et al., *Transformations of Consciousness*.
48. J. Rubin, *Psychotherapy and Buddhism* (New York: Plenum Press, 1996), 49.
49. Rubin, *Psychotherapy and Buddhism*, 51.
50. Rubin, *Psychotherapy and Buddhism*, 69.
51. Rubin, *Psychotherapy and Buddhism*, 75.
52. Rubin, *Psychotherapy and Buddhism*, 197.
53. See Blackstone, *Empathic Ground*.
54. Blackstone, *Empathic Ground*, 1.
55. Blackstone, *Empathic Ground*, 18.
56. Blackstone, *Empathic Ground*, 62.
57. Blackstone, *Empathic Ground*, 26.
58. Blackstone, *Empathic Ground*, 34.
59. Blackstone, *Empathic Ground*, 58.
60. Blackstone, *Empathic Ground*, 71–72.

61. R. C. Zaehner, *Mysticism Sacred and Profane* (New York: Oxford University Press, 1980), xiii.

62. Zaehner, *Mysticism Sacred and Profane*, 118, 150.

63. See P. Tillich, *The Courage to Be* (New Haven: Yale University Press, 1958); *The Meaning of Health* (Chicago: Exploration Press, 1984).

64. C. Brickman, *Aboriginal Populations in the Mind* (New York: Columbia University Press, 2003), 159.

65. Brickman, *Aboriginal Populations in the Mind*.

66. W. James, *A Pluralistic Universe* (Cambridge: Harvard University Press, 1977), 140.

67. James, *A Pluralistic Universe*, 145.

68. See D. W. Winnicott, *Playing and Reality* (New York: Penguin, 1980).

References

Alexander, Franz. "Buddhistic Training as an Artificial Catatonia." *Psychoanalytic Review* 18, no. 2 (1931): 129–141.

Bion, Wilfred. *Attention and Interpretation*. New York: Jason Aronson, 1983.

Blackstone, Judith. *The Empathic Ground*. Albany: State University Press of New York, 2007.

Bouyer, L. "Mysticism: An Essay on the History of the Word." Pp. 42–56 in *Understanding Mysticism*. Edited by Richard Woods. Garden City, N.Y.: Image Books, 1980.

Brickman, Celia. *Aboriginal Populations in the Mind*. New York: Columbia, 2003.

Browning, Don. *Religious Thought and the Modern Psychologies*. Philadelphia: Fortress, 1987.

Cooper, Paul. "The Disavowal of the Spirit: Integration and Wholeness in Buddhism and Psychoanalysis." Pp. 231–46 in *The Couch and the Tree*. Edited by Andrew Molino. New York: North Point Press, 1998.

———. "Buddhist Meditation and Countertransfernce: A Case Study." *American Journal of Psychoanalysis* 59, no.1 (1999): 71–86.

———. "Unconscious Processes: Zen and Psychoanalytic Versions." *Journal of Religion and Health*, 39, no. 1 (2000): 57–69.

De Certeau, Michel. "Mysticism." *Diacritics* 22 (1992): 11–25.

Deikman, Arthur. "Deautomatization and the Mystic Experience." Pp. 240–60 in *Understanding Mysticism*. Edited by Richard Woods. Garden City, N.Y.: Image Books, 1980.

Eigen, Michael. *The Psychoanalytic Mystic*. Free Association Press, 1998.

Engler, Jack. "Therapeutic Aims in Psychotherapy and Buddhism." Pp. 17–52 in *Transformations of Consciousness*. Edited by Ken. Wilber, Jack Engler, and Dan Brown. Boston: Shambhala, 1986.

———. "Being Somebody and Being Nobody: A Reexamination of the Understanding of Self in Psychoanalysis and Buddhism." Pp. 35–80 in *Psychoanalysis and Buddhism*. Edited by Jeremy Safran. Boston: Wisdom Publications, 2003.

Engler, J. "Reply: Can We Say What the Self 'Really' Is?" Pp. 86–100 in *Psychoanalysis and Buddhism*. Edited by Jeremy Safran. Boston: Wisdom Publications, 2003.

Epstein, Mark. *Thoughts without a Thinker*. New York: Basic Books, 1995.

Erikson, Erik. *Young Man Luther*. New York: W.W. Norton, 1962.

———. "The Galilean Sayings and the Sense of 'I.'" *The Yale Review* 70 (1981): 321–62.

Fingarette, Herbert. *The Self in Transformation*. New York: Harper and Row, 1965.

Fowler, James. *Stages of Faith*. San Francisco: Harper and Row, 1981.

Freud, S. *The Standard Edition (SE) of the Complete Psychological Works of Sigmund Freud. 24 vols*. Translated and edited by James Strachey. London: Hogarth Press, 1953–1974.

———. "Civilization and Its Discontents." *SE* 21 (1961): 64–148

———. "The Future of an Illusion." *SE* 21 (1961): 5–58.

———. "New Introductory Lectures." *SE* 22 (1964): 3–183.

Freud, S., and Oskar Pfister. *Psychoanalysis and Faith: Dialogues with the Reverend Oskar Pfister*. Edited by Heinrich Meng and Ernst Freud. Translated by Eric Mosbacher. New York: Basic Books, 1963.

Fromm, Erich, D. T. Suzuki, and Richard de Martino, eds. *Psychoanalysis and Zen Buddhism*. New York: Harper, 1960.

Fuller, Robert. *Spiritual but Not Religious*. New York: Oxford, 2001.

Homans, P. *Jung in Context*. Chicago: The University of Chicago Press, 1995.

———. "The Psychology and Religion Movement." Pp. 66–74 in *The Encyclopedia of Religion*. Edited by Mircea Elaide. New York: Macmillan, 1987.

Horney, K. *Final Lectures*. Edited by D. Ingram. New York: W.W. Norton, 1991.

———. "Free Associations and the Use of the Couch." Pp. 35–36 in *The Couch and the Tree*. Edited by Andrew Molino. New York: North Point Press, 1998.

James, W. *The Varieties of Religious Experience*. New York: The Modern Library, 1929.

———. *A Pluralistic Universe*. Cambridge: Harvard University Press, 1977.

Jonte-Pace, Diane, and William B. Parsons, eds. *Religion and Psychology: Mapping the Terrain*. London: Routledge, 2001.

Jung, Carl. *Memories, Dreams, Reflections*. New York: Vintage, 1961.

———. *Two Essays on Analytic Psychology*. Princeton: Princeton University Press, 1972.

Kakar, Sudhir. *The Analyst and the Mystic*. Chicago: The University of Chicago Press, 1991.

Katz, Steven, ed. *Mysticism and Philosophical Analysis*. New York: Oxford, 1979.

Kohut, Heinz. *The Search for the Self: Selected Writings of Heinz Kohut*, 1950–1978. edited by Paul Ornstein. Vol. 1. New York: International Universities Press, 1978.

———. *Self Psychology and the Humanities*. Edited by C. Strozier. New York: W.W. Norton, 1985.

Kripal, Jeffrey. *Kali's Child*. Chicago: The University of Chicago Press, 1995.

———. *Roads of Excess*. Chicago: The University of Chicago Press, 2003.

Lacan, Jacques. "God and the Jouissance of Women." Pp. 37–48 in *Feminine Sexuality*. Edited by Juliet Mitchell and Jacqueline Rose. New York: W.W. Norton, 1982.

MacDonald, Mary. "Spirituality." Pp. 8718–8721 in *The Encyclopedia of Religion*, 2nd edition. Edited by Lindsey Jones. New York: Macmillan, 2005.

Meckel, Dan, and Robert Moore, eds. *Self and Liberation*. New York: Paulist, 1992.

Meissner, William. *Psychoanalysis and Religious Experience*. New Haven: Yale, 1984.

Molino, Andrew, ed. *The Couch and the Tree*. New York: North Point Press, 1998.

Morel, Ferdinand. *Essai sur l'introversion mystique*. Geneva: Albert Kundig, 1918.

Parsons, William B. *The Enigma of the Oceanic Feeling*. New York: Oxford, 1999.

———. "Themes and Debates in the Psychology-Comparativist Dialogue." Pp. 229–53 in *Religion and Psychology: Mapping the Terrain*. Edited by Diane Jonte-Pace and William B. Parsons. London: Routledge, 2001.

———. "Psychology of Religion." Pp. 7473–81 in *The Encyclopedia of Religion*, 2nd edition. Edited by Lindsey Jones. New York: Macmilllan, 2005.

———. "Psychoanalytic Spirituality." Pp. 83–97 in *Spirituality and Religion: Psychoanalytic Perspectives*. Edited by Jerome Winer and James Anderson. Catskill N.Y.: Mental Health Resources, 2007.

———. "Psychologia Perennis and the Academic Study of Mysticism." Pp. 97–124 in *Mourning Religion*. Edited by William B. Parsons, Diane Jonte Pace, and Susan Henking. Charlottesville and London: University of Virginia Press, 2008.

———. "Psychoanalysis Meets Buddhism: The Development of a Dialogue." Pp. 179–209 in *Changing the Scientific Study of Religion: Beyond Freud?* Edited by Jacob Belzen. New York: Springer, 2009.

Principe, Walter. "Toward Defining Spirituality." *Studies in Religion*, 12 (1983): 127–41.

Rieff, Philip. *The Triumph of the Therapeutic*. New York: Harper, 1966.

———. *The Feeling Intellect*. Chicago: The University of Chicago Press, 1990.

Rizzuto, Ana-Maria. *The Birth of the Living God*. Chicago: The University of Chicago Press, 1981.

Robertson, Rolland. *Meaning and Change*. New York: New York University Press, 1978.

Rubin, Jeff. *Psychotherapy and Buddhism*. New York: Plenum Press, 1996.

Safran, Jeremy. *Psychoanalysis and Buddhism*. Boston: Wisdom Publications, 2003.

Schmidt, Leigh. "The Making of Modern Mysticism." *The Journal of the American Academy of Religion*, 71 (2003): 273–302.

Schwab, Raymond. *The Oriental Renaissance: Europe's Rediscovery of India and the East, 1680–1880*. Translated by Gene Patterson-Black and Victor Reinking. New York: Columbia University Press, 1984.

Sharf, Robert. "The Zen of Nationalism." Pp. 107–161 in *Curators of the Buddha: The Study of Buddhism under Colonialism*. Edited by Donald Lopez. Chicago: The University of Chicago Press, 1995.

Suler, John. *Contemporary Psychoanalysis and Eastern Thought*. Albany: State University Press of New York, 1993.

Teresa of Avila, St. *The Interior Castle*. Translated by K. Kavanaugh and O. Rodriguez. New York: Paulist Press, 1979.

Tillich, Paul. *The Courage to Be*. New Haven: Yale, 1958.

———. *The Meaning of Health*. Chicago: Exploration Press, 1984.

Weber, Max. *The Protestant Ethic and the Spirit of Capitalism*. New York: Charles Scribner's Sons, 1958.

Wilber, Ken, Jack Engler, and Dan Brown, eds. *Transformations of Consciousness*. Boston: Shambhala, 1986.

Winnicott, Donald. *Playing and Reality*. New York: Penguin, 1980.

Wulff, David. *Psychology of Religion: Classic and Contemporary*. 2nd edition. New York: John Wiley and Sons, 1997.

Zaehner, Richard C. *Mysticism Sacred and Profane*. New York: Oxford, 1980.

CHAPTER FIVE

Freud and Neuroscience: A Return to Origins

Kelly Bulkeley

Introduction

Sigmund Freud developed psychoanalysis on the basis of a neurological model of human mental functioning that he laid out in the *Project for a Scientific Psychology* (1895) and chapter 7 of *The Interpretation of Dreams* (1900).[1] Unfortunately, many scholars and clinicians who value Freud's theories try to dismiss or downplay the neurological roots of psychoanalysis. They question whether Freud himself remained committed to his nineteenth century speculations, and they regard his writings of this time as "the early Freud," lacking the literary sophistication and analytic insight of later cultural texts like *Civilization and its Discontents* (1930). In this perspective, Freud's scientific rhetoric merely reflected the modernist worldview his revolutionary ideas were destined to overcome. Taken to its extreme, this approach would encourage cleansing Freud's works of all references to science, the brain, or physical matter, the better to appreciate the essence of psychoanalysis as a theory of language and culture.

Meanwhile, critics of psychoanalysis have also pointed to the apparent gap between Freud's early career as a neurologist and his later theories, but they see it as a reason to reject psychoanalysis as outmoded pseudoscience. Many of Freud's critics view his scientific rhetoric as nothing but that, a deceptive tapestry of clever assertions adopting the posture of science but lacking an objective, verifiable basis in empirical fact. In its extreme form, this reading of Freud portrays him as a charlatan who leveraged his professional status as a psychiatrist to justify fanciful speculations that strayed farther and farther away from any foundation in real brain science.

In neither of these two approaches are Freud's original interests in the neural underpinnings of psychological life examined with a fair and respectful eye. This chapter aims to renew the neurological dimension of psychoanalysis, connecting the early years of Freud's career with contemporary advances in brain/mind science in order to develop a fresh understanding of psychoanalytic theory for the study of religion. The overarching claim here is that we can strengthen the interpretive power of present-day psychoanalytic theories of religion by recovering and updating the neuroscientific themes in Freud's work.

Freud the Neurologist

In 1873, at the age of eighteen, Freud enrolled at the University of Vienna to study medicine. His decision to become trained as a medical doctor reflected his strong interest in applying scientific principles to problems in human life. During his time at the University of Vienna Freud received instruction from the eminent German physiologist Ernst Wilhelm Von Brucke, who taught his students about Darwinian evolution and the dynamic biological qualities of all forms of life. These ideas made a big impact on Freud, establishing an evolutionary framework in his mental outlook for the rest of his life. He graduated in 1881 with his medical degree, and for the next few years he worked in Brucke's laboratory doing painstaking physiological research on the nervous systems of fish and other species, generating empirical evidence to aid the cause of promoting Darwin's theory of natural selection.

Between1885 and1886, Freud received a traveling fellowship to train and perform research at the Salpetriere psychiatric clinic in Paris with Jean Martin Charcot, whom many regarded as the leading neurologist in all Europe at that time. From Charcot Freud learned about the powerful role of clinical observation in the diagnosis of neuropathology, and he gained a greater appreciation for the distributed, nonlocalized nature of higher mental functions. Rather than simplistically equating neuroanatomical locations with psychological functions, Freud followed Charcot in identifying complex interactions between mental problems and brain pathologies. Those interactions do have a material substrate in the brain, Charcot taught, but the best way to study them is to examine how they function (or malfunction) in actual life, not just in a controlled laboratory setting.

During his pre-*Interpretation of Dreams* career phase Freud made several contributions to neurology, including important findings on agnosia (loss of the ability to recognize people and objects), aphasia (loss of abilities for oral and written language), and the cellular structure of the brain (what he called "contact barriers" between brain cells soon became known as "synapses" between neurons[2]). There can be no question that Freud belonged to the neuroscientific mainstream of his time. He knew as much as anyone in the late nineteenth century about the physiological workings of the human brain. When he chose to pursue a private medical practice in psychiatry he did so not as a rejection of science but because (a) he wanted to follow Charcot's methodological advice about studying the brain via detailed clinical observation and (b) he needed to provide financial support for his new wife (Freud married Martha Bernays in 1886) and their growing family. Continuing his work as a laboratory researcher could satisfy neither of these needs. Thus psychoanalysis grew organically from Freud's early investigations in neurology, as a continuation and refinement of the interests that originally inspired his professional career.

Seen in this methodological light, Freud's later turn to psychoanalysis represented an affirmative step forward in brain-mind science, not a retreat from it. What matters most, Freud came to believe, were the dynamic networks that are distributed *between* various neural regions and not localized in any one specific anatomical area. According to Mark Solms and Karen Kaplan-Solms, two leading figures in the psychoanalytic approach to neuroscience,

> It is of crucial importance for us to note that Freud first reached these conclusions not in relation to hysteria or any other neurosis, but, rather, in relation to *aphasia*—that is, in relation to a syndrome that only occurs in the context of a definite organic lesion. In other words, these were conclusions that Freud arrived at while he was still a fully fledged *neurologist*. They did not mark a break with neurology, but, rather, a break with a particular research tradition *within* neurology (the narrow localizationist tradition), which, he believed, was incapable of accommodating the complex clinical reality that Charcot had taught him to respect above all else.[3]

Brain-mind scientists today are engaged in a similar debate between those who favor a modularist view of discrete, anatomically localized brain functions (e.g., Steven Pinker, J. Tooby, and L. Cosmides) and those who advocate a holistic view of integrated psychological networks distributed throughout the brain (e.g., V. S. Ramachandran). Psychoanalysis has more in common with the latter perspective and is perhaps more likely to be perceived as pseudoscience by people who take the former view. It would be wrong, then, to say that Freud's work is incompatible with present-day neuroscience. The truth is, Freud's work may be incompatible with *some forms* of current neuroscientific theory, but it has the potential to fit better with others. Since there is at present no monolithic consensus among neuroscientists about how the brain-mind system works, the question remains open as to the best way of modeling and understanding the full range of its activities. Psychoanalytic ideas remain viable contenders in the effort to meet that challenge.

Psychoanalytic Theory in Light of Contemporary Neuroscience

This section focuses on two particular aspects of psychoanalysis as they relate to the findings of contemporary neuroscience: the unconscious and dreaming. These do not represent the only topics for a new integration of psychoanalysis and neuroscience, but for the purposes of this chapter they offer good illustrations of the general issues that arise when pursuing any such integration.

The Unconscious

The distinction between consciousness and the unconscious was not original to Freud, but he was arguably the first modern thinker to make it the cornerstone of a new psychological theory.[4] According to psychoanalytic historians J. Laplanche and J.-B. Pontalis, "If Freud's discovery had to be summed up in a single word, that word would without doubt have to be 'unconscious.'"[5] He made it the mission of psychoanalysis to explore the full range and extent of unconscious psychological functioning, first in his clinical work with individual patients and later in his cultural studies of religion, art, and collective social life. In both his general audience works (e.g., *Introductory Lectures on Psychoanalysis*) and his technical writings (e.g., *Mourning and Melancholia*) Freud always emphasized the unfathomable depths of the unconscious and its surprisingly widespread influence on people's conscious lives. He never tired of reminding his readers and listeners that consciousness represents but a tiny fraction of the mind's overall magnitude and power.

Contemporary scientists who study unconscious mental processes usually acknowledge their debt to Freud, though with varying degrees of generosity. Neuroscientist Joseph Ledoux, who has done important work on the brain systems involved in emotional processing, gives credit where he believes credit is due: "Emotional responses are, for the most part, generated unconsciously. Freud was right on the mark when he described consciousness as the tip of the mental iceberg."[6] Research by Ledoux and others on the nonconscious aspects of feeling, evaluation, and instinctive responses (e.g., fight/flight, disgust, arousal) bear obvious connections with psychoanalytic theory, yet few neuroscientists today take more than a passing interest in exploring these connections.

More typical is the attitude adopted by those who study the cognitive aspects of the unconscious, i.e., the myriad thought processes and information-processing operations that occur outside ordinary awareness. For them, Freud is irrelevant. To take one example, cognitive psychologist John Bargh says, "People are often unaware of the reasons and causes of their own behavior. In fact, recent experimental evidence points to a deep and fundamental dissociation between conscious awareness and the mental processes responsible for one's behavior: many of the wellsprings of behavior appear to be opaque to conscious access. . . . [A]t best, we have imperfect conscious access to the basic brain/mind processes that help govern our own behavior, broadly defined (i.e., from the motoric to the social and motivational levels)."[7] This is the same essential claim Freud made a century ago, and yet no attempt is made to investigate the possible connections between psychoanalytic theory and contemporary findings. Why not? Because psychoanalysis has fallen out of date. In the introduction to *The New Unconscious*, an edited volume including research by Bargh and others, the psychologist James Uleman is blunter in dismissing Freud's work as merely of historical interest with no relevance for the research agenda of present-day scientists:

> Many of Freud's ideas had already been expressed artistically in the literature and drama of the nineteenth century, and he regarded Dostoevsky as the greatest psychologist of that century. Freud's great contribution was to gather, elaborate, systematize, and refine these ideas, in an attempt to build a scientific approach to unconscious processes. In doing so, he put the unconscious on the intellectual and cultural map, and gave the term itself currency. . . . [But] the psychoanalytic unconscious is widely acknowledged to be a failure as a scientific theory because evidence of its major components cannot be observed, measured precisely, or manipulated easily. The theory's complexity renders it largely unfalsifiable. . . . [I]t does not provide an influential framework for understanding unconscious processes in academic or scientific circles.[8]

In the view of Bargh, Uleman, and others who focus on unconscious cognition, Freud's ideas are unhelpful because they cannot easily be tested in controlled psychological experiments. Furthermore, Freud's mythological references to the inner tensions of human mental life (e.g., the Oedipal complex,

Eros versus Thanatos, primary narcissism) do not fit well with the computer metaphors and information-processing language favored by these researchers. Their goal in studying the cognitive unconscious is to devise empirically based theories in which "goals, motivations, and self-regulation are prominent, without the conflict and drama of the psychoanalytic unconscious."[9]

This kind of distinction should be taken by other scholars as tactical, not ontological. It reflects a pragmatic choice as to which aspects of unconscious psychology are more amenable to certain kinds of research methods. It does not mean that psychoanalytic ideas are wrong or that human mental life is free of dynamic tensions, only that psychoanalysis is incomplete in its portrait of the unconscious, which, as Bargh, Uleman, et al. have amply demonstrated, has far more depth, range, and complexity than even Freud realized. At the same time, a purely cognitive theory of the unconscious would be incomplete as well. The "conflict and drama" described by psychoanalysis is real and needs to be included, though of course revised in light of current research.

A more charitable attitude toward Freud comes from neuroscientist V. S. Ramachandran, whose work focuses on the brain-mind implications of phantom limb syndrome and other rare forms of psychopathology:

> When I began this research about five years ago, I had no interest whatsoever in Sigmund Freud. (He might have said I was in denial.) And like most of my colleagues I was very skeptical of his ideas. The entire neuroscience community is deeply suspicious of him because he touted elusive aspects of human nature that ring true but that cannot be empirically tested. But after I had worked with these [neurological] patients, it soon became clear to me that even though Freud wrote a great deal of nonsense, there is no denying that he was a genius, especially when you consider the social and intellectual climate of Vienna at the turn of the century. Freud was one of the first people to emphasize that human nature could be subjected to systematic scientific scrutiny, that one could actually look for laws of mental life in much the same way that a cardiologist might study the heart or an astronomer study planetary motion. We take all this for granted now, but at that time it was a revolutionary insight. . . . Freud's most valuable contribution was his discovery that your conscious mind is simply a façade and that you are completely unaware of 90 percent of what really goes on in your brain. And with regard to psychological defenses, Freud was right on the mark. Can anyone doubt the reality of the "nervous laugh" or "rationalizations"? Remarkably, although you are engaging in these mental tricks all the time, you are completely unaware of doing so and you'd probably deny it if it were pointed out to you. Yet when you watch someone else doing it, it is comically conspicuous—often embarrassingly so.[10]

To sum up, then: current neuroscientific research suggests that Freud accurately anticipated some of the key features of unconscious psychology, although his theories extend far beyond what scientific experiments can verify. Nevertheless, the role of the unconscious in human mental life is even more firmly established today than it was during his time.[11]

In light of this, psychoanalytic theories of religion that refer to the unconscious will find strong general support from contemporary brain-mind science. Despite the occasionally anti-Freud rhetoric, the latest research is providing a wealth of insight into the nature and functioning of the unconscious, with direct implications for the study of religious beliefs, practices, and experiences. For example, could it be that people who engage in intensive practices of prayer, meditation, or yogic exercise have developed the non-pathological ability to alter the normal boundaries of access to the unconscious mind? What happens when the processes of the unconscious are highly stimulated, or dramatically diminished, in religious rituals? To what extent do the cultural features of a religion (e.g., its symbols, myths, moral codes) influence the development and maintenance of unconscious cognitive activities? These are the kinds of questions that may become better understood with the aid of new integrations of psychoanalysis and neuroscience.

Dreaming

Freud's father died in 1896, grieving him deeply and prompting an intensive period of analyzing his own psychopathological symptoms (shifting emotions, strange fantasies and memories, disturbing dreams).[12] Still following Charcot's teachings about clinical observation, Freud applied his mentor's method to himself. He described his sufferings in numerous letters to Wilhelm Fliess, the ear and nose specialist from Berlin who was Freud's closest friend during these years. In his letters Freud examined his turbulent psychological experiences in great detail, along with possible explanations of their causes. He shared with Fliess the various physical ailments and neurotic symptoms that had been plaguing him, and he confessed that "the chief patient I am preoccupied with is myself."[13] Early in 1898 Freud mentioned to Fliess that he had begun writing a book on dreams, which he finished in the fall of 1899. In the preface to the second edition (1908) of *The Interpretation of Dreams* Freud acknowledged that the book held great personal significance for him. Looking back on the process of writing it, he found it to be "a portion of my own self-analysis, my reaction to my father's death—that is to say, to the most important event, the most poignant loss, of a man's life."[14]

From the union of Freud's personal mourning and Charcot-influenced neuroscientific methods, psychoanalysis was born.

The Interpretation of Dreams retained its vital importance in Freud's thinking throughout his career. In 1908 he said, "During the long years in which I have been working at the problems of the neuroses I have often been in doubt and sometimes been shaken in my convictions. At such times it has always been *The Interpretation of Dreams* that has given me back my certainty."[15] In 1930, when he reflected on his life's many achievements, he concluded that this book contained "the most valuable of all the discoveries it has been my good fortune to make. Insight such as this falls to one's lot but once in a lifetime."[16] Although most readers skip over chapter 1 to get to Freud's famous "Irma" dream in chapter 2, the long opening chapter represents what is still today one of the most comprehensive surveys of nineteenth century scientific research on dreams and dreaming.[17] As already mentioned, chapter 7 provides a physiological explanation of dreaming using the (overly-mechanistic) terms that would be familiar to his neuroscientific contemporaries. In this way Freud framed *The Interpretation of Dreams* as a mainstream scientific monograph on a specific aspect of brain-mind functioning. To emphasize the neuroscientific importance of his topic he added in the 1908 second edition a sentence to chapter 7 that has become perhaps the best known line of the whole book: "*The interpretation of dreams is the royal road to a knowledge of the unconscious activities of the mind.*" (italics in the original)[18]

For the first half of the twentieth century, Freud's ideas about dreams held considerable sway over psychologists in Europe and North America. But starting in the 1950s researchers began using new laboratory monitoring technologies (e.g., the electroencephalograph, or EEG) to examine with greater precision the correlations between dreaming and brain-mind functioning in sleep. The initial findings showed sleep to be more complex than Freudian theory could account for. Specifically, the close association of rapid eye movement (REM) stages of sleep with dreaming cast doubt on the psychoanalytic idea that dreams are caused by pent-up instinctual demands, since REM sleep is an automatic process of the human brain that occurs regardless of whether or not people are frustrated in waking life. Critics of psychoanalysis saw an opportunity here because the central role of dreaming in the psychoanalytic enterprise meant that this new source of scientific evidence called into question the whole conceptual framework of Freud's ideas. If Freud was wrong about dreams, maybe he was wrong about everything.

The strongest voice in this line of attack came from J. Allan Hobson, a psychiatrist and neurophysiology researcher. In his 1988 book *The Dreaming Brain: How the Brain Creates Both the Sense and the Nonsense of Dreams*, Hobson reconstructed the scientific study of dreaming on non-Freudian grounds. "Because psychoanalysis is so dominant a theory," he says in the introduction, "its critical treatment is an essential theme of this book."[19] Hobson regarded Freud as merely the latest practitioner of ancient superstitions: "the prophetic tradition of dream study can be seen in its modern as well as its antique form. The wise man, the priest, or the psychoanalyst knows the dream code and can thus predict the future while deciphering both the past and the present."[20]

Hobson combined EEG studies of REM sleep with new findings on neurochemistry to offer an "activation-synthesis" hypothesis of dream formation in which random neural firings in the brainstem during REM sleep are sent to the reasoning parts of the brain which try to create semi-meaningful narratives from the chaotic input. As he said in an earlier paper with Robert McCarley, "such features as scene shifts, time compression, personal condensations, splitting, and symbol formation may be directly isomorphic with the state of the nervous system during dreaming sleep. In other words, the forebrain may be making the best of a bad job by producing even partially coherent dream imagery from the relatively noisy signals sent up to it from the brain stem."[21] In Hobson's view there is no need for disguise or censorship to explain the strange qualities of dreaming. All the psychological features can be attributed to the deficiencies of mental functioning during REM sleep. "I differ from Freud in that I think that most dreams are neither obscure nor bowdlerized, but rather that they are transparent and unedited."[22]

Hobson acknowledges in *The Dreaming Brain* and his other writings that dreams may still convey personally significant information and may at times stimulate extraordinary efforts at meaning-making. But the main thrust of his research is aimed at debunking the practice of dream interpretation and comparing the process of dreaming to a mental illness like psychosis. His work has succeeded in spreading the idea among intellectuals and the general public that science has proved that dreams are nonsense. And by proving that dreams are nonsense, it seems to prove that psychoanalysis must be nonsense, too.

Once again, the anti-Freud agenda leads some neuroscientists to overstate the significance of their research data. Of course modern sleep laboratory findings have advanced our understanding far beyond Freud's model. But Hobson's brainstem reductionism[23] does not adequately account for the facts that some dreams are reported from nonREM stages of sleep, while REM sleep does not always produce a dream. Hobson's theory depends on the identity of REM sleep and dreaming: the former explains the latter. If, however, dreaming and REM sleep are *not* isomorphic, then Hobson's refutation of Freud fails.

That would not necessarily prove Freudian dream theory is right, but at least it would cast aside the popular misconception that modern neuroscience has shown psychoanalysis is wrong.

The pioneering evidence on this point comes from Mark Solms, a psychoanalytically trained clinical neurologist who examined the waking and dreaming experiences of 361 people suffering from various forms of brain damage. By using standard methods of correlating pathologies in the brain with changes in mental functioning, Solms was able to develop a portrait of which neural systems play the most important roles in generating dreams. His findings, which have been further supported by brain imaging studies,[24] suggest that brainstem activities during REM sleep may be a *trigger* for the experience of dreaming, but dreaming itself does not require or automatically follow from REM:

> [T]he neural mechanisms that produce REM are neither necessary nor sufficient for the conscious experience of dreaming. . . . [N]ormal dreaming is impossible without the active contribution of some of the highest regulatory and inhibitory mechanisms of the mind. These conclusions cast doubt on the prevalent notion—based on simple generalizations from the mechanism of REM sleep—that 'the primary motivating force for dreaming is not psychological but physiological'. If *psychological forces* are equated with *higher cortical functions*, it is difficult to reconcile the notion that dreams are random physiological events generated by primitive brainstem mechanisms, with our observation that global anoneira [loss of the ability to dream] is associated not with brainstem lesions resulting in basic arousal disorders, but rather with parietal and frontal lesions resulting in spatial-symbolic and motivational-inhibitory disorders. These observations suggest that dreams are both generated and represented by some of the highest mental mechanisms.[25]

Solms has shown that important parts of the brain not directly involved in REM sleep are crucial for dreaming to occur. Much more research is needed to specify the nature of those neural systems and their interactions with waking consciousness, but already we can see that a strictly deterministic, unidirectional model such as the one proposed by Hobson cannot accommodate the latest neuroscientific data.[26]

At the same time, Solms' findings must be considered in the context of his fervent pro-Freud interests. As a translator of Freud's writings and a prominent advocate of psychoanalytic theory, Solms seems as equally determined to prove Freud right as Hobson is to prove Freud wrong. Thus Solms neglects to account for the many flaws in psychoanalytic dream theory: dreaming does not necessarily function as a guardian of sleep; children's dreams are not always transparently wishful; adult dreams do not always contain references to early childhood memories and fantasies; day residues are not always present in dreams; not every dream represents the fulfillment of a wish. According to social psychologist G. William Domhoff in his review of current scientific research on dreaming, "at the very least, traumatic dreams and recurrent dreams show that wish-fulfillment dreams are only a subset of all possible dreams."[27] If Solms' goal is to reassert the primacy of the psychoanalytic theory of dreams, he has not succeeded. However, if his work is taken as a new contribution to the scientific understanding of a phenomenon that Freud called "the royal road" to knowledge of the unconscious, then Solms has given us valuable data to consider.

Indeed, he may have given us more than he intended. Although Solms takes no interest in the content of dreams, several of his patients reported dreams with vivid imagery and religious symbolism (e.g., being by chased by horrible creatures, watching one's own funeral, standing before the pearly gates of heaven, encountering vampires, deceased relatives, black dogs, snakes). For religious studies scholars who use psychoanalysis to explore mystical experiences, Solms' research confirms Freud's insight that dreaming uses symbols and metaphors found in art, folklore, and myth. This opens the way to a new consideration of dream symbolism in relation to cultural creativity and religious life.[28]

Psychoanalysis and Religion, Revisited

This final section pulls back from the focus on specific areas of neuroscientific research to outline in broad strokes what a new psychoanalysis of religion might look like, one that has been brought into active dialogue with contemporary brain-mind science.

It will be evolutionary. As noted earlier, Freud took a strong early interest in Darwinian ideas. Throughout Freud's career, from neurology to psychoanalysis, he viewed his work through an evolutionary lens. Although his theories of cultural transmission depend on a faulty explanation for the inheritance of acquired traits (i.e., Lamarckian rather than Mendelian), Freud always remained closely tethered to the basic premises of Darwin's work. This was especially true in his attitude toward religion, which he regarded as primitive in both personal development (as a form of mental childishness) and in human history (as a primitive stage in the rise of civilization). Ironically, Freud's view are virtually identical to those found in several recent books offering sharply critical attacks on mainstream religion based on the latest findings of brain-mind science (e.g., Richard Dawkins's *The God Delusion*;

Daniel Dennett's *Breaking the Spell*). Dawkins et al. do their best to distinguish their brand of materialist atheism from Freud's, but the continuities with the psychoanalytic theory of religion are nevertheless striking. Both Freud and Dawkins et al. use an evolutionary-based psychology to analyze the negative impact of religion on people's mental growth and social behavior. Both are scornful of fundamentalists, moralists, and mystics. Both proclaim their atheism proudly and put their ultimate faith in human reason and scientific ingenuity.

Not all psychoanalytic theories of religion need to focus exclusively on the critical refutation of problematic beliefs and practices. But Freud's "hermeneutics of suspicion" has a valuable role to play in the study of religion, and his basic arguments appear even stronger today in light of recent developments in evolutionary psychology. Particularly in the study of topics like ritual practices, moral taboos, and beliefs about supernatural beings, the psychoanalytic critique of religion becomes all the more powerful when combined with current research on the evolved (and evolv*ing*) nature of the human brain-mind system.

It will be relational. Freud remained adamant in his hostility to religion all his life. However, many of his followers saw a positive potential for religion to promote psychological development and well-being. In contrast to Freud's emphasis on growing *out of* one's belief in God, they considered the possibility of growing *into* a more mature relationship with the divine, in whatever form a person conceptualizes that ultimate reality. Still using Freud's basic concepts and principles, psychoanalysts like C. G. Jung, Erik Erikson, D. W. Winnicott, Heinz Kohut, and Ana-Marie Rizzuto found that certain aspects of religion could provide valuable support for the achievement and maintenance of mental health. More than that, they argued that religion can provide people with a beneficial sense of meaning and potential that goes beyond what secular science can offer. Much of their thinking centers on the relational qualities of human development, from the mother-infant bond through early family life to friendships, love, procreation, and cultural generativity. Several works in recent years have focused directly on the religious implications of these relational ideas, including James Jones's *Contemporary Psychoanalysis and Religion* and John McDargh's *Psychoanalytic Object Relations Theory and the Study of Religion*. Jones and McDargh accept Freud's critique of religion, but they bring psychoanalytic ideas about relationality into conversation with a more sophisticated and nuanced understanding of religion in all its variegated forms.

Slowly but surely, neuroscientists are beginning to reach similar conclusions, in recognition that brain-mind development cannot be understood strictly in terms of what happens inside a single person's skull. Despite the tendency of Western psychology to focus on the individual in isolation from social context, scientists today are coming to a new appreciation of relational experience as a driving force in neurological growth. Indeed, a subdiscipline called "social neuroscience" has arisen to seek a better accounting of how the brain-mind system is influenced by people's relationships with other people, other forms of life, their physical environments, their ideals, and their ultimate beliefs about the cosmos. Research is only just beginning in these directions, but already we have strong evidence that the brain responds in very fast and precise ways to particular social perceptions, devotes tremendous resources to the analysis and evaluation of interpersonal situations, and controls its own processing activities by imitating the behavior of significant others in the social world.[29] A future merger of ideas from relational psychoanalysis and social neuroscience could provide a better way of explaining the potentially beneficial impact of religion by connecting it to the healthy functioning of those brain-mind systems involved in social cognition and behavior.

It will be holistic. The modularity versus holism dichotomy mentioned earlier remains a challenge for present-day neuroscientists, and thus for psychoanalytic theorists who want to draw upon neuroscience, too. Without denying the gains in knowledge made by a modular approach,[30] it has become clear there is no "God spot" in the brain, no single anatomical location where religious beliefs reside or where religious experiences happen. Rather, the many different dimensions of human religiosity indicate a widely distributed network of neural systems with far-ranging interactions that defy simple analysis. The task for future neuroscientists is to develop better models for these holistic aspects of brain-mind functioning, processes in which the emergent qualities of the whole become greater than the sum of the parts. As Solms says in relation to dreaming, "complex mental faculties such as reading and writing (and, we might add, dreaming) are not localized within circumscribed cortical centers. . . . [They] are subserved by complex functional systems or networks, which consist of constellations of cortical and subcortical structures working together in a concerted fashion."[31] According to the argument developed in this chapter, Freud created psychoanalysis for exactly this reason, to enable the application of clinical neuroscientific methods in the analysis of complex mental processes whose dynamics cannot be exhaustively explained by reference to modular brain functions. A newly revised psychoanalytic study of religion will use this method to explore the holistic qualities of religious life, looking closely at the discrete parts but also seeking to account for their interactions across many areas of experience.

It will be mystical. Contemporary neuroscientists tend to be uncomfortable with the mystical implications of their work, but that does not make the implications go away. Most significantly, neuroscience has demonstrated that our sense of external reality is in fact an elaborate creation of our own minds. According to Nobel Prize winning biologist Eric Kandel, "[O]ur knowledge of the world is based on our biological apparatus for perceiving the world. . . . [P]erception is a *constructive* process that depends not only on the information inherent in a stimulus but also on the mental structure of the perceiver."[32] The spiritual malleability of this mental structure has been demonstrated by brain-imaging studies of people who are meditating and praying.[33] Such studies show remarkable shifts in the regional activities of the religious practitioners' brains, shifts that show the potential to intentionally create and exist in psychological states very different from the one produced by ordinary brain functioning. Unfortunately these brain-imaging studies have often been misinterpreted as evidence in favor of a perennialist theory that all religious experiences share the same core feature of pure consciousness or absolute unitary being. Such a notion cannot adequately account for the multiplicity of different unusual brain states documented by the studies themselves. In fact, the best scientific data suggest a radical pluralism of possible brain-mind experiences.

This discovery opens up enormous opportunities for the psychoanalytic study of religion, particularly on the topic of mysticism (as pursued in Sudhir Kakar's *Shamans, Mystics, Doctors*, William Parsons' *The Enigma of the Oceanic Feeling*, and Jeffrey Kripal's *Roads of Excess, Palaces of Wisdom*). The psychological experiences of mystics, visionaries, prophets, and dreamers offer a powerful means of gaining insight into those dimensions of brain-mind functioning that elude laboratory methods of analysis. In some cases the mystical experience may involve a regression to earlier patterns of cognitive activity and social behavior; other cases may show a transformation to new, more mature patterns; perhaps most cases will display both regressive and transformative features. By linking these changes to current scientific knowledge about the neural networks involved in the creation and maintenance of a sense of reality, psychoanalysis can build a much stronger case for both the harmful and adaptive aspects of religion.

Conclusion

The story of neuroscience in the coming years will likely be one of increasing appreciation for the spontaneous creativity, adaptive flexibility, and relational dynamics of the human brain-mind system. Inevitably this will motivate neuroscientists to pay closer attention to the richly varied phenomenology of religion. A revised and updated psychoanalytic theory can help bridge neuroscience with the study of religion by taking advantage of Freud's "mixed discourse," his conceptual language combining physical forces and psychological meanings. As Paul Ricoeur argued forty years ago in his seminal study of psychoanalysis as a philosophy, Freud developed this mixed discourse in recognition of the intimate, irreducible relationship between the brain and the mind, between neurology and psychology.[34] This kind of interdisciplinary conceptual framework is exactly what the present state of brain-mind science is lacking. After a century in eclipse, the early neuroscientific themes of psychoanalytic theory may come to the fore once again.

Notes

1. Freud finished *The Project* in 1895 but did not publish it for many years afterwards. *The Interpretation of Dreams* was published in November 1899, but Freud asked that the year be postdated to 1900 so the book would become part of the new century.
2. Ledoux (1992), 38–39.
3. Solms and Kaplan-Solms (2000), 18–19.
4. Henri Ellenberger's work (1970) remains the best guide to the pre-psychoanalytic history of this concept.
5. LaPlanche and Pontalis (1973), 474.
6. Ledoux (1996), 17.
7. Bargh (2005), 38.
8. Uleman (2005), 4–5.
9. Uleman (2005), 6. The one exception in *The New Unconscious* is chapter 16, "The Unconscious Relational Self" by Susan M. Andersen, Inga Reznik, and Noah S. Glassman, who take the Freudian concept of transference as a general cognitive process of using significant others as templates for perceiving, evaluating, and responding to new people and situations.
10. Ramachandran and Blakeslee (1998), 152.
11. A final quote on this point, from neuroscientist Antonio Damasio in *The Feeling of What Happens* (1999): "The world of the psychoanalytic unconscious has its roots in the neural systems which support autobiographical memory, and psychoanalysis is usually seen as a means to see into the tangled web of psychological connections within autobiographical memory. Inevitably, however, that world is also related to the other kinds of connections. . . . The unconscious, in the narrow meaning in which the word has been etched in our culture, is only a part of the vast amount of processes and contents that remain nonconscious, not known in core or

extended consciousness. In fact, the list of the 'not-known' is astounding. Consider what it includes:

1. all the fully formed images to which we do not attend;
2. all the neural patterns that never become images;
3. all the dispositions that were acquired through experience, lie dormant, and may never become an explicit neural pattern;
4. all the quiet remodeling of such dispositions and all their quiet renetworking—that may never become explicitly known; and
5. all the hidden wisdom and know-how that nature embodied in innate, homeostatic dispositions.

Amazing, indeed, how little we ever know."(228)

12. This section draws on Bulkeley (1997), 15.

13. Masson (1985), 261.

14. Freud (1965), xxvi.

15. ibid.

16. ibid., xxxii.

17. For additional information about the dreams beliefs and practices of this period, see Vande Kemp (1981).

18. Freud (1965), 647.

19. Hobson (1988), 11.

20. Hobson (1988), 10.

21. Hobson and McCarley (1977), 1347.

22. Hobson (1988), 12.

23. See also Domhoff (2001).

24. Maquet et al. (1996, 2000), Nofzinger et al. (1997, 2002), Braun et al. (1997, 1998).

25. Solms (1997), 153, 241–42, italics in original.

26. Hobson's later work on the "AIM" model attempts to provide a more flexible, multi-dimensional approach (2000), but it retains the emphasis on brainstem activation and cholinergic neurotransmitters as decisive factors in the psychology of dream experience.

27. Domhoff (2003), 140

28. See Bulkeley, *Dreaming in the World's Religions* (2008).

29. See "The Unconscious Relational Self,"Andersen et al. (2005).

30. Kandel et al. (2000).

31. Solms (1997), 97–98.

32. Kandel et al. (2000), 383, emphasis in original.

33. Azari et al. (2001), Lazar et al. (2000) , Lou et al. (1999), Davidson et al.(2003), Newberg et al. (2001).

34. Ricoeur (1970).

References

Andersen, Susan M., Inga Reznik, and Noah S. Glassman. "The Unconscious Relational Self." Pp. 421–81 in *The New Unconscious*. Edited by R. R. Hassin, J. S. Uleman, and J. A. Bargh. New York: Oxford University Press, 2005.

Azari, Nina, Nickel Janpeter, Gilbert Wunderlich, Michael Niedeggen, and Harald Hefter. "Neural Correlates of Religious Experience." *European Journal of Neuroscience* 13 (2001): 1649–52.

Bargh, John A. "Bypassing the Will: Toward Demystifying the Nonconscious Control of Social Behavior." Pp. 37–58 in *The New Unconscious*. Edited by R. R. Hassin, J. S. Uleman, and J. A. Bargh. New York: Oxford University Press, 2005.

Braun, A. R., T. J. Balkin, N. J. Wesensten, R. E. Carson, M. Varga, P. Baldwin, S. Selbie, G. Belenky, and P. Herscovitch. "Regional Cerebral Blood Flow Throughout the Sleep-Wake Cycle." *Brain* 120 (1997): 1173–97.

Braun, A. R., T. J. Balkin, N. J. Wesensten, F. Gwadry, R. E. Carson, M. Varga, P. Baldwin, G. Belenky, and P. Herscovitch. "Dissociated Pattern of Activity in Visual Cortices and Their Projections during Human Rapid Eye-Movement Sleep." *Science* 279 (1998): 91–95.

Bulkeley, Kelly. *An Introduction to the Psychology of Dreaming*. Westport: Praeger, 1997.

———. *Dreaming in the World's Religions: A Comparative History*. New York: New York University Press, 2008.

Byrd, Randolph C. "Positive Therapeutic Effects of Intercessory Prayer in a Coronary Care Unit Population." *Southern Medical Journal* 81 (1988): 826–29.

Damasio, Antonio. *The Feeling of What Happens: Body and Emotion in the Making of Consciousness*. San Diego: Harcourt, 1999.

Davidson, Richard J., et al. "Alterations in Brain and Immune Function Produced by Mindfulness Meditation." *Psychosomatic Medicine* 65 (2003): 564–70.

Dawkins, Richard. *The God Delusion*. New York: Houghton Mifflin, 2006.

Dennett, Daniel. *Breaking the Spell: Religion as a Natural Phenomenon*. New York: Viking, 2006.

Domhoff, G. William. "A New Neurocognitive Theory of Dreams." *Dreaming* 11, no. 1(2001): 13–33.

———. *The Scientific Study of Dreams: Neural Networks, Cognitive Development, and Content Analysis*. Washington, D.C.: American Psychological Association, 2003.

Ellenberger, Henri. *The Discovery of the Unconscious*. New York: Basic Books, 1970.

Freud, Sigmund. *Civilization and its Discontents*. Translated by J. Strachey. New York: W. W. Norton, 1961. Original edition, 1930.

———. *The Interpretation of Dreams*. Translated by J. Strachey. New York: Avon Books, 1965.

———. *Introductory Lectures on Psychoanalysis*. Translated by J. Strachey. New York: Liveright, 1966. Original edition, 1916/1917.

Gay, Peter. *Freud: A Life for Our Time*. New York: W. W. Norton, 1988.

Hassin, Ran R., James S. Uleman, and John A. Bargh, eds. *The New Unconscious*. New York: Oxford University Press, 2005.

Hobson, J. Allen. *The Dreaming Brain*. New York: Basic Books, 1988.

Hobson, J. Allan, and Robert McCarley. "The Brain as a Dream State Generator: An Activation-Synthesis Hypothesis of the Dream Process." *American Journal of Psychiatry* 134 (1977): 1335–48.

Hobson, J. Allan, Edward Pace-Schott, and Robert Stickgold. "Dreaming and the Brain: Towards a Cognitive Neuroscience of Conscious States." *Behavioral and Brain Sciences* 23, no. 6 (2000): 793–842.

Jones, James. *Contemporary Psychoanalysis and Religion: Transference and Transcendence*. New Haven: Yale University Press, 1993.

Kakar, Sudhir. *Shamans, Mystics, Doctors: A Psychological Inquiry into India and Its Healing Traditions*. Boston: Beacon Press, 1982.

Kandel, Eric R., James H. Schwartz, and Thomas M. Jessel, eds. *Principles of Neural Science*. Fourth ed. New York: McGraw-Hill, 2000.

Kaplan-Solms, Karen, and Mark Solms. *Clinical Studies in Neuro-Psychoanalysis: Introduction to a Depth Neuropsychology*. Madison: International Universities Press, 2000.

Kripal, Jeffrey J. *Roads of Excess, Palaces of Wisdom: Eroticism and Reflexivity in the Study of Mysticism*. Chicago: University of Chicago Press, 2001.

Laplanche, J., and J.-B. Pontalis. *The Language of Psychoanalysis*. Translated by D. Nicholson-Smith. New York: W.W. Norton, 1973.

Lazar, Sara W., George Bush, Randy L. Gollub, Gregory L. Fricchione, Gurucharan Khalsa, and Herbert Benson. "Functional Brain Mapping of the Relaxation Response and Meditation." *NeuroReport* 11, no. 7 (2000): 1581–85.

LeDoux, Joseph. *The Emotional Brain: The Mysterious Underpinnings of Emotional Life*. New York: Touchstone, 1992.

———. *Synaptic Self: How Our Brains Become Who We Are*. New York: Penguin, 1996.

Lou, Hans C., Troels W. Kjaer, Lars Friberg, Gordon Wildschiodtz, Soren Holm, and Markus Nowak. "A 15O-H20 PET Study of Meditation and the Resting State of Normal Consciousness." *Human Brain Mapping* 7 (1999): 98–105.

Maquet, P. "Functional Neuroimaging of Normal Human Sleep by Positron Emission Tomography." *Journal of Sleep Research* 9 (2000): 207–31.

Maquet, P., J. M. Peteres, J. Aerts, G. Delfiore, C. Degueldre, A. Luxen, and G. Franck. "Functional Neuroanatomy of Human Rapid-Eye-Movement Sleep and Dreaming." *Nature* 383 (1996): 163.

Masson, Jeffrey Moussaieff, ed. *The Complete Letters of Sigmund Freud to Wilhelm Fliess*. Cambridge: Harvard University Press, 1985.

McDargh, John. *Psychoanalytic Object Relations Theory and the Study of Religion: On Faith and the Imaging of God*. Lanham: University Press of America, 1983.

Newberg, Andrew, Eugene D'Aquili, and Vince Rause. *Why God Won't Go Away: Brain Science and the Biology of Belief*. New York: Ballantine, 2001.

Nofzinger, E. A., D. J. Buysse, J. M. Miewald, C. C. Meltzer, J. C. Price, R. C. Sembrat, H. Ombao, C. F. 3rd Reynolds, T. H. Monk, M. Hall, D. J. Kupfer, and R. Y. Moore. "Human Regional Cerebral Glucose Metabolism during Non-rapid Eye Movement Sleep in Relation to Waking." *Brain* 125 (2002): 1105–15.

Nofzinger, E. A., M. A. Mintun, M. B. Wiseman, D. J. Kupfer, and R. Y. Moore. "Forebrain Activation in REM Sleep: An FDG PET Study." *Brain Research* 770 (1997): 192–201.

Parsons, William B. *The Enigma of the Oceanic Feeling: Revisioning the Psychoanalytic Theory of Mysticism*. Oxford: Oxford University Press, 1999.

Pinker, Steven. *How the Mind Works*. New York: W. W. Norton, 1997.

Ramachandran, V. S., and Sandra Blakeslee. *Phantoms in the Brain: Probing the Mysteries of the Mind*. New York: Quill, 1998.

Ricoeur, Paul. *Freud and Philosophy: An Essay on Interpretation*. Translated by D. Savage. New Haven: Yale University Press, 1970.

Solms, Mark. *The Neuropsychology of Dreams: A Clinico-Anatomical Study*. Mahway: Lawrence Erlbaum, 1997.

Tooby, John, and Leda Cosmides. "The Psychological Foundations of Culture." In *The Adapted Mind: Evolutionary Psychology and the Generation of Culture*. Edited by J. H. Barkow, L. Cosmides, and J. Tooby. New York: Oxford University Press, 1992.

Uleman, James S. "Introduction: Becoming Aware of the New Unconscious." Pp. 3–15 in *The New Unconscious*. Edited by R. R. Hassin, J. S. Uleman, and J. A. Bargh. New York: Oxford University Press, 2005.

Vande Kemp, Hendrika. "The Dream in Periodical Literature: 1860–1910." *Journal of the History of the Behavioral Sciences* 17 (1981): 88–113.

PART THREE

PHILOSOPHICAL RECONSIDERATIONS

CHAPTER SIX

Freud and Philosophy of Religion after Metaphysics

Gregory Kaplan

Freud, perhaps surprisingly given his manifest hostility to religious illusions, could help us to reengage philosophy of religion after metaphysics, that is, once we have stopped latently considering illusions hostile to our lives.[1] Freud's legacy for philosophy of religion arguably regards a kind of salvation, redemption, or liberation that *learns* from misprisions, errors, and bonds rather than *disavow* them.

We might consider reopening philosophical questions of whether Freud's account of religion presupposes naturalism and engages in reductionism. Taking Spinoza's naturalism and Husserl's reductionism as touchstones, a comparison to Freud's own conception—and critique—of philosophy indicates that psychoanalysis may not qualify as a "rigorous science" but nor does it abandon the explanation. Likewise, Freud's own appeal to natural conditions hardly disqualifies a "progress in spirituality." A reexamination of Freud's transference concepts will yield tentative conclusions about how something "more," a "remainder" simultaneously expresses and institutes psychic and social life.

Freud arguably inspires a philosophy of religion after metaphysics. A "surplus" of life, or "*more* than life" not only constitutes life, as in the creation of God, but also takes part, participates in that very life.[2] While power acts on life, it also activates the subjectivity of the subject who subjects to its terms.[3]

A trauma or disruption inaugurates consciousness; therefore, as Judith Butler puts it, "ego is other than itself."[4]

Philosophers of religion could opt for either side of the Freud wars. Was he a scientist? An artist? A technician? On the one hand the Freud who emphasizes the scientific procedure that he theorizes is viewed as a reductive naturalist. While it has not fared well over time, this reading of Freud has offered the prospect of inspiring cognitive neurophysiology as well as exposing itself to caricature.[5] On the other hand, the reading of Freud that emphasizes the therapeutic event that he practices views him as a nonreductive nonnaturalist; this Freud has—sometimes reluctantly—inspired the practice of psychoanalysis from Melanie Klein to Julia Kristeva.

Living requires an effort; it is an achievement, not a given. Moreover, it is accomplished more or less properly. However, its meaning is not necessarily derived from an external source. How would the meaning of life result from the achievement of living? What is the appropriate style of living that bestows meaning onto life?

Aristotle, probing the question in his *Nichomachean Ethics*, organizes the practical virtues toward an end, a final purpose, or *telos*. Contemplative life which, according to Aristotle, is done "for its own sake," marked by its "self-sufficiency," has the ironic effect of reorganizing the practical life that is oriented toward carving a space of leisure necessary for contemplation. [6] Yet since the practical virtues now point beyond themselves to some other goal, there opens up a gap, a reluctance within ethically virtuous life. Discontent unsettles the practical virtues, because the very limited formation of a life around determinate forms of life gives rise to fantasies of escape from life.

There are two ways to satisfy an urge, fulfill a desire, or compensate for a lack: (1) Hold an intentional belief and take action; or (2) repress and fantasize. Aristotle champions the former; Freud dissects the latter. Of course the first also arises in modern philosophy with Descartes and Hegel. For Descartes and Hegel, the subject fully present to itself, thought (consciousness, conceptuality) contained by itself (substance, essence). Hegel completes the dualism of subject and object in Descartes by giving the subject an objective form in history and giving the object a subjective meaning in consciousness. In contrast with the proposed Idealist resolution of need into a substance or essence, Freud's early model of mind worked from the idea that a pleasure principle seeks to discharge the tension building up in the (neural) networks transmitting energy through unfulfilled desired, unmet wants.

The compulsive repetition of a traumatic event, however, cannot be explained by the wish fulfillment of standard dreaming. No one *wants* to relive a horrific episode; nevertheless, perhaps one *must*. "They are repeated, under the pressure of a compulsion."[7] What drives this compulsion before the pleasure principle? Death, or "an urge inherent in organic life to restore an earlier state of things." As a result, Freud conjectures, "organic striving" itself reaches a "final goal," if properly interpreted. "If we are to take it as truth that knows no exception that everything living dies for internal reasons—becomes inorganic once again—then we shall be compelled to say that 'the aim of all life is death.'"[8] Freud is tempted here unfortunately to supplement his insight that there is no principle to organize experience "beyond the pleasure principle" with the "principle" of death. What remains of serious interest, however, as Lear notes, is the internalization of an aggression directed outward. It is a "disturbance of the fabric of life" which "can never be lived without remainder."[9] The unconscious does not motivate so much as attack motivation itself by reopening the wounds of a trauma.

Inasmuch as desire wants, paradoxically, the energy needed to satisfy or repress, it gives life "too much of too much," writes Lear. The unconscious mind is "self-disrupting."[10] The unconscious is not a standing reserve of hidden thoughts, but a rupture or hiatus taking place within, and thereby sustaining, its own effects of *dis*ordering life. Psychoanalysis aids the breaking up of those *dis*orders—orders which disrupt—that have accrued under the pressure of internalized aggression.

Having spent the bulk of *The Ethics* demonstrating the need for every effect to have a cause, Spinoza finally introduces a distinction between the existence of the body and the eternity of the mind. As a body, the striving to persist or *conatus* terminates in death. After its destruction, however, "something [of the mind] remains, which is eternal."[11] For, as Richard Mason writes, "in understanding how nature is, how we are part in it, we acquire a view which is less bound by duration and more derived from a perspective of eternity."[12] Undoubtedly, things have causes or reasons of necessity. (Whether the appropriateness of doubt is caused by a dream or by a demon, even Descartes concedes the necessity of causation, much to Hume's chagrin.) The necessity of things is just their *causa sui*, or self-causation. However, that does not specify what reasons there are, only presupposes that there are reasons. [13] Nevertheless, furthering reason increases self-determination, and thus what remains of the mind after the physical state deteriorates or gets destroyed. Pierre-Francois Moreau pithily remarks, *J'éprouve ma finitude, donc mon éternité*, "I realize my finitude, and thus my eternity." The feeling of eternity does not consist in the acquisition of certain knowledge about essences. Rather, this feeling arises from the freedom—and pressure—allotted the position we finitely inhabit. Finitude is not a limit of knowledge, as Descartes may have assumed. On Spinoza's account, finitude partakes of infinity. Infinity enhances, rather than negates or supplants, finitude.[14]

We may therefore characterize Spinoza as a nonreductive naturalist. Nothing exists outside nature. Nature explains itself. However, nature is itself infinite, irreducible. Nature and God are the same irreducible inclusivity of living. Spinoza accordingly does not reduce nature to a collection of finite things, since nature also comprises infinite activity. Although he insists that the explanation of an effect reaches its end in a natural cause, he does not promise any final or complete description of all natural effects (see *Ethics* III, 2, note). Nevertheless, understanding a description relies on an explanation of sorts, for understanding properly involves comprehending greater regions of life, not fewer.[15]

Wayne Proudfoot makes a pertinent distinction between descriptive reduction and explanatory reduction. The latter is analytically required, since explanations reach a terminal point subject to criticism, whereas the latter are not legitimate since there is in principle no end to the possible descriptions of an experience. Freud takes a similar position inasmuch as he intuits the principle that there are no principles beyond the pleasure principle. Nevertheless, Freud insists on the prospect of reaching some breaking point through analysis that discovers an "interest or force" that exerts power over the pleasure of life.[16] Death is the natural event that provides a clue of this "return" to "origins."

Yet, reduction also takes nonnaturalist forms, which means they do not reduce descriptively to nature, but do reduce to any number of plausibly conflicting interpretations (to adapt Ricoeur's turn of phrase), as Edmund Husserl's philosophical writings aptly demonstrate. Specifically, Husserl's project of *reduction* seeks to free consciousness from the artificial limits imposed by naturalism, psychologism, and historicism. These latter methods implied that thought was limited by extraneous confines, whether mental or social. Intentionality would therefore not participate in the world so much as reflect upon it. This reflection would require evidence. The search for evidence demands that consciousness look outside of itself, toward what appears to it: "to the things themselves." Pre-predicative experience is nothing more or less than "the self-evidence of objects." The reduction of consciousness finds at this deepest level an opening onto an infinite expanse of possibilities limited only by sensation and imagination.

Erlebnis is an "ambiguity" straddled between real and unreal, noema and noesis.[17] To Husserl, pre-predicative meaning comprises horizons; the transcendental delineates structure. This nonintentional passivity comes from outside of conscious structures. Husserl promulgates a nonnaturalist reduction.

Reduction for Husserl is more like clarifying, almost metaphoric for a soup-reduction that boils off the waste or irrelevancies and leaves only the essence.

Ricoeur points out the challenge that Freud levels at phenomenology. Husserl's reduction drills down into the sedimented layers of knowledge (episteme) that build over unreflective or preconscious beliefs (*doxa*). Phenomenology makes conscious the preconscious. One of three "masters of suspicion," Freud questions the freedom of the self-awareness presumed by explanatory reduction.[18] Even explanatory reduction cannot be trusted if consciousness can falsify or deceive itself, if our mechanisms fall victim to deceptive practices. No validating criteria may therefore place a check on descriptive reductions. Freud introduces, on Ricoeur's reading, "the novel problem of the lie of consciousness and consciousness as a lie."[19] What does psychoanalysis reduce to the unconscious mind? How does psychoanalysis reduce it? As Ricoeur puts it, psychoanalysis is "an antiphenomenology which requires, not the reduction to consciousness, but the reduction of consciousness" to something outside of it.[20]

Freud introduces into naturalism two features of reduction: (1) the depth psychology of the unconscious, which is not even accessible in the manner of a horizon or eidetic structure, and (2) intrinsic conflict. Much naturalism had relied on a cohesive field of mindfulness that organizes manifold experience (e.g., Hobbes, Hume). Whereas natural desires vary in pressure, they do not carry different values. Moral motivation seems, however, to provide an overriding limit, a superior authority over natural desire. Kant posed a challenge to naturalism: how could freedom act in accord with its own law if it were conditional upon the senses and their impulses or inclinations? Kant proposes that freedom not only transcends but virtually repels desirous inclinations. In this respect, the freedom of will helps to balance the loss of innocence and the disillusionment of experience. "Just as mourning impels the ego to give up the object declaring the object to be dead and offering the ego the inducement to live, so does each single struggle of ambivalence loosen the fixation of the libido to the object by disparaging it, denigrating it and even as it were killing it off."[21] Reduction to nature has explanatory force because the effect has a cause. However, the reduction of nature fails to describe every possible variation. Morally, nature is reduced to freedom.

Guilt registers the difference between human behavior tracing back to nature and human imagination deriving from nature. Freud consequently answers Kant's moral challenge to naturalism in his account of guilt. The sense of guilt burdens natural desires with a moral demand. The moral demand of guilt arises in the course of resolving the Oedipus complex. First, parental authority gets internalized. The psyche takes up or introjects the voices of parents. Amongst those voices are the ones of seduction and condemnation. Second, the aggression directed toward the rival parent who competes for the affections of a desired object (or seducer) is taken over by the superego and redirected toward the ego which must now pay for the guilt accrued from its newfound recognition of that rivalry.[22] The love instinct coincides in the libido with the death instinct. What separates and relates them is the ego, or in Kant's language, will. Freud seems to echo Nietzsche's acerbic remark about the smell of cruelty in the categorical imperative.[23]

If anything, guilt marks a shift, a dis-ease of consciousness—whether affected by the unconscious or the law of freedom. How shall we understand this shift? What shifts, exactly; from and to where? A reductive transfer operates at the symbolic level, whereas a naturalized transfer occurs at the physical level.

Transfer in Husserl's writing takes meaning from one place and puts it into another. Consciousness is a mobile center within a horizon. Husserl writes, "In their intentions, [acts] necessarily imply an infinite horizon of inactive [inaktuelle] validities which function with them in flowing mobility. The manifold acquisitions of earlier active life are not dead sediments; even the background (for example, that of the perceptual field), of which we are always concurrently conscious but which is momentarily irrelevant and remains completely unnoticed, still functions according to its implicit validities."[24] Consequently, it is not essential to thematically recollect the "first time" a given sense was instituted in consciousness, since the sense is repeatedly confirmed or, rarely, disconfirmed. This is precisely the meaning of evidence, which "institutes" an "abiding possession" of sense that returns in the structure of the intended object and its horizons. "To the extent that there is givenness beforehand, there is such a transfer" of sense. The habituality attached to the ego's ongoing experience of its surrounding world provides the "grounds" for ordinary sense-acquisition and sense-bestowal.[25]

The transfer that Nietzsche tracks in his *Genealogy of Morals* suggests a more naturalistic than reductionist flavor. There he exposes the "transfer" of legal contract of debt (*Schuld*) into the moral burden of guilt, being in the wrong.[26] As a result of reading Freud's concept of the transference genetically in the vein of Nietzsche's *Genealogy of Morals*, we might correct Freud's tendency to view death as the aim or final cause of life. We might instead view death as the efficient cause of (more) life; perhaps, as Leonard Lawlor states ironically, "death is actually life itself."[27]

The "compromise formation" which Freud theorizes provisionally, perhaps even superficially resolves a conflict among instincts and between instinct and guilt. However, unremembered occurrences in the past still apply pressure in the present. Transference repeats what is not remembered. If the repetition is noticed and reconfigured, however, then the transference reduces, clarifies or dissolves the screen memory. As Freud puts it, "The transference thus creates an intermediate region between illness and real life through which the transition from the one to the other is made. The new condition has taken over all the features of the illness, but it represents an artificial illness which is at every point accessible to our intervention."[28] On Eric Santner's apt reading, the primal scene is neither a natural occurrence nor a cultural event, but an "enigmatic message" which the self hears. He calls "undeadening" this spacing or hiatus established "by a kind of unconscious transmission that is neither simply enlivening nor simply deadening."[29]

Given the death instinct or natural hostilities of life, which Hobbes had elaborated, how does civilization last? Much like the psyche sustains itself by internalizing a voice (superego) that comes to discipline itself (ego) by containing its desires (id), so too society introjects the punishing limit of morality. The superego places a check on incessant desires so they do not overwhelm the social weal. To Freud then conscience does not replace natural determination with moral motivation; rather, nature employs conscience to preserve its life in society. Guilty conscience is perhaps less a signal of freedom than a mark of Cain. How free is the voice of freedom? To Kant the natural inclination of desire, because determined by external forces, comprised a "foreign impulse" against which the rational subject would need to defend its independence: "he does not . . . ascribe them to his proper self, that is, to his will" choosing independently.[30] The internalized voice dictates the maxims of self-rule. Yet, according to Freud, that voice had effectively incorporated the commanding parents. Freud points out the motivations we have—releasing the pressure of guilt, for one—to maintain the illusion of freedom.

An idea characteristic of psychoanalysis, writes Freud in *Civilization and Its Discontents*, "tells us that conscience (or more correctly, the anxiety which later becomes conscience) is indeed the cause of instinctual renunciation to begin with, but that later the relationship is reversed. Every renunciation of instinct now becomes a dynamic source of conscience and every fresh renunciation increases the latter's severity and intolerance." [31] Guilty conscience not only serves to limit the wanton discharge of instincts, it also gives shape and form to the very self or subject it condemns. The most important question, precisely formulated by Butler, is this how resistance can come from/within attachment? Perhaps more importantly, how can the resistance break down and let the attachment remain—or let it go.[32]

Is breaking down resistance its own reward or does it aim for a worthwhile transformation? How could we make the most of living—even entertaining life "too much"? In Spinoza's words, "supreme contentment of spirit follows from the right way of life."[33] What that way requires, though, is nothing like a detachment from nature. Utter independence, what Spinoza calls "absolute control," is not within our reach.[34] Since narcissism haunts the assertion of free will, however categorically deduced, Ricoeur emphasizes the contingent, conflictual exercise of freedom. Indeed, "evil . . . consists less in a transgression of a law than in a pretension of man to be master of his life."[35] Freud theoretically concurs, however much it would appear otherwise in his practice. In Freud's official prose, psychoanalysis does not aim "to make pathological reactions impossible, but to give the ego freedom to decide one way or the other."[36] It proceeds haltingly, not decisively. Thus Norman O. Brown has fittingly renamed the Oedipal complex an Oedipal project, because "the essence of the Oedipal complex is the project of becoming God—in Spinoza's formulation, *causa sui*."[37] Viewing the Oedipal as a project of becoming and not a state of being, Freud is documenting the psychological provision of a physical-theological condition.

Nature "includes a kind of internal excess," as Santner puts it; "the 'heroic' break with nature is immanent to nature itself."[38] What brings living to life is the "too much" that comes from/within a "too little." As an offering to the philosophy of religion after metaphysics, Freud's thought—of guilt and transference, among other things—enriches "a conceptual basis for a notion of liberation that is unrelentingly immanent," as Kenneth Surin and many others have compellingly urged.[39]

Notes

1. See Mark Wrathall, ed., *Religion after Metaphysics* (Cambridge: Cambridge University Press, 2003).

2. Eric Santner, *The Psychotheology of Everyday Life: Reflections on Freud and Rosenzweig* (Chicago: Chicago University Press, 2001), 10.

3. See Judith Butler, *The Psychic Life of Power* (Palo Alto: Stanford University Press, 1997), 84.

4. Butler, *The Psychic Life*, 195.

5. See Freud's 1895 "Project for a Scientific Psychology" and Kelley Bulkeley in this volume.

6. Aristotle, *Nichomachean Ethics*, X7.11a27–b26; see Jonathan Lear, *Happiness, Death, and the Remainder of Life* (Cambridge: Harvard University Press, 2002).

7. Sigmund Freud, *Beyond the Pleasure Principle*, in *Standard Edition*, ed. James Strachey (New York: Norton, 1981), XVIII: 21.

8. Freud, *Beyond*, 36–38.

9. Lear, *Happiness*, 96; see Freud, *The Ego and the Id*, in *The Standard Edition*, ed. James Strachey (New York: Norton, 1981), XIX: 56.

10. Lear, *Happiness*, 127.

11. Spinoza, *Ethics* V, 23.

12. Richard Mason, *The God of Spinoza: A Philosophical Study* (Cambridge: Cambridge University Press, 1997), 245. Mason's account is controversial, and I defend it elsewhere; for our purposes it depicts a faithful "Spinozist" position, however textually accurate or not. Without going into detail, I suspect a pragmatist would gain more from reading Spinoza's *Treatise on the Emendation of the Intellect*, which treats learning *in media res*, than Descartes' *Discourse on Method*. From a vantage similar to process theology, see Philip Clayton, *The Problem of God in Modern Thought* (Grand Rapids, Mich.: Eerdmans, 2000), 392–401.

13. Mason, *God*, 65–66.

14. Pierre-Francois Moreau, *L'expérience et léternité* (Paris: Presses Universitaires de France, 1994), 546–59.

15. "Enclaves of unintelligibility are barren rather than fertile," see Mason, *God*, 259, 41, 253–54, and passim.

16. Wayne Proudfoot, *Religious Experience* (Berkeley: University of California Press, 1985), 203.

17. See Edmund Husserl, *The Essential Husserl*, ed. Donn Welton (Bloomington: Indiana University Press, 1999), 331; and Husserl, *Ideas Pertaining to a Pure Phenomenology and to a Phenomenological Philosophy* (Dordrecht: Kluwer, 1983), Book I, Section 36.

18. Paul Ricoeur, *Freud and Philosophy* (New Haven: Yale University Press, 1977), 32.

19. Paul Ricoeur, *The Conflict of Interpretations: Essays in Hermeneutics* (Evansville: Northwestern University Press, 2007), 99.

20. Ricoeur, *Conflict*, 237.

21. Freud, "Mourning and Melancholia," in *The Standard Edition*, ed. James Strachey (New York: Norton, 1981), XIV: 257. On Freud's revised theory of instinct, see *New Introductory Lectures on Psychoanalysis*, James Strachey, ed. (New York: Norton, 1989), 91–100, 118–120.

22. See John Deigh, *The Sources of Moral Agency: Essays in Moral Psychology and Freudian Theory* (Cambridge: Cambridge University Press, 1996), 113–159.

23. Nietzsche, *Genealogy of Morals*, II.6.1.

24. E. Husserl, *The Crisis of the European Sciences and Transcendental Phenomenology*, (Evansville: Northwestern University Press, 1970), 149.

25. Edmund Husserl, *Cartesian Meditations* (Dordrecht: Kluwer, 1995), 111–113. "Each everyday experience involves an analogizing transfer of an originally instituted objective sense to a new case, with its anticipative apprehension of the object as having a similar sense" (*Cartesian Meditations*, 141).

26. Nietzsche, *Genealogy of Morals*, book 2, section 8.

27. See Leonard Lawlor, *Implications of Immanence* (New York: Fordham University Press, 2006), 137 and 10 on Jacques Derrida, *Speech and Phenomena* (Evansville: Northwestern University Press, 14–15.

28. Freud, "Remembering, Repeating and Working Through," in *Standard Edition*, ed. James Strachey (New York: Norton, 1981), XII: 154–55.

29. Santner, *Psychotheology*, 35–36, see 106.

30. Immanuel Kant, "Groundwork of the Metaphysic of Morals" in *Practical Philosophy*, ed. Mary Gregor (Cambridge: Cambridge University Press, 1999), 92, 104.

31. Freud, *Civilization and Its Discontents*, in *The Standard Edition*, ed. James Strachey (New York: Norton, 1981), XXI: 129, see Lear, *Happiness*, 197–198, and Butler, *Psychic Life*, 55, 81.

32. Butler, *Psychic Life*, 88.

33. Spinoza, *Ethics* V, 10, scholium.

34. Spinoza, *Ethics*, V, preface.

35. Ricoeur, *Conflict*, 438.

36. Freud, *Ego*, 51n.

37. Norman O. Brown, *Life Against Death: The Psychoanalytical Meaning of History* (New York: Viking Press, 1959), 118.

38. Santner, *Psychotheology*, 136.

39. Kenneth Surin, "Rewriting the Ontological Script of Liberation," in *Theology and the Political*, ed. Creston Davis, John Milbank, and Slavoj Zizek (Durham: Duke University Press, 2005), 262.

References

Brown, Norman O. *Life Against Death: The Psychoanalytical Meaning of History*. New York: Viking Press, 1959.

Butler, Judith. *The Psychic Life of Power*. Palo Alto: Stanford University Press, 1997.

Clayton, Philip. *The Problem of God in Modern Thought*. Grand Rapids, Mich.: Eerdmans, 2000.

Deigh, John. *The Sources of Moral Agency: Essays in Moral Psychology and Freudian Theory*. Cambridge: Cambridge University Press, 1996.

Freud, Sigmund. *The Standard Edition*. Edited by James Strachey. New York: Norton, 1981.

———. *New Introductory Lectures on Psychoanalysis*. Edited by James Strachey. New York: Norton, 1989.

Husserl, Edmund. *The Crisis of the European Sciences and Transcendental Phenomenology*. Evansville: Northwestern University Press, 1970.

———. *Ideas Pertaining to a Pure Phenomenology and to a Phenomenological Philosophy*. Dordrecht: Kluwer, 1983.

———. *Cartesian Meditations*. Dordrecht: Kluwer, 1995.

———. *The Essential Husserl*. Edited by Donn Welton. Bloomington: Indiana University Press, 1999.

Kant, Immanuel. *Practical Philosophy*. Edited by Mary Gregor. Cambridge: Cambridge University Press, 1999.

Lawlor, Leonard. *Implications of Immanence*. New York: Fordham University Press, 2006.

Lear, Jonathan. *Happiness, Death, and the Remainder of Life*. Cambridge: Harvard University Press, 2002.

Mason, Richard. *The God of Spinoza: A Philosophical Study*. Cambridge: Cambridge University Press, 1997.

Moreau, Pierre-Francois. *L'expérience et léternité*. Paris: Presses Universitaires de France, 1994.

Proudfoot, Wayne. *Religious Experience*. Berkeley: University of California Press, 1985.

Ricoeur, Paul. *Freud and Philosophy*. New Haven: Yale University Press, 1977.

———. *The Conflict of Interpretations: Essays in Hermeneutics*. Evansville: Northwestern University Press, 2007.

Santner, Eric. *The Psychotheology of Everyday Life: Reflections on Freud and Rosenzweig*. Chicago: Chicago University Press, 2001.

Surin, Kenneth. "Rewriting the Ontological Script of Liberation," in *Theology and the Political*. Edited by Creston Davis, John Milbank, and Slavoj Zizek. Durham: Duke University Press, 2005.

Wrathall, Mark. *Religion after Metaphysics*. Cambridge: Cambridge University Press, 2003.

CHAPTER SEVEN

"The Jewish People Does Not Dream": The Paradoxes of Identification, or Martin Buber and Sigmund Freud on the Meaning of Judaism

Bettina Bergo

for Dominique Scarfone

Introductory Remarks: The Jewish People Does Not Dream

This chapter unfolds a curious claim by Philippe Lacoue-Labarthe and Jean-Luc Nancy; to wit, "the Jewish people does not dream."[1] If dreaming and phantasy exemplify the psychoanalytic phenomenon of "identification"—which is an individual and social phenomenon, and one that bedeviled Freud as he traced its origins and work in culture—and if the first *bona fide* identification is with the Father,[2] then the Jews do not quite "dream."

> "The Jewish people does not dream," we understand this expression in two registers: (1) This people does not identify with the Father in the oniric mode, or in the mode of an immediate adhesion to the *figure* (or phantasm, or phantom) of the Father. [Nevertheless], if it is the people and the religion of the Father, then it is this in an *other* sense, call it as "vigil" and as "vigilant." (2) This people—or its "analysis"—escapes the royal road of psychoanalysis (i.e., that of dreams) up to a certain point. It requires, as Freud's *Moses* put it, the importing (*Eintragung*) of the concept of the unconscious into collective psychology and, consequently, a re-elaboration of that concept.[3]

My purpose in this chapter is to explore the meaning of identification in light of myths and the Judaic innovation, which consists of a foreclosure on representation. Lacoue-Labarthe and Nancy understand foreclosure informally, as an act of symbolic exclusion or shutting out. Unlike Lacan's *forclusion*, they do not insist that what is shut out never reaches consciousnesss.[4] Foreclosure reorganizes what is imaginable in a given community, and this influences ritual action and memory. The foreclosure of representation has surprising effects on the way in which we envision our identity, as I will show by reading Martin Buber on Genesis 3 (eating from the tree of knowledge). Throughout, I will be comparing Buber's reading with Lacoue-Labarthe and Nancy's arguments concerning mythic identifications. As part of a larger project whose goal is to rethink the unconscious as affectivity largely independent of positive or thetic representation, Lacoue-Labarthe and Nancy are exploring the conjoined origins of psychic and social structures in their work *L'inconscient est destructuré comme un affect* [The Unconscious Is Destructured like an Affect].

Mythic and narrative events like taboos and expulsions imitate social and psychic functions, including foreclosures notably—whether these bear on representations, bodies, or on symbolic territories. What holds these exclusions together under a common concept is that foreclosure works like the taboo on incest. It has a negative and a positive normativity. Negatively, the foreclosure of representation prevents identification with "fathers" or personifiable powers, in oneiric or ritual modes which entail ecstasies and fusion. Such identification extends from cults of the ancestors to animism, henotheism, and hero-god myths. It also extends into art and fantasy.

Positively, the foreclosure of representation sometimes opens to an impulse toward representation.[5] This positive pressure does not drive us toward *mimetic* representations, such as those conceived to imitate 'reality' or the 'gods', etc. There is, at virtually every epoch of human history, a mimetic and a differential representation. Differential representation gives form to what Derrida called the "trace." I am calling "differential representation" a narrative or figurative operation by which a trace (recounted or drawn) has the effect of opening up the surface on which it is drawn, by introducing a very simple difference. This difference, once introduced, changes the surface or narrative context, and the subject perceiving or reading it grasps that the ground and the author of the mark are not reducible to each other. A similar phenomenon is found in psychoanalytic therapy with schizophrenics, for whom it is essential that their fusion with an imaginary figure be opened up to admit a third differentiating element: the analyst, society, or the father. As we will see, the foreclosure of dreaming, explored by Lacoue-Labarthe and Nancy, joins the profound message of Genesis 3 in Buber's reading. There, eating of the fruit of the Tree of Knowledge of good and evil—not to mention Adam and Eve's expulsion from the Garden—exemplifies both the foreclosure of identification and the introduction of a differentiating trace. It bears out Lacoue-Labarthe and Nancy's claim that Judaism introduced this innovation into its mythology early on, creating a religion largely devoid of ancestor cults, animism, semi-divine heroes. Virtually an anti-religion, Judaism foreclosed identification with the Father "in the phantasmatic mode." This means that, in Judaism—i.e., in the culture and thinking structured by the Torah and its commentaries—a limit and something like a finite modality is set out as inaugural. These separate humanity as a whole from divinity—despite residual resemblances, communication, or gifts. Moreover, this limit, sketched as early as the myth of the Garden, posits mortality, as death and as separation, at the heart of religion and its symbolic institution of society and politics.

Whether this limit is unique to Jewish monotheism or not seems to me of secondary importance, for the moment. Some historical interpretations have argued that the separation made Jewish cultural and religious survival possible.[6] The limit breaks, in any case, with religions (whether polytheistic or temporarily monotheistic) in which gods are conceived on a human model, where ancestors influence community decisions, and humans accede to divinity by rites, deeds, or the death of heroes. In the Jewish beginning, then, is a limit. The limit sets the activity of separation in motion and opens to an ordered creation of new combinations—as if it worked like a cultural geometry. In many biblical narratives, we are confronted with practical and conceptual limits on phantasmatic identifications of different sorts; the same identifications by which Greek tragedy conceived the incipience of the human political community out of the peaceful relations between the gods of Olympus or through the struggle between heroes and the anonymous force of *Anankè* or fate. However, from the Judaic limit arose a sociality and a politics of a different sort. It was structured neither by mythic nor totemic social identifications; nor was it beset by problems arising from conflicting paternal identifications.[7]

Buber's Biblical Humanism

In contrast to "Greek Humanism," Martin Buber defined the rebirth of the Jewish community textually, as a "Biblical Humanism" (1933, 1941).[8] This rebirth is expressed in a tone redolent of Nietzsche (whom Buber read carefully), as "the rebirth of its normative primal forces." These forces are located in the capacity to hear the paradoxical word of the Jewish Bible; a word that is paradoxical because it encompasses universality (as the possibility of identification for the nations) and particularity (the question of some kind of identification in separation). Moreover, the word is simultaneously transcription, trace, and voice; a speaking-to that is always repetition, which is why a midrash holds that the Torah was composed before the creation of the world. Biblical humanism is for Buber a calling for Jews. But while humanism has roots in religious and mythical thought, Jewish humanism introduces the supplementary foreclosure of representational transcendence—the same transcendence that makes possible an "immediate adhesion to the figure" of any great Other. As I noted, this anti-fetishistic reflex makes it appear almost anti-religious.

Buber exemplifies what it means to hear the paradoxical word in his reading of Genesis 3 in a later essay entitled "The Tree of Knowledge" (1953).[9] There, Buber rethinks life forces in an exegetical context. In the Garden narrative, the original force that is the will to know finds itself definitively limited without in turn engendering reactive forces. Buber calls the initial will to know a "human demonism."[10] The great challenge is to disable that will without disabling a love of knowledge or engendering new forces in a reactive will.

For Buber, the genius of the Garden narrative lies in conceiving mortality prior to sexuality or morality. The Tree of Knowledge stages the meaning of the will to know for a finite, created being. Irreducibly, this will to know aims at omniscience which is one aspect of will to power. Without urging that we disabuse ourselves of the idea of truth, as Nietzsche had done, Buber insists that for created beings, truth amounts to a knowledge of the opposed poles of the world's being. Although translations of the Bible have expressed this as "knowledge of good and evil," we should avoid the evaluation that is superimposed on it. For Buber, omniscience means an exhaustive knowledge of worldly binaries like fullness and lack, hope and despair, fusion and dissociation; those moving elements that form the grammar of myths and a frame for cultural identities.

Buber unfolds his conception of finite truth on the premise that human experience is disjunctive. Forces we unleash, and forces that act upon us, can set us into a position of "yes-saying" *or* into one of "no-saying," whereby we are either open to transcendence-in-separation or distance ourselves from it. Buber is not interested in the question of the ontology of "sin," or in "the fall of man." Yes-saying "can present itself to the experience and perception of man, while [he is] in the no-position." This would mean to feel and to know oneself separated from the good or from God. But "not [so,] the no in the yes-position."[11] Humans realize this "when [man] recognizes a condition in which he finds himself whenever he has transgressed the command of God, as the 'evil' and the one he has thereby lost and which . . . is inaccessible to him, as the good."[12] The no and the yes positions are existential and moral, individual and collective. In themselves, they are not exclusive to Judaism.

Knowledge of and movement between the two positions are both historical states, and immanent ones, as illustrated by the narrative of Adam and Eve. Following their expulsion from the Garden, this narrative unfolds as "a process in the world":

> at this point, the process in the human soul becomes a process in the world. Through the recognition of oppositeness, the opposites which are always latently present in creation break out into actual reality; they become existent . . . the first humans, as soon as they have eaten of the fruit, 'know' that they are naked . . . they feel the natural state of unclothedness in which they find themselves to be an ill or an evil . . . and by this very feeling, they make it so . . . [13]

In this hermeneutic circle, the values and acts that we see in Adam and Eve's shame are explained by the recognition that being is processual, and worldly processes concern time and space as finite continuities. The knowledge Adam and Eve gained about the opposites that structure being is a human knowledge determined by human time and human space, and shaped by the actions we take on our evaluations. In God, Buber argues, these opposites stand together, which leaves unanswered their ontological status in light of God: "He encompasses them, as He is absolutely superior to them; He has direct intercourse with them."[14] This is because God is not a being in the sense of a creation; perhaps not a being at all. There is no purposive unfolding or "becoming" in Buber's reading of the Other, though it may be possible to speculate about a dialectic of forces in creation.

Humans are the agents and sites of this dialectic of created being. The decisive separation between humans and God lies in the *mode* by which the opposed forces and positions in existence come to pass. For Buber, when the narrator of Genesis 3 has God say that man "is become as one of us, to know good and evil," the narrator ironizes that man now knows existence and, being finite, cannot help reactively unleashing a terrible dynamic of opposed forces.[15] This knowledge is not creative, then, because it is the knowledge of a finite creature situated in space and time; the language "become as one of us" combines irony with a rueful compassion.[16] For the ambitious creature could not grasp its new "unlike-likeness," any more than it could hold fast to the "yes" and the "no" positions at the same time. This "unlike-likeness" expresses a hiatus between the creator and the created, finitude and infinity. In the Garden narrative lies the discovery of the meaning of finitude, the human historical condition that admits of unlike repetitions, fabulation, and myths of identity. What it cannot do is to leap over the hiatus.

Cyclical and linear according to its modes, mortality engages humans in a history and a care for the succession of generations. The fact of mortality—and notably the fact that Adam and Eve are expelled from the Garden before they can eat from the Tree of Life—argues for the good fortune implicit in embodied mortality, at least so far as a finite thing is concerned when it wills to surpass its limits.

Humans thus ate from but one of two trees in the Garden. Adam and Eve were driven out before they could consume the fruit of the Tree of Life; for, a finite creature that eats its way to eternal life is demonry, Buber argues. "Demonry" expresses the idea of a being that could live out its *conatus* and drive to know forever, without ever holding together the opposites it first encountered in its Edenic paradise.

By this logic, while human mortality is tragic, (especially in the form of the death of the other, as Levinas has observed), it is also redemptive and for that reason, not above irony, as we will see. "For [man], as the being driven round amid opposites, [death] may become a haven, the knowledge of which brings comfort," writes Buber.[17]

> This stern benefaction is preceded by the passing of sentence [the announcement of tragedy is inscribed in the act of justice]. It announces no radical alteration of that which already exists; it is only that all things are drawn into the atmosphere of oppositeness. . . . From the *seat*, which had been made ready for him, man is sent out upon a *path*, his own . . . into the world's history . . . [18]

Through these events, death becomes the source of time's value and inaugurates the reckoning of a hitherto absurd notion called "history." No thinking, philosophical or religious, that fails to address death as limit and institution, can grasp, in a way that is free from phantasmatic identification, the significance of human sociality, and the necessity of a pragmatic limitation of the drives. We might say that, for the Greeks too, the political problem par excellence was that of limiting the coalescence of disparate drives within a group or a tyrant. Plato's mythic body of the tyrannical ruler (Republic, book IX), with its multiple heads, replays the difficulty of limiting drives and their inevitable conflict in the absence of the foreclosure of mythic identifications. But this limitation has to be flexible enough to avoid a complete divorce between the life energies carried by those so-called drives and their beneficial sublimations.

Buber argues that the sources of Genesis 3 come from other religions—including the Avestic stories of the jealousy of the gods. But Genesis 3's innovation is that the one God is not jealous of his creation, precisely because this God is *not* conceived on the model of humanity. This God would escape our grasp, arising as it does in the movement of inscription (as a trace that produces differences) and later, in the sociality deployed through the prophetic call. Anthropomorphic conceptions of gods may entail human-like responses on their part (jealousy, anger, repentance). But this modeling of identification—wherein the gods look and act like us, send our contemplation back to us, and thereby celebrate a collective self-sacralization that vitiates the existential limits set by death and the (death of the) human other. If there is no "knowledge" either of death or the other as such, the endless repetition of rebirths, ancestor or totemic worship, and anthropomorphic divinities suggest that this limit called death is never so serious. Life is reborn out of life; through the hero, humans pass between the below position and the above position with assurance. Yet there appears to be an existential need to lighten the anxiety of uncognizable limits, and this has implications for the understanding of monotheism and its relationship to other practices of sacralization. Hermeneutic inscription, enacted in and as a given community under foreclosure, effectively takes the place of phantasmatic identifications, Dionysiac dreaming, and acts of sacred fusion. Here, in any case, the separation already implicit in the narrator's irony "man is become as one of us"—an irony that arises from the implicit negation that this impossibility states[19]—adheres to the oppositions of being within the economy of mortality and finitude. What is finite cannot become infinite. The infinite (God or voice) knows but is not subject to what structures finitude itself: space-time, historicality, and indeed, the demonry or drive quality of willing to know and to be infinite.

Identification as Incorporation and the Transformation of the Voice

When Lacoue-Labarthe and Nancy claim that "the Jewish people does not dream," they are carrying Buber's meditation on finitude and the dialectic of forces a step further. Buber understood that a thoroughgoing identification with the God (or the Father) could only be phantasmatic. Lacoue-Labarthe and Nancy explore the implications of the foreclosure of such identifications in light of cultural sublimation. With the containment or foreclosure of phantasmatic identification, a different "law" becomes possible. Like all laws, this law effects differences. Culturally and historically, it gives the repetition of events a different quality, an ethico-gestural quality in which no one stands above the "law" because no one, be they shaman or seer, ascends to or otherwise incarnates the transcendental object. I do not mean that there is no ethical normativity in cultures whose religious practices ritually realize phantasmatic identifications. However, this enactment has implications for their conceptions of time and the cosmos. It is enough to say, for now, that following the (new) law is not equivalent to identifying phantasmatically with the Father. In this nonequivalence, it is the law that becomes open to completion; open therefore to the community, just as it becomes a site for the reinterpretation of the community. Everyone subject to the law thus brings to it his part of its understanding: the human reception of the law becomes a practical infinite.[20] But this infinite is neither fusional nor vertical. It ramifies.

The second consequence of "not dreaming" is the limitation set on phantasmatic elaborations about the immortality of the soul and the survival of the dead. Nothing eradicates the memory and desire that immortalize an ancestor, but his fetishization may be subverted if it is subject to questioning, or to irony. This entails the symbolic limitation of repetitions that, in mythic logic, become tragic because they enact an enduring malaise tied to agonizing loss, like a ghost whose law and words insist, determining the destiny of the group. When we look at the repetition compulsion of Freud's "Wolf Man," we find that each male authority incarnated the Wolf Man's subjugation by his father. So much for the psychological level; but we should recall the tragic conviction characteristic of Greek tragedy: Whatever you do, whether it is to avenge my name or to escape that responsibility, you shall only repeat the course of events that is your fate.[21] These illustrations show the widespread operation, and phantasmatic efficacy of the "not-quite-dead" (parents, ancestors, heroes; all objects of identification) in their relation to the living, who may lose their own lives in that "infernal" relation. The symbolic foreclosure of such immortalities makes possible the creation of a community that is not defined by identification as "we are *x* being," or "we carry within us, as our destiny, Him who was our Father."

Together, the formal abandonment of ancestor cults, spectral forces taken as presences—and the nonfigurability of God (iconically or in name)—forces the *work of finitude* to take place. It does so by way of three factors: (1) the task of continuous interpretation; (2) the configuration of a full if diachronous time as repeating holy days that inflect the past into the future, without destroying everyday time; and finally, (3) through a messianic temporality of generations to come, in which a promise of justice persists as it changes (along with the conditions of pardon and return), although without taking form as *parousia* or fulfilled presence. These are the basic aspects of the modification made possible by the foreclosure of "dreaming." There is a dialectic between them.

In "The Tree of Knowledge" Buber insists that it was no punishment to be banished from the Garden of Eden. Yet his claim seems strange. In the Garden, Adam walked with God. Adam was both creature *and* adult. However, his peculiar temporality remained an open question. For that reason, Adam was initially more than human and less than human—like a phantasy. In fact, he is there, in this figuration of prehuman time, curiously less a "being," less "existent" than when he "becomes" finite. Garden humans are at once inbreathed dust *and* immortals (provided they do not sin). Other immortals or semi-mortals show up in Genesis, and their commerce with humans is also catastrophic. However, if to be human is to be possessed of a finite temporality without being wholly condemned by it, and if the beginnings of one's humanity are accompanied by a *logos* that is reason and communication, then how could the Garden Creature—though he had names for animals—grasp that existence "is" in the mode of "finite becoming"? And what would it mean to Adam or Eve to envision eating something forbidden, something that would make them "like" God? Certainly, *incorporation* is the material ground of any identification, but they understood neither finitude nor identification and its dangers. The Garden beings knew neither the desire that characterizes creatures with bodies, nor the difference between them and that voice called Elohim, and certainly not the separation that identification denies.

Perhaps expulsion was better than an act of mercy (since finitude became the property of humans when they could not eat of the Tree of Life—thankfully so, given their contradictory "divine" knowledge). It was better than mere mercy, because the narrative expulsion forced the creation of a fledgling community that took shape through a dialectic of identification and dis-identification which, for Nancy as for Freud, permitted an alternative (a less metaphysical) conception of social existence. The foreclosure of identification, as the first premise of negative theology, is coextensive with a social *logos* of human interrelations, coming to pass in the presence of an unfigurable "transformer": the present-absent Third party.

This third position is doubly, and divergently, exemplified in the unknowable One and in the Law. It exemplifies two types of diremption: humans and their creator, humans and the (interpretable) structures of behavior (Law). But the Third party has a third sense as well. It denotes the position of the mythical narrator of Genesis, about whom Buber argues that "he" was aware of the irony implicit in the origin that was the expulsion from the Garden.[22] The *human* genesis is thus *not* the creation of Adam, but the coming-into-humanity-as-finite of the two proto-humans, thanks the "magical" increase in their "knowledge," brought about by the simplest of assimilation-identification: eating. This magical increase of knowledge is the beginning of the knowledge of becoming—which lies both within and outside of human powers. As magic, it will be foreclosed (hence, the expulsion). Now, the knowledge of becoming is also the knowledge of passing out of being, or death—the death of the other person. So it was hardly tragic that the pair could not eat of the tree of Eternal Life, because possessing the *knowledge* of death is the only way through which humans grasp non-becoming, *stasis*, and correlatively, eternity as negation and promise; although this is not knowledge as truth or adequation between mind and thing. Without this ethical knowledge, the Garden Adam is more infinite than finite, undecidably mortal and immortal. For human beings, who are *born* rather than created, there is more value in knowing *that* one dies than in *possessing* immortality with no understanding of becoming or mortality. Thus the narrative voice of Genesis, as well as that of Buber commenting it, both stand in the position of the Third. We see this clearly when Buber writes, "In this lamentable effect of the great magic of becoming like God, the narrator's irony becomes apparent; an irony whose source was obviously great suffering through the nature of man."[23] A vast afterward could be opened by the question of the work and surreptions of narrative irony; especially when it glimmers through shifts in the work done by the Third party. Such shifts are possible as the inscription of absence into a narratological voice, standing in for and in some sense supplementing, that of "the Name"—or the author.

Nakedness and Becoming

The immediate, perceptible consequence for Adam and Eve of their eating the fruit of knowledge was a paltry discovery: their reciprocal nakedness. Against any "wild psychoanalysis," Buber writes that the "recognition of this fact, the only recorded consequence of the magical partaking, cannot be adequately explained on the basis of sexuality, although without the latter it is, of course, inconceivable."[24] His arguments in this passage imply that the expulsion was a divine second thought—not as the direct consequence of eating the fruit—as though God sought to protect them from the deadly combination of shame and the *hubris* of knowledge. At the moment when their eyes are opened, it is not clear what the consequences of their act will be. The serpent promised god-likeness. But Eve, Buber tells us, "intensified God's prohibition" with her surprising response to the serpent, "touch it not, else you must die."[25] Since it was not clear what god-likeness *or* death might be, how can it be clear that Eve intensified the prohibition? Stranger, she did not simply mimic the injunction either, since, when Adam received it, Eve had not yet been created. And again, if to die means to disappear or to cease to be, then this too remains only an abstract possibility for creatures whose bodies are suspended in the *nunc stans* of the Garden. The vertiginous play of perspectives here, between the mortal, the demonic, the divine, and the "Adamic," opens conundrums that can be worked out only after the introduction of a foreclosure. That is, after the separation figured simultaneously as a decision of the absent Father (the voice) and the expulsion from paradise into finite space-time.

The immediate outcome is nakedness. But this nakedness is not quite the sight of another body, whose exposure might excite desire. Nakedness amounts to an "unnatural uncoveredness" that elicits shame and resembles the nakedness of the serpent (Genesis 3:1). The all-too-human exposure, in nakedness and shame, seems unthinkable in a nondomesticated animal (which invites questions about the serpent). Still, shame is not (yet) guilt. It is closer to phenomenological descriptions of those affective moments in which "we are unable to make others forget our basic nudity."[26] As such, fundamental nudity belongs to the finitude of human flesh, which deepens the irony Buber attributed to the narrator. Having become "as gods," our new, divinized (or de-devinized?) beings have become more human, shamefaced and exposed to each other, as well as to the absent One who always saw them naked—at least until the moment He lost sight of Adam's whereabouts![27] If it is divine to suffer in one's exposure, then Adam and Eve have become more divine. If it is not divine to suffer in this way, then their knowledge has brought them only into the "demonic" state that more readily typifies the human condition, and which Freud referred to as a condition governed by *Triebe* (drives). The act of consumption, understood as *Verkörperung* or incorporation, is in mythic logic a mimetic act that repeats a sacrificial rite that devours and perpetuates an ancestor or totem animal as the divinity. Here, consumption leads to "knowledge" and, had Adam and Eve eaten of the Tree of Life, this would have led to their incarnation—or the parodic replication—of the Father himself.[28]

The consequence of *Verkörperung* is wonderfully described in Freud's *Totem and Taboo* and in *Moses and Monotheism*. There, anxiety and shame arise from the transgression that denudes, strips bare. But the transgression, always a kind of murder or usurpation, brings about a perverse equalization—whether this be the creation of a band of brothers (who eliminated the father), or two humans who come "to know" what the Father alone knew (without knowing it in quite the way he did). It is remarkable that the first textual illustration of the uncrossable separation between being and becoming, infinity and finitude, is repeated through a host of biblical narratives (cf. the Deluge, Genesis 6:1; the Tower of Babel, Genesis 11:1), as though this lesson required repetition in variations, because it belonged to a complex gesture of ethical and social import.

A perplexity remains with the *re*-cognition implicit in seeing the Other as naked. What role does this re-cognition play in the origin of a human subject? To answer this question, another one must first be explored: How is existence, understood as change and becoming, known to the creature who ate the fruit of the Tree of Knowledge? To understand this, I need to make an etymological detour. Thereafter, I will return to the connection between the French philosophers, Buber, and Freud's Moses.

Erum: Being Naked, Yet Shrewd

Before the events described in Genesis 3, Adam and Eve are characterized as *Arummim*.[29] *Arummim* is the plural of *Arum* (here, "naked") for which a recognized alternative spelling is *Erum*. It is said at the end of Genesis 2 that these two beings who were "one flesh," "felt no shame."[30] From the opening of chapter 3, the *Arum* theme unfolds in all its equivocity; and this, by way of superlatives. "Now the serpent was the shrewdest of all the wild beasts that the Lord God had made" (Genesis 3:1). "Shrewdest," here, means simultaneously "most naked," "fleshly" because without fur or feathers, *and* "crafty," "cunning," "cautious," or "prudent." *Erum* takes *all* these senses. Because it is the naked "wild beast" that speaks to Eve, we might say that in matters of knowledge and morality, the serpent was more readily the interlocutor of the humans than the humans were to each other, or even to God. The serpent was clearly shrewder than the two innocents, and some commentaries argue that it must have gone about upright, since the curse placed on it was what obliged it to slither about on its belly (Genesis 3:14). Thinking this way, the serpent becomes simultaneously proto-human in its reason and its nakedness (like them, it was almost a featherless biped), and better than human in its synthetic knowledge of the meaning of death and "divine perception."[31]

The acquisition of knowledge by humans results in the curse on the serpent itself—and its demotion to the rank of something worse than cattle. The curse on Adam is in fact a curse upon the ground over which he moved and which he would have to toil. In the case of the serpent, the curse is set directly upon a being and on its body (it now slithers on its belly). In the case of the humans, it is a curse on the nature of the work that the new human has to perform. The difference between these two curses is crucial, because if religion arises, as Hermann Cohen pointed out, as contemporaneous with reason and with the essence of the Law, then there existed an upright being that spoke and knew, and yet was not clearly assimilable to humans *or* to angels, the serpent. The one thing this creature lacked was that it was not explicitly created "after our likeness" (Genesis 1:26). This means that a being could exist who knew and spoke, yet was less divine than those two who initially did *not* know the forces of life and could not communicate with the refinement that such knowledge procured. In fairness, it is only in Genesis 3:22—i.e., after the pronouncement of God's threefold curse—that the tradition integrated the second aspect of the Eden allegory: the presence of *two* forbidden trees.

If we pursue the question of nakedness this time in light of the shame that Adam and Eve did not initially feel, then we find another interpretive path. This one Buber opens through his analysis of the meaning of "knowledge of good and evil." If "good and evil" amount to Being, or better, to Life understood as omnipresent binaristic forces (pain and pleasure, benefit and discomfort, fullness and emptiness), then this knowledge may well be possessed *affectively* before it is represented as an object of reason.[32] In other words, we stand in relation to what-is through our various modes of sensibility and affectivity. So far as these open us to existence or to what-is, it is not absurd to consider them "attunements," like Heidegger's *Stimmungen*, among which are joy, boredom, and *Angst*[33]—and to which Levinas will add enjoyment, shame, fatigue, and nausea. These affective attunements, whatever their number, can only be suspected of our early "humans," Adam and Eve. If anything, what we find is delight and the *apatheia* that receives imperatives without fear or pondering. After that comes the shame that fears evil, shame before a God (or Father) transformed, and anxiety—something like the anxiety of responsibility. Even here, these modes of "knowing" have little representational content outside the perception of an enduring lack. There is nothing elaborately moral present. Yet the spectacle of their nudity is also not an aesthetic one. Stricken with mortality, the flesh has not so much become ugly as its vulnerability elicits shame and redoubled anxiety. The haste with which Adam and Eve cloaked themselves in leaves and retreated to a position of invisibility which alone could assure some restoration of their lost wholeness, implies that the Third party has consequently become more fixed, more explicitly seeing, and potentially punitive (but we are seeing things, now, through their eyes). The "God" who now sees them as naked, always saw them thus, only now they realize it. What must have been his perplexity to find the two suddenly striving for invisibility and hiding!

The sad irony is that this God not only must now evict his creatures, he must institute a symbol of foreclosure. That is the function of the "fiery ever-turning sword," which guards the Tree of Life from the creatures' eventual return (Genesis 3:24). Henceforth, Adam and Eve will see the third precisely as a Third: as separated, whole, the source of a law revealed to them in reason and shame. By virtue of separation-foreclosure, they also see in each other a Third party. To be the Other, in a moral sense, a human being is a naked face, a gaze, and an interruption of the forces of which he has become aware.[34] But to be the Other is also to be a Third; one like-me who is not like-me, and above all who judges me. At this point, Lacoue-Labarthe and Nancy's reflection points us in a direction that runs parallel with Buber's thought.

The Psychoanalytic Counter-Narrative: The Birth of Anxiety in Transgression and Traumatism

For Freud, anxiety was "the paradigm of affect."[35] This is true despite the important changes he introduced into his arguments about its meaning. Thus, in 1897, when he was still tied to neurology and a theory of energetics, Freud wrote the never-published *Entwurf zur einen wissenschaftlichen Psychologie* [Outline for a Scientific Psychology]. At that time, he had encountered anxiety to such an extent and in such a range of forms that he attempted to reduce it to a unitary mechanistic model: anxiety signaled excesses produced by endogenous and especially exogenous stimuli, invariably seeking release through the musculature (in movement). As he evolved his psychoanalysis, anxiety came to light as the primary symptom of that polymorphic condition, hysteria, which Freud had encountered in Jean-Martin Charcot's clinic at the Hôpital de la Salpêtrière. In his first *topos* (i.e., primary and secondary processes), then, anxiety was the sign of repression and its efficacity as a foreclosure. As Freud wrote to his friend, Wilhelm Fliess: "What, now, does normal repression furnish us with? If free, it can lead to anxiety; if psychically bound, [it leads] to rejection, that is to say, to the *affective basis* of a multitude of processes of development, such as morality, shame, etc."[36]

By 1926, the mature Freud had reconceived the "subject" of psychoanalysis by integrating his first topic into the second one (i.e., the *Ich*, *Es*, and *Über-ich*). In so doing, he inverted the relationship of repression to anxiety, having encountered a plethora of cases where anxiety signaled no discernable repression. Freud then argued that anxiety was more than the affective basis of a host of developmental processes. Anxiety preceded repression in its origin, and it could exist independently of repression. As the neurophysiological turmoil of the neonate, anxiety even preceded the formation of the Ego. It arose as the physiological reaction to the danger of suffocation. His 1933 "New Introductory Lectures," which present psychoanalysis in its final form, define anxiety as a reaction to traumata, the first of which was birth.[37] Trauma anxiety will repeat over the course of the emergence of the Ego, and continue afterward, thanks to the retroactive intensification of earlier incidents carried into the present. This is where *Moses and Monotheism* takes it up. There, trauma anxiety is extended to the prehistory of the species itself:

> mankind as a whole also passed through conflicts of a sexual-aggressive nature, which left permanent traces, but which were for the most part warded off and forgotten; later, after a *long period of latency*, they came to life again and created phenomena similar in structure and tendency to neurotic symptoms . . . the phenomena of religion.[38]

In humans' prehistory—which is the history figured in Buber's study of the myth of expulsion—the primary symbolic anxiety ("permanent traces") arose from the trauma experienced by the sons following their transgression, which was the violent elimination of the dominant male (Freud called him the *Urvater*). A logic of cultural recurrence mirrors the repetition-intensification found in individual neuroses.[39] This logic also contains an inexpungible nostalgia for the strange innocence in which the Third party ("God") is near but does not judge us. This is an innocence destroyed by the will to know and by the realization of mortality, which the Garden allegory figures as the expulsion.

We can interpret Freud's "permanent traces" as ingrained developmental memories or as the transmission of acculturated affects. Yet more important is the ongoing return of a repressed trace. Despite Freud's embrace of recapitulation theory ("ontogenesis reproduces phylogenesis") and his occasional Lamarckianism, it is *historic* transmission that is at stake. By historic transmission, I mean the passing on of cultural history, concentrated in parables and myths, as well as the transmission brought about by the repetition of behaviors engendered by a malaise in a family or a society. The remarkable thing here is that the people who would ultimately become "Jews" embodied the force and the desire that instituted the law of the Third in a monotheistic form. By Freud's account (working from archeological material), it was the

Jews who revived the religion of the Father-God and with it, the foreclosures figured by the Garden and normalized in the Mosaic proscriptions. In this respect, they had an original claim to the status of "not dreaming." Monotheism forecloses with peculiar power identifications with God and heroes, such as those we see in polytheism. According to the psychoanalytical account, the early Hebrews enacted what had become their cultural unconscious, by confronting the reforms proposed by their own priests, who were anxious to modify the absolute monotheism and embrace a more natural, almost imperial volcano-God called Yahweh. Anxiety would thus have persisted among the people like a demand that the unattainable Third be revived *in all his distance* (distance is an effect of foreclosure). Whether this anxiety was due primarily to Freud's "structure" or "return of the repressed"—here reenacted in the murder of Moses—or to the loss of the privilege of election by the one God, is unclear. What is clear is that the foreclosure of acts of anthropomorphic instating (e.g., a plurality of gods, divinized ancestors, sacred entities, and forces that figure human passions) characterizes the monotheism that Moses supposedly taught to a people who then preserved, unconsciously, his founding intuition.

If we follow Freud's speculation about the Egyptian Moses and those marginal nomads who perpetuated his abstract god, we confront a circle of origins: was it a logical-temporal repetition that motivated the demand to reinstitute this monotheism? If so, we should accept the hypothesis of Moses's own murder (and the persistence of guilt attaching to his memory). Or was it some anxiety, embedded in the popular imagination, that motivated the restitution of an all-powerful absent One who, despite his distance from humans, elected one people from among the nations? If election-in-distance does diminish *Angst*—about mortality, or facing political and cultural threats—then why was this 'option' not more prominent among the mythic choices made by early peoples? Was this rarity due to the psychic impact of the accompanying foreclosure on identification? Lacoue-Labarthe and Nancy abbreviate this foreclosure as being placed simply "on dreaming." But it applies to virtually every form of fetishization and hypostatization.[40] If we follow the parallelism Freud drew between the rites and narratives of religions, the practices of reenactment, partial remembering, and the transference characteristic of neuroses, we encounter yet another circle. This is the circle of anxiety itself. If anxiety is a privileged bridge between sensation and affectivity (mechanistic sensation and higher level emotions), then anxiety holds the body-mind parallelism in place, in what amounts to a discontinuous proximity (sensation is not affect, and conversely; but affect often accompanies, or even precedes, sensation). However, anxiety also evinces both cultural and subjective aspects: an entire cultural group can be beset with, and transmit, its anxiety.

In Freud's second topic, the primacy of this curious sensation-affect expresses the impossibility of positing an *archè* for the Ego, since there is at least one pre-egoïc affect that evolves with the emerging Ego and later appears to belong to the Ego. But the difficulty of stating when precisely "I" am there, when the Ego that inhabits its name takes form, was not Freud's intuition alone. Even if it was not thematized clinically, the narrative of the Garden and the expulsion *also* concerns the difficult *archè* of the human. Moreover, the perplexing, archetypal murder of the powerful male—who, in perishing, returns to haunt the sons and elicit from them a rejection of violence and inauguration of "legal" foreclosures—presents a comparable anxiety structure, albeit at a different level. This discontinuous repetition, like the repetitions of anxiety in the individual, seems to be the only affective "structure" thinkable in the absence of identifiable origins. If the earliest stages of social existence emerge thanks to the expulsion from paradise into mortality, foreclosure, and nakedness, then this sociability must be enhanced by an additional gesture—purely human this time—whereby the sons (of Adam) recognize that they are also brothers. That is, they come with difficulty to realize that they are not simply individuals elected by the father, but can also form a pact amongst each other.

Freud and Buber: The Work of Foreclosure

We thus face two circles of origin and two hypotheses about Judaism. Buber's reading of Genesis illustrates an initial foreclosure that will be repeated over the history of the Hebrew people. Freud's Moses sketches the psychological history of a God, or Father, occupying a unique structure of the Third party (sole legislator, unknowable, alone in electing his chosen), by virtue of foreclosures recorded in the people's narrative *and* carried by that people like a permanent mnemonic trace. The point of intersection of the two readings, Buber and Freud's (and with Freud, Lacoue-Labarthe et al.), lies in the work performed by foreclosure. Of course, the Genesis narrative and the story of Moses belong to two different layers of Jewish history. And the proscriptions on magic, representation, and polytheism stand in a certain tension to Freud's reading of *Verkörperung*, the primitive identification consisting of incorporations that pass from the eating the apple all the way to totemic meals and, ultimately, to the Christian eucharist. For Adam and Eve, eating the proscribed fruit is closer to magical consumption than it is to murder. In Freud's reconstruction, the two are connected through survivals of ancient cannibalism. To my mind, the connection has more to do with the incomprehensible but sensed outcome (by Adam and Eve) of this consumption. To become "as one of us" is, for a creature, to supplant its creator. Nevertheless, following the logic of foreclosure, the incorporation that elicited expulsion puts an end to such "dreaming" (the Garden is as much a dream as is the divinization of beings, Garden or worldly ones).

If we consider the two levels of drives, in a self and in a group (or a culture)—something Lacoue-Labarthe and Nancy's work encourages—then we understand their claim for the work of foreclosure. At an individual level, Freud pushes Buber's arguments by insisting that anxiety is the affect in which inside and outside, man and God, paradise and society, blur. Such indistinctions evoke anxiety and must be limited.[41] On the other hand, Lacoue-Labarthe and Nancy argue that the sociality of ethnic and political identifications is actually superposed on a more originary sociality through the logic of repetition. Again, murder can be compared with the taboo on the Tree of Life, because murder—of the paradigmatic strong male and as a deliberate act—entails "the social comprehension (or 'incomprehension') of death. It is itself the ambivalence of dissociation: the appearance of an Ego *in its disappearance*, the relation that arises *from the lack of a relation*."[42] According to Lacoue-Labarthe and Nancy, the deliberate sacrifice or murder of this Father turns on the knowledge that death is final, and it is what happens to *others*, leaving behind it the survivors whose act and new status forge the new pact uniting those who reassemble under a "social contract." Eating of the Tree of Knowledge is also decided in the affective indeterminacy of anxiety (i.e., Eve knew neither what knowledge of all things would mean nor what death was), with a peculiarly social outcome: the succession of generations, or human history. The sociality of the brothers forged by murder is ambiguous and unforeseen. However, it must rest on something like a prior sociality thanks to which the choice was made—in the "first" place—to forego election by the strongest male for the sake of a more horizontal social organization.

Murder (and perhaps expulsion) thus bespeaks something like a will to sociability, which congeals in the refusal of tyranny, natural or political. This will and this act restore what the expulsion from the Garden made possible, a "primitive horde."[43] Both murder and expulsion evince the aporia of origins, with the primitive horde standing in a dialectical relationship to the ancient "Father." And it is curious that, in all but a brief essay he sent to Ferenczi, Freud maintained (in *Totem and Taboo* [1912] and in *Moses and Monotheism* [1939]) that in the beginning was the strong male[44]—who nevertheless lorded it over "the whole horde," itself *already* in existence, if unreflectively.[45]

Freud's published works de-emphasized the original (social) horde in favor of the community under a strong male. He did not reckon with something like the group consciousness of a social identity, because the proverbial sons are defined in light of one who was not really their biological father (paternity being a causality they did not know), but simply their tyrant. Whatever the circumstances of their survival, however, Freud does argue that it was the expulsion of the sons that introduced them to a new, and unstable, "state of nature." He observes, "they [the parricides] were forced to live in small communities."[46] These small communities were presumably without strong males, at least for a time. All of that was insufficient to transform what Freud refers to as "sons" into "brothers." Only the overcoming of the father and the partaking of his body assured that further evolution. "The cannibalistic act thus becomes comprehensible as an attempt to assure one's identification with the father by incorporating a part of him."[47]

Chiasmatic, the two levels of sociality take shape through a decisive act of vengeance following the *initial* expulsion by the Father. If the sociality of brothers, post-sacrifice, in no way protects them against the return of the Father, a vague consciousness of the threat of judgment persists; and when a father-substitute returns, as he certainly will, it will likely be as a father-son, i.e., as a "mortal," already marked by the possibility of murder. The innovation of Jesus—really, that of Paul—carries a trace of the foreclosure of the position of absolute Father. If this innovation revives a "phantasy of salvation,"[48] it carries with it henotheistic ambiguities (Jesus, man-God next to the Father), which the expulsion from the Garden had foreclosed. If the messianic supplement is found first in the Hebrew prophets, it is also found transformed in Paul's Father-Son synthesis, which Freud suspected was the only remaining mode of return for the Father. If this is the unique return of the erstwhile Father,[49] then it is such because it is the effect of a mnemonic trace, something like a cultural *impensé* that has no need to be transmitted in a naïve Lamarckian fashion (despite Freud).[50] As a blurring of divine and human, the new-old Father, who is also a Son, reopens the possibility of fusional or fetishistic identifications. These are identifications similar to those we find in myths and epics peopled by semi-divine heroes. And there begins the worst conundrum.

Oedipus and Moses: Paradoxes of Paternity

When Lacoue-Labarthe and Nancy argue that Oedipus might replace Moses as "history's only real Father, a father who accepts himself as such,"[51] they are resisting Freud's vector-like logic of repetition, whose paradox is to have posited an origin (archaic murder), despite its dating from a time immemorial. Instead, Lacoue-Labarthe and Nancy emphasize that one becomes a father only in becoming *conscious* that one has sacrificed or murdered one's own father, their claim being that Moses was an *unconscious* father. Now, one becomes conscious only through the repetition of the same (or the similar), through whose social traces a certain awareness congeals, initially as a shared affect, then through actions. Through the work of repetition (and resistance in psychoanalytic theory), they argue that only the recognition of repressed violence opens to a sociality able to identify itself as ethnicity or as a micropolis. This parallels Freud's theme of *Durcharbeitung*, working or talking through a neurotic condition (i.e., our condition as human beings). Yet the mature Freud saw something different in "the return of the father-son" avatar. He speculated that the source of Christian anti-Semitism lay precisely in a certain Christian notion of recognition: Christians had "murdered God; as against the Jews who, at least according to a standard version of the story of Moses, would not admit that they murdered God (as the archetype of God, the primeval father, and his reincarnations)."[52]

Thus, *either* one forecloses access to God ab initio, and unravels the structure of identification (i.e., identification as "occupying the place of the other," which implies murder, latency, revivification of a memory, and the repetition of identification), *or* one reenacts the process, thereby reopening the ancient dilemmas. That is the choice, unless consciousness of the murder *also* forecloses identification. Clearly, it does this selectively. The case of Oedipus is interesting as a "hero" who, inhabiting the monstrosity of his flaw (to defy *'Ανάγκη* or natural necessity, and fail at it), presaged the end of the repetitions in his disappearance en route to Colonnus.

Tragedy, Irony, and the *Witz*

Is the return of the son the condition sine qua non of socio-ethnic "paternity"? Or does the son represent a supplementary acquisition, which makes fatherhood simultaneously social and temporal through the continuity and stabilization of generations? Clearly, for Freud, the depth, which "in the Jewish religion resulted from the murder of its founder,"[53] is not shared by Islam (and presumably not by Paul's Christianity of resurrection, either). That sets Freud apart from Lacoue-Labarthe and Nancy's claims for Oedipus' superiority to, or equality with, Moses. Does not the essential force of catharsis, which the representation of Oedipus enables, turn on identification with him, however tormented? It would seem that this identification is not fetishistic. If Lacoue-Labarthe and Nancy are right in suggesting that Freud glimpsed a model of deferred identification in "the Jewish story,"[54] this is because the Jewish story he had in mind, as the model of Jewish social identification, carried irony. It was thus related to the *Witz* about which he wrote during the "triumphalist" period of psychoanalysis (1905–1910). The *Witz* expresses a particular sort of social identification in which the author of the joke is a member of his or her target group. The ironic or comedic quality comes from this group's collective personality; it is a *Sammlungsperson*, from which the joker is able to take some distance (like a lightened version of the rhetorical *metalepsis*, reporting a story which has been reported to you). The *Witz* short-circuits a direct or vectorial *mimesis* by preserving distance. It does this, thanks precisely to the proximity between the satirist and his or her object. In this gesture of self-ironization, an identification *à part* takes place, which opens to thought. Humor is thus like the irony that Buber observed of the narrator of Genesis; the distancing effects are similar.[55]

Buber's insistence on the ironic tone of the narrative voice in Genesis 3 brings about a comparable distance and return. There is no way to identify fetishistically with the Father when confronting the Third party who is Elohim/Adonai. For Buber, the expulsion from the Garden opens to a history that is human first, and becoming-a-people, second; that is, the first "murder" (by incorporation), followed by foreclosure (by expulsion), recapitulates an original sociality (unmediated identification with an indeterminate entity: a voice), only to open to the new social structures of kin and tribe (of brothers). All too human, we suppose. However, as Freud adds in regard to Moses—and the Gospels—these are stories told about Jews among Jews.[56]

Unmediated fusional identification was not the lot of the Jews, who returned to the monotheism of Moses, after the sacerdotal compromise in their religious practices (1350 and 1215 BCE).[57] Forces among the people presumably impelled this return, which was the revival of their original "obscure and incomplete tradition" of radical monotheism.[58] For Freud, this is the return of the repressed, but it differs from such returns in Greek tragedy. Something more is underway, as this "repressed" contains a unique stimulus toward ethical norms and self-respect. At the heart of the return-restoration of the primeval Father[59] is a temporal lag that Freud compares to latency in individuals' psychosexual development. This latency separates subjects from the thrall of the drives as from their initial identifications.[60] Now, the value of developmental latency parallels the (latent) time of discovery essential to the *Witz*. The surprise of the joke lies in the sudden discovery that the addressor has cloaked himself with a story, of which he is the part standing in for the whole or *Sammlungsperson*, which is also the comic object.

In Buber's reading of Genesis 3, the loss of the father is figured spatially first, as it occurs thanks to the expulsion, which orders space into sacred and profane sites while instituting the repeating and self-differentiating time of generations. This temporality must be understood on two levels. First, because it is anything but the "all at once" time Buber attributes to divine knowledge, diachronic time is social *and* biological; it echoes the time of the narrative itself. In an ironic sense—made possible by the repetition imperative characteristic of the narrative (to be told and retold)—it is always the time of the Garden, always the time of foreclosure. Here, the foreclosure *is* the narrative (moment) that recounts (and incorporates) its incipience as a narrative ("I am telling you this story because I am, like you, a part of the generations begun thanks to the expulsion"). Second, if the temporality of ethnic sociality is unleashed by a traumatic loss, we have learned, through Freud, that trauma may be exogenic or endogenic (i.e., birth) in origin, but it will persist as though it were each time exogenic—like the incursion or imprinting of an external force.

Whether we consider the trauma of the murder of the Father or that of the expulsion and foreclosure of immortality, the anxiety that characterizes the return of the repressed inaugurates a strange urge for self-identification. This is because anxiety is similarly characterized by a repeating time that has no origin. After mistaking anxiety for a mere symptom, Freud acknowledged that anxiety precedes the consolidation of the Ego, and its recurrence isolates the Ego, as though its identifications could never fully ground it. Anxiety repeats the trauma of an origin at which the Ego had not yet developed. With each repetition, anxiety changes by virtue of its attachment to different objects. As Freud argued in *Inhibitions, Symptoms and Anxiety* (1926), through the repetitions of anxiety "a danger-situation" is "a recognized, remembered, expected situation of helplessness."[61] But the shock it repeats proves immemorial, because indefinitely retraceable. "It is unrecognizable because it consists of ever-changing cathexes (*Besetzung*) that can be 'recognized' only by being displaced . . . disfigured (*ent-stellt*). And it is immemorial, because the 'actual' situation of helplessness resists the bifurcation into past and future that is the condition of memory and anticipation."[62] Identification flowing from anxiety might prove fetishistic or ironic, in its origin and its repetitions it reflects a striving to stabilize the anxious Ego.

Anarchism and the Circle of Origin, or: Why the Jewish People Does Not Dream

The complex of repetition and displacement with no determinate *archè* characterizes the latency and recurrence found in Freud's hypothesis of the

Vatermord. The displacement that encourages recognition corresponds to a prohibition that excludes mimetic attributions (becoming "as gods"). The circle of origin, replaying itself and lacking a fixed starting point, is thus preserved. Almost despite himself, Freud discerned a circle of origin in anxiety and in the murder of the father. I believe he would have appreciated Buber's glimpsing it in the situation of presence-absence and transgression, which occasioned the (ironic) expulsion. More important than a de facto murder of a powerful male, which, Freud insisted, occurs in every culture, is the social and contractual impetus (Lacoue-Labarthe and Nancy call it a "social drive") that motivates the weaker males to associate in opposition to the proto-father. No accident, then, that Freud pursued his study of Moses and of the phenomena of identification together, even as he protested his ineptitude in the dubious domain of nineteenth century mass psychology, "where we do not feel at home."[63] In all three cases, the anarchy of the narrative origin comes to light. But this circle and these displacements in repetition are significant. The danger (of loss and traumatization) to which anxiety reacts is real, even if irrecoverable. And it cannot be "self-identical."[64] So, too, the danger that the return of the repressed implies for individual and social psyches. Eating from the Tree of eternal life would have destroyed this time of repetition, which is the time of mortality—there is no time of eternity that is narratively meaningful, short perhaps of death). Sense requires the self-structuring of narrative acts. The first moment, spatialized as the Garden, serves as the site of humans' unconscious proximity to divinity, which Buber called the "yes position." But this principle is a null site without traces. There is no initial trace of separation here for two reasons: first, the paternal commands in the Garden are as incomprehensible to the proto-humans as the "father" is (until he judges, he is almost their companion, a present-absent voice). Second, there is no viable "subject" and the object (God) is unfigurable, though not thanks to any prohibition on representation.

Evaluations are incomprehensible to beings that live beyond good and evil in undifferentiated communion with Buber's "yes" and "all." But the irony of a beginning that is not really a beginning, precisely here, is unmistakable. Our first humans are physical adults who, when they lose their spiritual status as children (with no need for adulthood so long as they are "in God"), enter into an adulthood without fullness, in which desire is fragmented (i.e., they are exposed, naked, ashamed; the earth from which they are made is cursed). That is why the expulsion—which Lacoue-Labarthe and Nancy call the stuff of "maternal identification"[65]—inaugurates a history. And this history recapitulates narratively a prehistory that was pre-narrative without presence, dialogical and minimally semiotic (Adam's naming animals), without reflective judgment. All of this supposes a more substantive, figurable alterity to which an Ego could oppose itself.

Lacoue-Labarthe and Nancy present their own version of this insight. "That the subject *might be born* [*naisse*] (rather than being constituted, or structured, in a word, posited for itself) means that it is deferred indefinitely. Moreover, the anxiety of this birth is also the phylogenetic event, or element, par excellence: if anxiety repeats, it is not through heredity . . . The community of [human] birth is the anxiety of the dissociation of identity."[66] This deferral at the heart of the "birth" of the subject corresponds to a kind of social unfolding in which ethnic or tribal identity stands under a double question. In Moses's case, the question is that of identification. For the Mosaic monotheistic tradition, identity is won through the return of repressed (latent and forgotten) material, in which election (ethical identification) *and* its refusal (in the murder of Moses) assure social identification and a distance from identity. In the case of Buber's Adam and Eve, the acquired supplement of knowledge from the Tree changes little about their condition. They do not come "to know" all things, because they cannot "know" as gods do, in the eternal now. That said, this supplement forces them and their progeny to reenact the condition (will to knowledge) *as well as* the nostalgia for an unconsciousness of it. All of this with more or less anxiety and awareness.

Conversely, the foreclosure—whether it takes the form of expulsion or the taboos on violence and the creation of pacts—inaugurates sociality within finitude rather than in the dream life of fusion with the eternal. According to Lacoue-Labarthe and Nancy this is why the Jewish people "does not dream." The vigil they preferred to the idea of phantasmatic identification resembles Buber's vigil, which consists of listening to the voice in the biblical word, rather than representing or imbibing it. On the other hand, the return of the primeval father in "mass psychology" suggests that early identifications, even if temporarily neutralized by trauma (murder) and latency, persist to such an extent that when the son (or sons?) returns, he will return *in the guise* of something like a father. This complicates the trajectory of identification, arguing that no foreclosure is simply enduring.

"If there was no such leader [among the colonized Jews], then Christ was the heir to an unfulfilled wish-fantasy; if there was such a leader, then the Christ was his successor and his reincarnation." Taken together, the foreclosure of dreaming and identification, and the return of the repressed murder, suggest that no religion that follows Mosaic monotheism can be simply a "son-religion."[67] While Freud can say that Paul's innovation consisted in reinstating the universality of Judaism, at the price of abolishing a restriction,[68] it remains that the repetition that took the form of Christianity created a contradiction. To obtain universality, that "one characteristic of the old Aton religion," election and its sign (circumcision) had to be abolished. If we read this with Freud's observations on the Jewish *Witz*, that would suggest that Paul's innovation did not leave Jewish sensibility unaffected. Election had long had an ethical signification, but election by an *unreachable* father held open the possibility of irony and necessitated the codification of practices through which identification was not magically obtained, but socially organized. Enter the paradoxical son, and election proceeds according to a "pneumatic" principle, justified by corporeal resurrection.

Lacoue-Labarthe and Nancy approached the difficulties of identification from the perspective of time and affectivity. For them, the foreclosure of dreaming gives rise to anxiety which, in Buber, would be a vigil. As they argue: "The affection [being-affected] that constitutes identity only takes place in the withdrawal of identity. [But] withdrawal does not mean absence, that is, a presence simply removed. No foregoing identity here can be removed. To withdraw is not to disappear and, properly speaking, it is no modality of being [*et ce n'est à proprement parler aucun mode d'être*]. What does this mean, if not to assert that "withdrawal is like an act of appearing, disappearing. Not only of appearing *in* disappearing, but of appearing *as* a disappearing, in the event of disappearing itself."[69] And that is precisely how anxiety repeats, like Alice in Wonderland's Cheshire Cat and its appearing-disappearing grin.

Identity is neither simply an intentional movement nor an affective vector. It is real events without begin ones that are "objective." That is, if to be an event means that something has "to be" as a thing or an entity. Our authors give it a term that is metaphoric in inception, but literal in operation: "inscription."[70] "Inscription" denotes traces left behind in some material. That it might be read or accessible to deciphering is not the primary condition of inscription. Inscription should instead be understood as the process of in-scribing, like the 'writing' of trauma in or on a body that suffers and develops paralysis or anaesthetic points. Here, what is "initial form" need never be repeated identically in order to recur. To be sure, there is a difference between the tragic irony of the expulsion and a traumatized body. However, both carry with them a yearning for wholeness and a resistance (to death, and to an inaugural event, whether creation or birth)—even as this wholeness disappears under foreclosure. These paradoxical events suppose fragments of narratives even as they unravel when we take them up and examine their structure. Now, Buber's interpretation of Genesis 3 was motivated by his vision of the renewal of Judaism.[71] Freud's reading of Moses both defends Jewish specificity and sets it into an open-ended "phylogenesis" of trauma, whose densest instance is the Jewish one. This is because, without promising salvation, it labors under the contradictory strains of a community of brothers, the struggle against the return of the primeval Father, and the ongoing discussion of what it means to set justice in the space left open by his disappearance.[72] Perhaps Buber's renewal is not Freud's vindication, but both require a decisively historic sensibility. Consonant with the drive to incorporate knowledge of good and evil and to abjure mortality is the profound anxiety that accompanies the passage from dreaming to non-dreaming. Sometimes this anxiety engenders strategies for surpassing the trauma of an origin deferred. If Paul resurrected the Father by transforming the son into a son-father, messianic tendencies in Judaism have opened onto other apostasies. Sabbataianism celebrated another such son-father, whose paternal function was promulgated by his self-styled "prophet," Nathan of Gaza.[73] Buber's concern to harness the forces for renewal,[74] which embrace ethical election while refusing identifications that include mimesis and incorporation (including the phantasy of incorporating the maternal breast, which precedes identification with the father), depend on narrative transmission (including a narrative "unconscious" that repeats aspects of itself in words). Yet this carries no historical assurance with it. The challenge lies in the recognition of the paradoxes of identity, and a symbolic order (stories, maxims, myths) that makes possible the reenactment, without fetishism, of social ties rooted in identification.

Notes

1. Philippe Lacoue-Labarthe and Jean-Luc Nancy, "Le people juif ne rêve pas," in Adélie and Jean-Jacques Rassial, eds., *La psychanalyse est-elle une histoire juive? Colloque de Montpellier, B'nai B'rith* (Paris: Éditions du Seuil, 1981). Hereafter *PJNRP*. A shorter English version appeared as "The Unconscious Is Destructured like an Affect (Part I of 'The Jewish People Does Not Dream'), trans. Brian Holmes, *The Stanford Literature Review*, 6 (1989): 91–209. Both pages are cited, where appropriate.

2. Capitalizing the Father here signifies that the first identification is relational and as if divisive, with a being as much phantasmatic as phenomenal. The Father, as we know, introduces the differentiation and separation, if only by being that which causes the mother's attention and desire to triangulate. Any idea of identification with the mother would have to be ulterior. The mother is imbibed, introjected; Freud rarely speaks of the child's relation to its mother as identification, and certainly not around the Oedipal stage.

3. Lacoue-Labarthe and Nancy, *PJNRP*, 194, 59. Translation modified.

4. I am grateful to Dominique Scarfone, author of *Oublier Freud? Mémoire pour la psychanalyse* (Montreal, 1999), for his remarks on "forclusion" (foreclosure), which

I reproduce here: "Lacan used 'forclusion' to translate Freud's *Verwerfung*. This term appears most prominently in the Wolf Man case, and it seems to refer to some 'radical rejection,' in Wolf man, of the very idea of castration. Not repression, but, utter *eradication* of something that, being so drastically suppressed, comes back from without, in the form of the famous hallucination of the cut finger. Lacan then used 'forclusion' in the specific context of the psychoses with the famous 'forclusion du nom du père' (foreclosure of the name of the father). 'Forclusion' thus has such a radical meaning that it *becomes paradoxical*: it is quite difficult even to think of this concept and, what is more, to think of it as a positive 'defense mechanism,' since we cannot easily conceive of the complete erasure of *any* signifier. Such a complete erasure does not seem conceivable; some trace, a gap at least, will remain." It is the paradoxical quality of what is radically repressed, yet also analytically reconstructible, on which Lacoue-Labarthe and Nancy are basing their interpretation of affect and identification, here.

5. See Marie-Lise Roux's engaging essay "La contrainte à la représentation" in *Psychanalyse et préhistoire*, ed. A. Fine, R. Perrron, and F. Sacco (Paris: PUF, 1994, *Revue française de psychanalyse*), 31–39.

6. See, for example, Friedrich Nietzsche, "The Antichrist" in *Twilight of the Idols/ The Antichrist*, trans. R. J. Hollingdale (London: Penguin Books, 1990), sections 25–26. Nietzsche's argument is that in order to survive the destruction of the first temple, Jews made their god unattainable, untouchable. If Yahweh began as a typical national god, it would be transformed gradually into a sovereign beyond humanity and history itself. "The old God *could* no longer do what he formerly could. One should have let him go. What happened? One altered the conception of him: at this price one retained him. Yahweh, the God of "justice"—no longer, at one with Israel; [no longer] an expression of national self-confidence . . ." Nietzsche, in this, is following relatively standard historical criticism of his age.

7. I will not attempt to determine the degree of difference between Jewish monotheism (which, as Buber recognized, also had its mythic narratives and heroes) and other religions, whether monotheistic or not. That determination exceeds the bounds of this chapter.

8. Martin Buber, *On the Bible: Eighteen Studies*, ed. Nahum N. Glatzer (New York: Syracuse University Press, 2000), 211–16. Hereafter *OB*.

9. Buber, *OB*, 14–21.

10. We should contrast human demonism with what Buber calls "divine demonism" when, in his "Moses" (1945), he comments on a passage from the J manuscript in which all distance between Yahweh and Moses disappears (Yahweh, there, attempts to murder Moses, cf. Exodus 4:24–26).

11. Buber, *OB*, 19.

12. Buber, *OB*, 19.

13. Buber, *OB*, 19.

14. Buber, *OB*, 18.

15. Buber, *OB*, 20.

16. While Buber will speak of irony, Freud will see the roots of the "Jewish-joke," and with an insight different from both of them, Hermann Cohen will argue that irony or humor grasps both the hiatus between the "ought" and the "is," and humans' forgetfulness of this hiatus. Humor and irony would thus represent an attitude of compassion, *and* social ethical feeling (cf. Robert Gibbs' insightful essay "Seeing the Unique God: Humor and the Sublime in Jewish Aesthetics" in *Man and God in Hermann Cohen's Philosophy*, ed. G. Gigliotti, I Kajon, and A. Poma (Padua, Italy: Cedam, 2003), pp. 219–232, see esp. 222).

17. Buber, *OB*, 21.

18. Buber, *OB*, 21.

19. Irony is also due to the metonymic process at work in the claim (such that knowledge of good and evil, which is but one aspect of being "like" God, is attained, while the other aspect, God's incomprehensibility in transcendence, remains beyond the knowledge of good and evil. Indeed, it is as though Buber's Adam and Eve understood that eating of the tree of good and evil were only part of a greater act of becoming like God—that process of phantasmatic identification which the serpent awakens (would the serpent represent a logic of repetition in which the finite is made infinite through cycles of return?)—they would have gotten around to the fruit of the tree of eternal life sooner or later. This "second tree" would represent the perfection of the creature that could only mean its ceasing to be a creature (death), or its becoming creator (of itself). The second option is logically ruled out, at least without passage through the first option (death). This logic is of course that of Dionysus, "the twice born."

20. Let us specify what fusional identification with the Father means. Within an oedipal logic, as we know, it is the father term that, like a trace, effectuates differentiation and the *mise à distance* between the child and the mother. Therefore, the foreclosure of identification with the father is either a secondary foreclosure, like a mark on the mark, *or* if it has equi-primordiality, then identification itself must be split into: pure fusion (mother-child, breast-mouth) and onset of identification (child-father, child-law). Both, in fact, are the case. Let us begin with the second. (2) Freud insisted that identification, properly speaking, begins with the figure of the father. It presupposes a minimal disengagement from the mother. But the story of Eden means that one cannot reproduce, using the father, the archaic scheme of mother-child fusionality. The *law* must preserve itself as law, not as me, nor as a figure. (1) Establishing identification as requiring minimal disengagement from a "prehistoric" fusion with the mother abrogates the question of whether there are primary versus secondary foreclosures. It may well be that the foreclosure of identification with the father "looks" like a mark placed upon the function of the father itself (i.e., mark on the mark) or, in fact, that this foreclosure simply protects the *integrity* of the division, or cut, introduced by the advent of the third party called the "father."

21. How much of an accident was it that the Rat Man ultimately died in World War I (with and for his military "fathers") on the battlefield—in the very same milieu in which he had encountered the first crushing instantiation of his father?

22. Needless to say this irony is not bitter; it would be virtually destroyed if the expulsion were tragic, that is, if it were somehow the goal or entelechy of finitude to become omniscient and temporally infinite.

23. Buber, *OB*, 19.

24. Buber, *OB*, 19.

25. Buber, *OB*, 15. The nature of this intensification is unclear since Eve is only repeating the command that Adonai / Elohim gives to Adam in Genesis 2:17. In fact, He says: "Yes, on the day where you eat of it, you will die, you will die." My translation from André Chouraqi, *La Bible*, (Paris: Desclée de Brouwer, 1989). Drawn from the Tanakh and the last edition of the *Biblia Hebraica Stuttgartensia*.

26. Emmanuel Levinas, *On Escape / De l'évasion*, trans. Bettina G. Bergo (Stanford, Calif.: Stanford University Press, 2003), 64. Levinas adds: "[Shame] is related to everything we would like to hide and that we cannot bury or cover up. The timid man who is all arms and legs is ultimately incapable of covering the nakedness of his physical presence with his moral person." The idea of a moral person covering a carnal being is related to the haste with which Adam and Eve construct loincloths.

27. Psychoanalyst Alain Didier-Weill argues, in his *Les trois temps de la loi*, that it is inconsistent to suppose that God literally "lost sight" of where Adam was hiding. Instead, he proposes something consonant with Buber's notion of the "yes" and "no" positions. Firstly, it is interesting that Adam hid himself; but the verses convey that Adam's anguish arises *with the God's question* to him: "Where are you?" Thus, Didier-Weill argues that, "because he believed he knew 'where' he was, Adam [thereby] learns that he is not there where he could be: whereas he believed, in effect, that he was there where he was hidden, behind his tree, he discovers, in anguish, two things: for one thing, that this hiding place is not really one, under God's gaze and, for another thing, that, despite that gaze which means to him 'I know where you are,' God nevertheless asks him, 'Where are you?' This dual insight (deductively attributable to Adam) shifts the meaning of the 'place of hiding' to a sort of null site, such that in humans, there might be some metaphoric site at, or in which the Other (or the Father) cannot clearly see 'where' one stands." Is this a place of desire, a place of a certain spontaneity, or is it, as Didier-Weill suggests, a part of ourselves that remains ignorant of what "we" want, supposing that in that ignorance "the Other does not know where I am"? The important thing is the invisible, metaphoric "point" created in this perplexing moment. For a short-lived instant, filled with anxiety, "that the Other might not know where I am provides the ego with the illusion of mastery by which he believes he is 'there' where he is hiding from the gaze." And, "As consistent as the hiding place may be, for example behind titles or social emblems, the ego may claim to know where it is"—a sense that is unraveled, not reinforced by the God's question, because there is no physical or geographical place in which such hiding would really dissimulate. Thus "the specular hiding place where Adam was concealed draws its consistency or solidity only from its disavowed unawareness: 'It is because the Other does not know where I am that I can remain where I am hidden'." But this is precisely what cannot continue, and the Other, who thus irrupts into what recent

psychoanalysis calls the 'real' (*my reality*, as it were, here), makes it all too evident that I am not so much hidden as I simply no longer know *where* I am. This is the only viable meaning of such a call. It explains the anguish that the call produces in Adam. See Alain Didier-Weill, *Les trois temps de la loi: Le commandement sidérant, l'injonction du surmoi et l'invocation musicale* (Paris: Éditions du Seuil, 1995), 200–202.

28. In psychoanalytic interpretations, the Father is there before the biological father, in the figure powerful domineering male who polarizes the community and evokes the ire of less powerful males.

29. Tanakh, 6.

30. בּוֹשׁ pronounced alternately "buwsh" or "boosh," is a primitive root; properly, to pale, i.e., by implication to be ashamed; also (by implication) to be disappointed or delayed—(be, or put to shame, be or cause to be confounded). Clearly, shame without the consciousness of fault or sin takes a meaning weaker than shame after the transgression. The present shame is closer to Levinas's description.

31. It was certainly a reversal that humans, after expulsion, should strike at the serpent's head—the seat of its reason—while all it could do was lunge at their feet. Where, after all, did the serpent *first* strike, if not at Eve's imagination?

32. What is radically original in the fact of being human is the way in which the human posits, before itself, the world in its autonomy. But we must add that: "to be-facing-the-world is not thinkable if there is not already a 'behavior-towards-it-qua-world,' which is to say, the sketch of a relational behavior. See Gabriel Marcel, « L'anthropologie philosophique de Martin Buber » in *Martin Buber : L'homme et le philosophe*, Gabriel Marcel, Emmanuel Lévinas et André Lacocque, Eds., (Brussels : Éditions de l'Institut de Sociologie de l'Université Libre de Brussels, 1968), 26. Hereafter abbreviated as *AP*. The phrases in single quotes are from Buber's *Schriften zur Philosophie* in his *Werke*, (Heidelberg: Kösel & Lambert Schneider Verlag, 1962), 414, my translation. Thanks to Gabriel Malenfant for noting this citation.

33. Heidegger derives a great deal of his insight into the *Stimmung* called *Angst* from Kierkegaard. Kierkegaard provides the first existentialist interpretation of the anxiety Adam felt in the Garden. This anxiety was due to his strange, affective awareness that he "was able." What precisely he was able to do was unclear to him and thus produced anxiety.

34. For Freud, writing between 1935 and 1936 (the unpublished third essay of his *Moses and Monotheism*), the emergence of the Third into consciousness, as separated and as omnipresent, could only have come to pass with a primordial transgression, like a murder. We tend to forget that, under the influence of Darwin and a certain Jung, the insistence of a species memory in human beings erupts from time to time out of latency, much the way a neurosis may erupt in an individual after a period of latency. This is a trans-cultural, trans-historic pattern of repetition. If Moses was indeed the high priest of the monotheistic Egyptian monarch, Ikhnaton, and if he prolonged the survival of Egyptian monotheism by introducing the notion of being chosen *as well as the foreclosures on representation we find in Judaism*, then it could only be his murder (a murder that repeated a gesture dating from primeval times, in which

the "father" was simply the powerful male who dominated other males and had access to any female desired) that propelled into latency both Moses' memory and the power of his teaching. See Freud, *Moses and Monotheism*, trans. Katherine Jones (New York: Vintage Books, 1967), essay 3, "Moses, his People, and Monotheistic Religion" [written before March 1938], 102ff. Hereafter MAM. For the discussion of prehistoric memory, repetition, and neurosis, see Freud, MAM, 107–115. The evidence for the murder of Moses, Freud finds in the recent work of Ernst Sellin, but also in Goethe's *Israel in der Wüste*, volume VII, cf. *Moses, Op. cit.*, p. 114.

35. Lacoue-Labarthe and Nancy, *PJNRP*.

36. Sigmund Freud, "Letter to Fliess No. 75," in James Strachey and Anna Freud, eds., *Complete Psychological Works of Sigmund Freud*, Vol. I [1886–1899]: "Pre-psychoanalytic Publications" (London: Hogarth Press, 1966), 269.

37. The incipience of anxiety would be the auto-intoxication of the neonate, upon its severance from the mother's body, and as yet without a developed Ego.

38. Freud, MAM, 101.

39. Freud writes: "Early trauma—defense—outbreak of the neurosis—partial return of the repressed material . . . I will invite the reader to . . . assume that in the history of human species, something happened similar to the events in the life of the individual" (Freud, MAM, 101).

40. This does not exclude the anthropomorphic qualities of Elohim/Adonai and of Yahweh. The "one" God may appear given to a host of passions, but that God nevertheless is neither "known" nor imitable, in part because the moral pendant of his affects is not questionable the way the Greek gods' judgments can be. We should keep in mind that the narratives of Genesis are not the sole material to which Nancy et al. are referring; they have in mind the Torah and certain Talmudic discussions.

41. See Samuel Weber, *The Legend of Freud: Expanded Edition* (Stanford, CA: Stanford University Press, 2000), 88. "The ambiguity of the problem is already clearly inscribed in the passage cited [from Freud]: the danger that the psyche confronts *approaches it from without* ('eine *von aussen nahende* . . . Gefahr'); but the 'excitation' that constitutes the immediate form of that danger *arises from within*, endogenically'. The difficulty of reconciling these two assertions will be to explain just how the psyche can 'notice' (*merkt*) a danger that is both exogenic in origin and endogenic in operation."

42. Lacoue-Labarthe and Nancy, *PJNRP*, 70, 205.

43. Freud, MAM, 114.

44. A document by Freud that was only discovered in 1985, among Ferenczi's papers, suggests that Freud was anything but sure about this order of priority. The document dates from 1915; it would therefore be a supplement to or correction of the arguments in *Totem and Taboo* (cf. Jean Laplanche, *Nouveaux fondements pour la psychanalyse* [Paris: PUF, 1994], chap. 1. In English, *New Foundations for Psychoanalysis*, trans. David Macey [New York: Blackwell Publishers, 1989]).

45. Freud, MAM, 102. "All primeval men, including . . . all our ancestors, underwent the fate I shall now describe. . . . The strong male was the master and father of

the whole horde, unlimited in his power, which he used brutally. All females were his property. . . . The fate of the sons was a hard one; if they excited the father's jealousy, they were killed or castrated or driven out. They were forced to live in small communities and to provide themselves with wives by stealing them from others. Then one or the other son might succeed in attaining a situation similar to that of the father in the original horde" (Freud, MAM, 102–3).

46. Freud, MAM, 103.

47. Freud, MAM, 103.

48. Freud, MAM, 110.

49. Freud, MAM, 111.

50. See Laplanche's excellent discussion of Freud as neither Lamarckian nor Darwinian; in Jean Laplanche, *New Foundations*.

51. Lacoue-Labarthe and Nancy, *PJNRP*, 70, 205.

52. Freud, MAM, 115.

53. Freud, MAM, 118.

54. Lacoue-Labarthe and Nancy, *PJNRP*, 194.

55. Buber understood this clearly enough. He recounts the story of Isaac, son of Yekel of Cracow who, because of a dream, travels to Prague to unearth a treasure. Once there, he encounters the captain of the guard who, for his part, had dreamed that he was to go to Cracow in order to find a treasure under the furnace of one Isaac, son of Yekel: "In that city, where half the Jews are called Isaac, and the other half, Yekel, I can see myself entering the houses, one after another, turning them upside down!" Buber ironizes on him who would not listen to his dream; the more so that Isaac went home with enough treasure to rebuild the *Schul*. But this is not the "perfectly asocial" dream described by Freud in his study of the *Witz*. It is rather the "perhaps" of the dreamed message; not to mention the irony that, if one paid it heed, one might come off enriched. See Martin Buber, *Le chemin de l'homme d'après la doctrine hassidique* (in the original *Der Weg des Menschen nach der chassidischen Lehre*), trans. Wolfgang Heumann (Monaco: Éditions du Rocher, 1989), 49–56.

56. Freud, MAM, 117.

57. Freud, MAM, 75, 85.

58. Freud, MAM, 89.

59. Freud will write: "The restoration of the primeval father, of his historical rights marked a great progress, but, the other parts the prehistoric tragedy also clamored for recognition. How this process was set in motion, it is not easy to say" (Freud, MAM, 109). Then, making a surprisingly Nietzschean inference, Freud adds: "It seems that a growing feeling of guiltiness had seized the Jewish people—and perhaps the whole civilization of that time—as a precursor of the return of the repressed material" (Freud, MAM, 109). Note here that the original event is described as a tragedy. It is in the repetition that the tragedy is transformed, at least in the Jewish case. And it is transformed diversely: for the Christians, into soteriology; for the Muslims, a heroic monotheism; other religions remained close to ancestor worship. The relationship between tragedy and irony is thus overdetermined and the guilt to which Freud re-

fers suggests that the return of the repressed is an explanation that largely excludes Nietzsche's historic and economic conditions in the *Genealogy of Morality*.

60. Freud, MAM, 100–1.

61. Freud, "Inhibitions, Symptoms, and Anxiety" in *The Standard Edition* (London: The Hogarth Press, 1953–1974), 92.

62. Freud, MAM, 87. Weber, *Legend of Freud*, 91.

63. Lacoue-Labarthe and Nancy remind us that Freud, holding fast to a logic of identity—of the Ego that, however torn between the instances through which it takes shape in the second Topic, retains a constancy as a subject—and to his entrenched "archeophilia" (attachment to a principle of origins), missed the curious quality of Jewish identity as a "path that would lead [him and us] beyond the identity principle" (195). They further suggest that this goes some way toward explaining "the failure, or at least . . . the suspension of the analysis of identification in Freud" (196)—a failure that went beyond his discomfiture before *Volkspsychologie*.

64. Weber, *Legend of Freud*, 96.

65. Speaking of the totemic meal, or incorporation—which Freud insists is of the dead father—our authors venture: "But what is really dissociated, and incorporated, is a food which repeats the common maternal substance. Freud notes this . . . without *seeing* . . . that in its most 'regressive', most 'interior' moment, in the moment of *assimilation* which brings the clan members together [repetitively]—and which dis-sociates them—the clan's identification is an identification with the Mother." While "at most we may speak of the maternal substance [here] . . . [m]aternal unity is separation, expulsion. This primordial indivision is what it is—maternal—[ultimately] through division alone" (*PJNRP*, 67, 202).

66. Lacoue-Labarthe and Nancy, *PJNRP*, 65, 200.

67. Freud, MAM, 111.

68. Freud, MAM, 112.

69. Lacoue-Labarthe and Nancy, *PJNRP*, 66, 201.

70. Lacoue-Labarthe and Nancy, *PJNRP*, 66, 201.

71. In a succinct study of his intellectual development, Pnina Levinson (Heidelberg) reminds us that, long emphasizing the difference between religiosity or faith, and religion, Buber was not concerned that biblical stories like this one were fables or myths, as such. The "demythification" popular among Christian theologians of his time (Bultmann) conferred no additional legitimacy to his Judaism. The Bible taught—notably through the prophets, but also globally—the lesson of *Teshuva*: conversion, return to justice, and a new sense of precisely what it means *to be a Jew*. Cf. P. N. Levinson, "Martin Buber: Sa vision du judaïsme dans la dialectique prêtre-prophète" in *Martin Buber: Dialogue et voix prophétique, Colloque international Martin Buber 30–31 octobre 1978* (Strasbourg: Centre de recherches et d'études hébraïques, Université des Sciences humaines de Strasbourg/Paris: ISTINA, 1980), 113ff.

72. Freud, MAM, 116. The question of justice is in fact tied to what the Jews *did indeed admit*, contrary to the Christian accusation of admitting no murder: i.e., the idea of castration, as sign, pact, and radical foreclosure; i.e., morality and law.

73. This was the centuries-long movement inaugurated by the life and "disappearance" of Sabbatai Tsvi, the seventeenth century "messiah." See Gershom Scholem's immense study, *Sabbatai Sevi: The Mystical Messiah* (Princeton, NJ: Bollingen Press, 1976).

74. Freud, MAM, 118.

References

Buber, Martin. "*Schriften zur Philosophie*" in *Werke*. Heidelberg: Kösel & Lambert Schneider Verlag, 1962.

———. *Le chemin de l'homme d'après la doctrine hassidique*. Monaco: Éditions du Rocher, 1989.

———. *On the Bible: Eighteen Studies*. Edited by Nahum N. Glatzer. New York: Syracuse University Press, 2000. [*OB*]

Didier-Weill, Alain. *Les trois temps de la loi: Le commandement sidérant, l'injonction du surmoi et l'invocation musicale*. Paris : Éditions du Seuil, 1995.

Freud, Sigmund. *The Standard Edition*. London: The Hogarth Press, 1953–1974.

———. *Moses and Monotheism*. Translated by Katherine Jones. New York: Vintage Books, 1967. [MAM]

Gibbs, Robert. "Seeing the Unique God: Humor and the Sublime in Jewish Aesthetics." Pp. 219–32 in *Man and God in Hermann Cohen's Philosophy*. Edited by G. Gigliotti, I. Kajon, and A. Poma. Padua, Italy: Cedam, 2003.

Lacoue-Labarthe, Philippe, and Jean-Luc Nancy. "Le people juif ne rêve pas." In Adélie and Jean-Jacques Rassial, eds., *La psychanalyse est-elle une histoire juive? Colloque de Montpellier, B'nai B'rith*. Paris: Éditions du Seuil, 1981. [*PJNRP*]

———. "The Unconscious Is Destructured like an Affect (Part I of 'The Jewish People Does Not Dream')." Translated by Brian Holmes. *The Stanford Literature Review* 6 (1989): 91–209.

Laplanche, Jean. *New Foundations for Psychoanalysis*. Translated by David Macey. New York: Blackwell Publishers, 1989.

Levinas, Emmanuel. *On Escape / De l'évasion*. Translated by Bettina G. Bergo. Stanford: Stanford University Press, 2003.

Levinson, P. N. "Martin Buber: Sa vision du judaïsme dans la dialectique prêtre-prophète" in *Martin Buber: Dialogue et voix prophétique, Colloque international Martin Buber 30–31 octobre 1978*. Strasbourg: Centre de recherches et d'études hébraïques, Université des Sciences humaines de Strasbourg/Paris: ISTINA, 1980.

Marcel, Gabriel. "L'anthropologie philosophique de Martin Buber" in *Martin Buber: L'homme et le philosophe*. Edited by Gabriel Marcel, Emmanuel Lévinas et André Lacocque. Brussels: Éditions de l'Institut de Sociologie de l'Université Libre de Brussels, 1968.

Nietzsche, Friedrich. *Twilight of the Idols/The Antichrist*. Translated by R. J. Hollingdale. London: Penguin Books, 1990.

Roux, Marie-Lise. "La contrainte à la représentation." Pp. 31–39 in *Psychanalyse et préhistoire*. Edited by A. Fine, R. Perrron, and F. Sacco. Paris: PUF, 1994, *Revue française de psychanalyse*.

Scarfone, Dominique. *Oublier Freud? Mémoire pour la psychanalyse*. Montreal: Boréal, 1999.

Scholem, Gershom. *Sabbatai Sevi: The Mystical Messiah*. Princeton, NJ: Bollingen Press, 1976.

Strachey, James, and Anna Freud, eds. *Complete Psychological Works of Sigmund Freud*, Vol. I [1886–1899]. London: Hogarth Press, 1966.

Weber, Samuel. *The Legend of Freud: Expanded Edition*. Stanford, CA: Stanford University Press, 2000.

CHAPTER EIGHT

Freudian Unconscious and Secularization of Judaism

Jean-Joseph Goux

Sigmund Freud did not discover the unconscious. It is false, as he pretends it to be, that the philosophers before him purely and simply identified consciousness and mental life. In England, France, and Germany, the existence of a mental unconscious life became a postulate and a subject of reflection a quarter of a century before Freud. Not only did Nietzsche in Germany ask, but also, as an example, Jean-Marie Guyau in France, asked, since the beginning of the 1880s, what consequences the existence of an unconscious mental life would have on the creation of a new ethic. An ethics that would not be founded on absolute ideals, or transcendent obligations, but which would take into account, life, life itself, conscious and unconscious, in a tension toward a much greater intensity.

But Freud, in an era where post-hypnotic suggestion, hysteria, and amorous fetishism were the object of an intense interrogation, deserves all the credit of bringing clarity in the description and theoretical interpretation of these phenomena. Most of all, Freud possessed the rare ability to combine two approaches that must have seen quite incompatible to many of his contemporaries: a scientific, rationalist, or positive approach that constituted the ethos of a majority of psychiatrists of this time, and an approach founded on another ethos, the one of interpretation. This last approach takes into account the symbols, the images, and it translates them to go toward other significations, or other levels of truth hidden behind the immediate meaning. This last approach seems contradictory with an objective and Cartesian view of the world founded on the naked truth. This approach is rather of a literary, aesthetic, or religious type. It is exactly what the positivist mind tries to eliminate. Therefore we find in Freud a fruitful combination, almost contradictory in the approach of psychological phenomenon. He is an unbeliever positivist, but he remains an interpreter of the hidden meaning of words, images, and signs. Freud develops an approach that we would name today hermeneutic. It is there that probably resides his great originality in regards to the dominant psychiatry of his time. Of course this concerns a very particular hermeneutic. Contrary to the religious exegesis, this hermeneutic does not seek to establish a meaning, to discover greater significations that would reveal a transcendental message. On the contrary this hermeneutic aims at reducing the illusions, demystifying and denouncing dissimulations; in one word, it is a hermeneutic of suspicion as Paul Ricoeur says so well.

There is no doubt that the Freudian discovery fits into the vast movement of decline, or of the withdrawal, of religious faith. In following the various deisms, theisms, or agnosticism of the Era of Enlightenment, the ninetneeth century—the century which was the one of Feuerbach, of Marx, of Nietzsche—was acquainted with a more explicit and a more radical and systematic affirmation of atheism. It is not only the absence of a supreme God that is proclaimed but, with it, the new and huge responsibilities that this "death of God" brings upon every human being. If God is dead, a new man must be born, more responsible, more conscious of himself and of his own strengths.

The Freudian discovery is precisely located in *this* conjuncture. Man ceases to make an appeal to the beyond where the divine is located. Man recognized that this hereafter is only the fantastic projection of his own inner resources. At the same time man scrutinizes and sounds out these resources, he goes to the bottom of himself, in the most hidden of this conscience and of his psyche. Not even with the hope of finding any sacred treasures, but to reveal the mechanisms of a psychology. He thus extends his quest of rationality and of intelligibility all the way to the regions that were, up to this present day, out of the reach from a scientific investigation.

Thus could be defined the boundaries of a historical conjuncture that has been propitious for the emergence of psychoanalysis: the withdrawal of all religious beliefs before the scientific mind. This withdrawal has two consequences: first of all, it strips bare the place of an unconscious life (recognized as the hidden and obscure source of illusory religious symbolism or images), then it imposes an exploration, by means of reason, of this interior dimension which reveals itself in its psychological nudity. The willingness to seek clarity has no more limits. Thus the dreams, the hypnosis, the delirium, the instincts, will become the object of a rational curiosity.

From this point of view, a certain type of question may be asked concerning the relationships between Freudian psychoanalysis and religion. This question does not concern the contribution of psychoanalysis to a better understanding of the various religions. But rather the relationships between the emergence of psychoanalysis and a certain overall historical conjuncture, in which is also included the religion of its founders. This is where the question of secularization intervenes.

In retrospect, if we consider the great innovative movements that mark the nineteenth century, we perceive better and better that the emancipation in regards to established religions, for example in Marx, Nietzsche, or Freud, did not occur as an absolute and radical break. This exit from the religions bears in the new points of view that it promotes, many assumptions or old conceptions, that continue to play a major part and maybe a guiding role (although quite often nonconscious) in the new, as revolutionary as it may be. There are many exits of the religious, exits that still are marked by the religious world from which they come. For example, it is easy, or rather easy to pinpoint in Marx's conception of History and in the driving force that the proletarian must play, and also in his critique of ideologies, a secularized transposition of the strength of Hebraic Messianism and of the critique of idols. Regarding Nietzsche, in spite of this vigorous proclamation of atheism and anti-Christianism, it will not be too difficult to see in the glorification of what he himself calls the great *redemptive (or redeeming)* personalities, a kind of secularized substitute of a God-man who may give a totally new meaning to the world and to life.

In other words, there is not only one atheism, but many atheisms that continue to bear the marks of religious beliefs, from which they came out. On the surface, these atheisms are the complete renunciation of ancient beliefs, but in reality and in depth, they continue to operate following patterns or interpretations, of emotional configurations, of expectations, that prolong the religious education that modeled the thinker. Indeed, it is not the purpose to deny the radical novelty, the modernity of these thinkers, to lessen the upheaval that they brought, down to simple transpositions. But we may not pretend to deal with truths of fact, as pure and simple discoveries, what they achieved and most of all in regards to a world of significations. We could even uphold (following Gadamer) that it is as much as the massive load of unthinkable preconceptions, than the radicalism of the complete blank they sought for, what gives strength and firmness to their thought.

Therefore, that is true concerning Marx and Nietzsche, is also, and possibly even more, in regards to Freud. His object compels him to stay in areas where the beliefs, the representations, are shaped nearer to the mysteries of the soul, to the background of psyche, that are precisely the ones that religious thinkers tackled, quite often with terror. The relationship between Freud and religion is not necessarily the closest when he explicitly speaks about religions. This relationship to religion is dissimulated in a certain manner to approach language, alterity, the unknown, desire, the image, etc. But it is evident that when Freud confronts the question of monotheism he casts a particularly revealing light on his works. It is his own epistemological unconscious that he analyzes.

I have no doubt that there are many ways, many approaches to address the question of relationships between Freudian psychoanalysis and secularization of Judaism. I would like only to sketch out a few thoughts regarding the clues that appear to me the richest in ramification, the one of iconoclasm.

I shall let what Freud stresses in *Moses and Monotheism* lead me, while trying to go further than his own perception.

> Among the precepts of Mosaic religion is one that has more significance than is at first obvious. It is the prohibition against making an image of God, which means the compulsion to worship an invisible God. I surmise that in this point Moses surpassed the Aton religion in strictness. Perhaps he meant to be consistent; his God was to have neither a name nor a countenance. The prohibition was perhaps a fresh precaution against magic malpractices. If this prohibition was accepted, however, it was bound to exercise a profound influence. For it signified subordinating sense perception to an abstract idea; it was a triumph of spirituality over the senses; more precisely, an instinctual renunciation accompanied by its psychologically necessary consequences.[1]

Freud ties what he calls "a dematerialization of God" to a vast historical movement in which we are able to find some equivalents in other cultures: the passage from matriarchy to patriarchy. But with the Hebrews this passage is radical: it imposes a withdrawal of every image of divinity and an upmost importance granted to written records. We are able to detect it also in the rite of circumcision which expresses the "will of the father," and in the transmission of "the name of the father," etc. Thus the most remarkable precept on which Freud insists in his last book is the iconoclastic prescription, the second commandment. And it is striking that he insists on the psychological aspect of this law: "*an instinctual renunciation*, accompanied by its psychologically necessary consequences."

What is this instinctual renunciation?

It is remarkable that the Decalogue, which is presented as the most dense compendium of divine laws, seems marked by an incredible absence: the one of the *prohibition of the incest* which is nevertheless considered by anthropologists and by Freud himself as one of the fundamental and founding laws of human society, or even more, according to Levi-Strauss as *the* law that enables the passage from nature to culture.

We can hardly, as it seems to me, avoid the hypothesis that a religious substitute or equivalent, or religious trace, of the ban of incest is present in the precepts of the Decalogue, and this, evidently, under the form of a ban to make an image of God. Without being identical, this iconoclastic prescription has a certain relationship with the universal ban of incest, and this could explain the singularity of a Freudian approach.

To sculpt an image of God is to produce a material image. *Materiality* and *mater* had been often associated, as shown in Latin etymology. But more generally one can say that any sensible image echoes with a sensual attachment which has ultimately its origin in the sensual attachment to the maternal figure. Conversely to tear oneself away from the enticements of the senses and direct one's thoughts toward the unrepresentable God is to turn away from the desire for the mother, to rise toward the sublime Father (although he never bears that name in the Torah) and respect his law. Here the Mosaic proscription acquires its full fundamental importance. The holy wrath of Moses, analyzed so minutely by Freud, this controlled holy wrath portrayed by Michelangelo in a sculpture that makes such an impression on the founder of psychoanalysis, leads us to the taboo of incest with the mother. And beyond this incestuous desire, to the threat of castration brandished in opposition to it.

The guilt that Freud admits to feel in front of this famous sculpture, as if he himself belonged, he specifies, to the idolatrous mob that bears the brunt of Moses's wrath, is enlightened both by the cultural roots of Freud and by the universal threat of paternal punishment that awaits a potential violation of this fundamental prohibition. Never more clearly than in this conjunction do we see the mutual reinforcement of Freud's heritage and the emotions of his personal drama. That Judaism was able to reduce the oedipal conflict to its minimal abstract structure, and to dramatize its significant elements with virtually no recourse to a mythology, sheds light both on Freud's own state of mind and on the cultural potential of this discovery of the oedipal drive as universal structure.

The fundamental prohibition against figuring the deity, making images, carving statues, would be a radical form—the Judaic form—of the incest prohibition. And the formidable rage loosed upon the idolaters by Moses would signify or remind them of the threat of castration attendant upon forbidden sexual desire or any kind of worship to the mother. Judaism, seen in this light, sets the stage for the central drama to be uncovered by the psychoanalytic approach. The Judaic scene simplifies and radicalizes, and in so doing highlights the significant articulations of an emotional constellation that the mythologies, with their endless family sagas, never emphasize in such a reduced form. Even in the Oedipus myth the interdiction as such does not appear.

Now, I wish to take a step in the direction of some historical facts concerning the pre-Mosaic religion, in order to confirm this interpretation by other means. Those people threatened by the sublime fury of the legislator of the Jews are not just any idolaters: they are those who dance and feast around the golden calf. Concerning the historical and mythical signification of the golden calf, Freud remains silent. But according to certain researches on the myths of this cultural era, all evidence points to the fact that this golden calf is a *golden cow*, an equivalent of the Egyptian Isis, the great goddess who on certain occasions (for example, at the winter solstice) was represented in the form of a cow, veiled in black. Similarly, the Phoenician god Baal, in the form a bull, mates with his sister, the wild cow, to whom a bull calf is born. There is no doubt, in any case, that this religious adoration of the golden calf was a sexual celebration, an orgy, which involved rituals of sacred prostitution. These rituals included an act of symbolic incest with the great mother goddess in order to obtain fertility.

If this mythological and symbolical context turns out to be true, then what Moses condemns when he castigates the idolaters is actually, in a historical perspective, the cult of female, maternal deities, and much more the fertile incest rites that come with this archaic cult. The law given to the Jewish people by Moses is first of all a radical banning of incest with the mother, not only in the real, so to speak, but also (and perhaps first of all), in its imaginary and sacred form. The banning of the sacred, religious, or symbolic form of incest, appears as the metaphoric banning of the "real" incest.

In place of the incestuous attraction of the golden cow, Moses advocates an invisible god. With his written law, Moses institutes a kind of blindness with regard to image, imagination, and phantasm—all of which are associated with sensuality and attraction for the dimension of the mother, may it be the real mother herself as well as the great mother goddess who is its religious amplification or collective transposition.

Doing so, Moses brings to completion the exodus from Egypt, the land of sphinxes, tombs, and hieroglyphs. He leads his people not merely out of the land that bears this name but also out the *inner Egypt*, land of the imagination and its invasive icons. Moses rejects colorful phantasmagorias, the incomprehensible labyrinth of polyvalent symbolic imagery, and sets himself before the void of the sanctuary, containing only the *writing* of the Law.

We might state, from this point of view, that Freud's psychoanalysis constitutes a second exodus from Egypt, in a secular and private form. Freud proclaims that image and phantasy are delusion, and that behind the seductive draperies of the imaginary, an enduring symbolic structure homologous to a language must be discovered. Psychoanalysis seeks not to interpret the image with another image endlessly, but finally to dissolve it, to reduce it, to repress its welling forth, by translating it into a clear and communicable language.

The Hebrews, as Freud reminds us, were obliged to find a writing other than hieroglyphic writing, for figural representation was forbidden to them. The letter representing the sounds of the voice replaces the direct image of the things or the metaphorical image of ideas that dominate the mode of writing used by Egyptians. In the same way Freud, instead of remaining in the thrall of oneiric imagery rich with strange symbolisms (with perhaps inexhaustible meanings) reduces all dreams to the *law* of a desire that can be verbally formulated. Likewise Marx, unimpressed by modern idolaters who fetishistically worship the enigmatic "hieroglyphs of commodities" and money, seeks the law of the value hidden beneath this phantasmagoria that he compares to a religious illusion. In two acts of refusal wholly parallel, in their intellectual realm, to the "exodus from Egypt," the founding act of Mosaic law, both of these great thinkers, these two analysts of phantasy, negate cryptophoric symbolism.

This radical extirpation of the prolific imaginary, in favor of the agency of the letter, effected by those who followed in Freud's footsteps, as Jacques Lacan, is fully in keeping with this devaluation of the imaginary by a writing that decrees law and name. The patriarchal value of the alphabetical letter sheds light on Lacan's extension of the symbolic order conceived as "l'instance de la letter." For Lacan the symbolic order is operative in the most trivial play on words, in the language mechanism of dreams, just as in the most holy "Name of the Father." All these signifying operations bear the mark of the preeminent alphabet that disqualifies and dissolves the imaginary horizon. This radical conception of the letter in Lacan's doctrine is fully coherent with the Freudian secularization of the mosaic scene.

The Lacanian interpretation by the letter (spoken or written) takes for granted the law of the father. It automatically demands that the patient sacrifice the imaginary and, with it the desire for the mother, the goddess—incest and paganism. The process of cure is already, by virtue of the mode of interpretation, governed by a hermeneutic decision originating from the iconoclastic commandment.

One can say that from the very start it is Moses who takes the analyst's chair and who repeats the second commandment to the patient, incessantly, in every interpretation of the patient discourse. The analyst fends off images, pictures, fantasies; he shatters gods, smashes idols. Whenever he speaks, he reenacts the iconoclastic gesture. Thus, the hermeneutic posture of the analyst postulates in advance the result that the patient will achieve, that the patient *must* achieve—if he does not flounder in the errors of his dreamy paganism. Mental circumcision is his access to the law of the father—whence the Judaic scene of Freudo-Lacanian analysis: the patient is the pagan, so to speak. His hysteria (his madness) is a frenetic dance around the Golden Calf (the cow of Isis) to the sound of the tambourine and the flute. His perverse (polymorphous, polytheistic) imagination is flooded with erotic fantasies, exotic gods that take shape in his imagination. He is possessed by netherworld divinities who take possession of his unhealthy dream. As for the analyst, he occupies the place instituted by Moses. He leads his patient forth from Egypt, driving the gaudily picturesque hieroglyphics of his fantasies home to the letter, driving every show of the imaginary to the strokes of an alphabet. From hieroglyph to letters: such is the movement, the coming out, and emancipation.

These few remarks, which would deserve a longer elaboration, bring me to a short conclusion. Psychoanalysis, as a practice as well as a theory, presupposes the process of secularization. It is not in the collective transfer toward the All-other that the most intimate effects of the subject are regulated (Feuerbach called them "his love secrets"), but in the private transfer of the analytical situation. The de-collectivization or de-socialization of God is without any doubt a historical condition prior to the invention of psychoanalysis as a theory and as a practice. The withdrawal of the socialized projections of the religions and the decline of a certain living relationship to the "other scene," out of which the religious could regulate certain symbolic procedures, show as consequences an interior and individual sedimentation that is identified as unconscious. It is not by chance that psychoanalysis was invented in a certain context of a religion opposing itself to all idolatrous or humanizing temptation, by an iconoclastic prescription that takes away all figure to the divine. This God All-other was needed in order to identify an unconscious that is also all-other in regards to consciousness.

Note

1. Sigmund Freud, *Moses and Monotheism* (New York: Vintage Books, 1939), 144.

~

Index

The Ability to Mourn (Homans), 68
abjection, 72, 78
Alacoque, Marie, 37
Alexander, Franz, 110, 123
Allport, G. W., 10, 18, 20
Almodovar, Pedro, 74–75
American Psychiatric Association, 39
anatta, 122–26, 129, 131, 137–38
anti-Semitism, 59, 63, 66, 76n19, 200
Aristotle, 170
Augustine, 3

Bakan, David, 60
Bargh, John, 151–52
Batson, C. D., 13
Beauvoir, Simone de, 137
Beckford, James, 88
Belzen, Jacob, ix, 41n1, 43n26, 46nn55–56, 47n66, 48n81, 49n93, 140n3
Bergo, Bettina, xi, 209n26
Bergson, Henri, 134
Bion, Wilfred, 117
Blackstone, Judith, 111, 124–26, 131–33
Blannbekin, Agnes, 37
Bourdieu, Pierre, 24
breast, 32, 206, 208
Brickman, Celia, 137–38
Brown, Norman O., 176
Browning, Don, 41n1, 112
Brucke, Ernst Wilhelm Von, 148
Buber, Martin, xi, 182–87, 189–98, 201–5, 207nn7–16, 208n19, 212n55, 213n71
Bucke, R. C., 128
Buddha, 116, 124
Bühler, Karl, 9
Bulkeley, Kelly, x, 162n12, 176n5
Butler, Judith, ix, 62–63, 68–69, 71–74, 79n68, 170, 175

Calvin, John, 116
Capps, Donald, 41n3, 78n48, 88–89, 101n16
Carroll, Michael, ix–x, 88–89
Charcot, Jean-Martin, 113, 148–49, 153–54, 194
Chodorow, Nancy, 91–93
Christ, 37, 61, 204. *See also* Jesus
Civilization and Its Discontents, 59, 147, 175
Cohen, Hermann, 193, 207n16
Cole, Michael, 46n57
Coltart, Nina, 119
common-core, 120–21, 123–24, 126–27, 132–36, 160, 161n11. *See also* mystics
Confessions (Augustine), 3
constructivism, 120, 122, 125–26, 132, 139–40. *See also* mystics
Contemporary Psychoanalysis and Religion (Jones), 158
Cooper, Paul, 111, 119, 124–25
Corbett, L., 13–14
Coser, Lewis, 97
Cosmides, Leda, 149
Crews, Frederick, 60

Damasio, Antonio, 161n11
Darwin, Charles, 148, 157, 210n34
Dawkins, Richard, 157–58
DeCerteau, Michel, 112–14, 121
Deikman, Arthur, 125
Demerath, N. J., 88
Dennett, Daniel, 158
Derrida, Jacques, 177n27, 182
Descartes, René, 170–71, 177n12
Diagnostic and Statistical Manual (*DSM*), 39, 60
Didier-Weill, Alain, 209n27
Dillon, Michele, 88
Dittes, James, 60
Domhoff, G. William, 157
The Dreaming Brain (Hobson), 154–55
Dzog-Chen, 132

Eckhart, Meister, 126
Eigen, Michael, 111, 119
Eliade, Mircea, 116
Ellenberger, Henri, 161
Ellison, Christopher, 98
Eng, David, 72
Engler, Jack, 111, 123–25, 129–31, 133, 137–38
The Enigma of the Oceanic Feeling (Parsons), 41n1, 140n1, 160
entheogens, 110, 134
Epstein, Mark, 111, 124–25
Erikson, Erik, 20, 27, 28, 78n48, 112, 117, 123, 133, 137–38, 140n7, 158
Eros, 152

Faith Born of Seduction (Manlowe), 38
feminism, 60, 72, 91–92, 108, 137
Ferenczi, Sándor, 198, 211n44
fetish, 62–63, 69, 71, 73, 184, 188, 196, 199–202, 206, 217, 223
"Fetishism," 62–63, 71, 73, 76n20
Feuerbach, Ludwig, 218, 224
Fingarette, Herbert, 111
Fliess, Wilhelm, 153, 194
Flournoy, Théodore, 113
Fowler, James, 112
Fromm, Erich, 20, 110–11, 123, 141n15
Fuller, Robert, 114, 119
The Future of an Illusion, 59, 62–64, 76n20, 88, 108, 110

Gadamer, H. G., 27, 219
Gay, Peter, 60
Genealogy of Morals (Nietzsche), 174
Gilligan, Carol, 91–93, 137
Gimello, Robert, 122–23
Giorgi, Amedeo, 9–10
Goethe's Country, 65
Goetz, Bruno, 109
Goux, Jean-Joseph, xi–xii
Guyau, Jean-Marie, 217
Gyamtso, Rinpoche Tsultrim, 125

Hackney, Charles, 98
Hamlet, 67
Hammarskjöld, Dag, 118
Handbook of the Sociology of Religion (Dillon), 88
Hart, Darryl, 98
Hegel, G. W. F., 170
Heidegger, Martin, 193, 210n33
Hisamatsu, Shin'ichi, 110, 129
Hitler, Adolf, 27
Hobbes, Thomas, 173, 175
Hobson, J. Allan, 154–56, 162n26
Homans, Peter, ix, 41n1, 60, 62, 68–70, 73, 74, 75, 77n43, 79n56, 117, 140n4
Hood, Ralph, 42n5, 45n42, 88–89
Horney, Karen, 110, 123, 141n15
Hume, David, 171, 173
Husserl, Edmund, xi, 169, 172–74
Huxley, Aldous, 134–35

incorporation, xi, 187–90, 201, 206, 213n65
Inhibitions, Symptoms and Anxiety, 202
instinct, 34, 64–65, 133, 151, 154, 174–75, 177n21, 219–22
Interpretation of Dreams, 109, 147, 153–54, 161n1
Introductory Lectures on Psychoanalysis, 150

Jacobs, Janet Liebman, 91–93
James, William, 3, 45n39, 78n48, 110, 111, 113–14, 120–21, 123, 128, 139–40, 141n11
Jesus, xi, 4, 87, 136, 199, 206. *See also* Christ
Jones, Ernest, vii, 70
Jones, James, 158
Jonte-Pace, Diane, ix, 141n16
Journal for the Scientific Study of Religion (*JSSR*), 88–89
Jung, Carl, 3, 4, 13–14, 18, 20, 67, 78n48, 107, 110, 117, 118, 127–29, 134–35, 138, 158, 210n34
Jung in Context (Homans), 68

Kakar, Sudhir, 117, 160
Kandel, Eric, 160
Kant, Emmanuel, 120, 139, 173–75
Kaplan, Gregory, xi
Kaplan-Solms, Karen, 149
Katz, Steven, 120
Kazanjian, David, 72
Kelman, Harold, 110
Kierkegaard, Soren, 210n33
Klein, Dennis, 60
Klein, Melanie, 170
Kohut, Heinz, 35, 38, 40, 117–18, 133, 158
Kondo, Akihisa, 110
Krause, Neal, 98
Kripal, Jeffrey J., 41nn3–4, 160
Kristeva, Julia, ix, 62, 68, 71–73, 75, 170
Kung, Hans, 60, 116

Lacan, 33–35, 117, 182, 206n4, 223–24
Lacoue-Labarthe, Philippe, 181–83, 187, 194, 196–201, 203–5, 207n4, 213n63
Laplanche, Jean, 150, 211n44, 212n50
Le Rider, Jacques, 69
Lear, Jonathan, 171
Ledoux, Joseph, 150–51
Levi-Strauss, Claude, 221
Levinas, Emmanuel, 186, 193, 209n26, 210n30
Levinson, Pnina, 213n71
Lin, Maya 79
Lipset, Seymour Martin, 96–97, 99, 102n26
Loss (Eng and Kazanjian), 72
Luther, Martin, 95, 99, 102n25, 123
Lyman, Stanford, 97

MacNeill, W. H., 23
Mahamudra, 132
Manlowe, Jennifer L., 38
Marx, Karl, 218, 219–20, 223
Maslow, Abraham, 18, 20
Mason, Richard, 171, 177n12
Matte-Blanco, Ignacio, 124
McCarley, Robert, 155
McDargh, John, 158
Meissner, William, 93, 112, 137, 140n7
melancholia, ix, 38–39, 61–75, 77n40, 78n48, 78n51, 79n67. *See also* mourning; "Mourning and Melancholia"
Memories, Dreams, Reflections (Jung), 128
Mitchell, Steven, 35, 125, 129
Mitscherlich, Margarete, 78
Mohammed, 126
monotheism, xii
Moreau, Pierre-Francois, 171
Morel, Ferdinand, 110, 113
Moses, xi–xii, 192, 196–97, 199–201, 203–5, 207n10, 210n34, 220–24. See also *Moses and Monotheism*
Moses and Monotheism, 59, 181, 191–92, 195, 198, 207n10, 210n34, 220
mourning, ix, 61–75, 78n51, 124, 140n8, 154, 173. *See also* melancholia; "Mourning and Melancholia"
"Mourning and Melancholia," 64–67, 73, 150
Mourning Religion (Parsons, Jonte-Pace, and Henking), 140n8
Mysticism Sacred and Profane (Zaehner), 134
mystics, x, 15, 18, 30, 37, 109–29, 134–39, 141n11, 158, 160. *See also* common-core; constructivism; perennialism

Nancy, Jean-Luc, 181–83, 187, 189, 194, 196, 198–205, 207n4, 211n40, 213n63
Nathan of Gaza, 206
naturalism, xi, 10, 169–74
Neulander, Judith, 92
neuroscience, 148–61, 161n11
Nichanian, Marc, 74
Nichomachean Ethics, 170
Nietz, Mary Jo, 91
Nietzsche, Friedrich, 174, 183–84, 207n6, 212n59, 217, 218, 219–20

oceanic feeling, viii, 110, 114–15, 120–22, 135
Oedipal, 63, 93, 95, 97, 100, 120, 151, 176, 206n2, 208n20, 221. *See also* Oedipus
Oedipus, viii, xi, 107, 111, 127–28, 136, 137, 173, 199–200, 222. *See also* Oedipal
"On Transience," 64, 65, 78n51
Orsi, Robert, 97–99
Ostow, Mortimer, 94–95
Otto, Rudolph, 78n48

Parsons, William, x, 41n1, 77n40, 140n1, 141n16, 160
Patai, Raphael, 92
Paul, Saint, 113, 126, 199–200, 204–6
penis, 62–63, 76n19. *See also* phallus
perennialism, 120–22, 125–26, 134, 160. *See also* mystics
Pfister, Oscar, 60, 68, 70, 77n40
phallus, 63, 78n51. *See also* penis
Pinker, Steven, 149
Plato, 109, 186
Plotinus, 117
Pontalis, J.-B., 150
positivism, 89
Project for a Scientific Psychology, 147
Proudfoot, Wayne, 172

Psychoanalytic Object Relations Theory and the Study of Religion (McDargh), 158

Ramachandran, V. S., 149, 152
Ramakrishna, 4, 15, 109
Rat Man, 208n21
Religie, melancholie en zelf (Belzen), 38–39
Religionswissenschaft, 5–8, 21, 29, 31, 42n12
Rice, Emmanuel, 60
Ricoeur, Paul, 34, 60, 161, 172, 173, 176, 218
Rieff, Philip, 60, 116–17
Rilke, Rainer Maria, 67
Rizzuto, Ana-Maria, 44n33, 45n38, 45n50, 60, 71, 93, 112, 138, 140n7, 158
Roads of Excess, Palaces of Wisdom (Kripal), 160
Rolland, Romain, 109, 114–15, 117, 121–22, 135
Rubin, Jeffrey, 111, 130–31, 133

The SAGE Handbook of the Sociology of Religion, 88
Salome, Lou Andreas, 67
Sanders, Glenn, 98
Santner, Eric, 77n43, 175, 176
Sato, Koji, 110
Schafer, Roy, 74
Schiller, Friedrich, 109
Schorske, Carl, 69
Schwab, Raymond, 109
Shamans, Mystics, Doctors (Kakar), 160
Shweder, Richard, 46n57
Silesius, Angelus, 117, 123
Smith, Christian, 98
Sociology of Religion, 88
Solms, Mark, 149, 156–57, 159
Speaking the Unspeakable (Jonte-Pace), 75n1
Spinoza, Baruch, xi, 169, 171–72, 176, 177n12
spirituality, x–xi, 9–10, 40, 111–21, 126, 128, 131, 134, 137–40, 169, 220
Stark, Rodney, 93–96, 98–99
Structure and Change in Economic History, 23
Suler, John, 111
Surin, Kenneth, 176
Suzuki, D. T., 110, 141n15
Symbolic Loss (Homans), 68

Teresa of Avila, 37, 113, 117
Thanatos, 152
Tillich, Paul, 112, 135–37
Tooby, John, 149
Totem and Taboo, 59, 107, 127, 191–92, 198, 211n44
totemism, viii, 183, 187, 191, 197, 213n65
transference, xi, 28, 111, 131, 161n9, 169, 174–76, 196
Two Essays on Analytical Psychology (Jung), 128

Uleman, James, 151–52
Underhill, Evelyn, 127
University of Chicago, 123
University of Leuven, 38
University of Vienna, 109, 148

Valsinger, Jaan, 46n57
Ventis, W. L., 13
Vergote, A., 36–37, 40
Vidich, Arthur, 97
vippassana, 123–25, 129
Vitz, Paul, 60
Vivekananda, 109
Von Unwerth, Matthew, 67

Weber, Max, 116–18
Wilber, Ken, 13

Winnicott, Donald, 38, 93, 139–40, 158
Wittgenstein, Ludwig, 16, 69
Wolf Man, 188, 207n4
womb, 34, 109, 110, 123, 127

Yerushalmi, Yosef, 60
yoga, 118–19, 153

Zaehner, R. C., 121, 134–36

About the Contributors

Jacob A. Belzen graduated with degrees in social sciences, history, philosophy, and religious studies. He is professor at the University of Amsterdam, has served in several national and international organizations in history and psychology of religion, and has published extensively in these fields. In 2001 he was elected a Fellow by the American Psychological Association and, in 2001, received the William James Award from the APA.

Bettina Bergo is "professeure adjointe" at the Université de Montréal. She is the author of *Levinas between Ethics and Politics* (1999) and coeditor of several collections, notably *Levinas' Contribution to Contemporary Thought* (Graduate Faculty Philosophy Journal). She has translated three works of Levinas; M. Zarader's *The Unthought Debt: Heidegger and the Hebraic Heritage* (2006); the collection *Judéités: Questions à Jacques Derrida* (2006), and Jean-Luc Nancy's *La Déclosion* (2005). The author of numerous articles on Levinas, Merleau-Ponty, feminism, and psychoanalysis, she is currently working on a history of anxiety, as sensation and affect, in nineteenth century philosophy and psychology.

Kelly Bulkeley, Ph.D. (University of Chicago), is a visiting scholar at the Graduate Theological Union and teaches in the Dream Studies Program at

John F. Kennedy University, both in the San Francisco Bay Area, and is a former President of the International Association for the Study of Dreams. He has written and edited several books on dreaming, religion, psychology, culture, and science, including *The Wilderness of Dreams* (1994), *An Introduction to the Psychology of Dreaming* (1997), *Visions of the Night* (1999), *The Wondering Brain* (2004), *Dreaming Beyond Death* (2006), and *Soul, Psyche, Brain: New Directions in the Study of Religion and Brain-Mind Science* (2005).

Michael P. Carroll is professor of sociology at the University of Western Ontario in London, Ontario. He has written six books and a number of articles on the sociology and psychology of religion, including *The Cult of the Virgin Mary: Psychological Origins* (1986). His most recent book deals with the Penitente brotherhood of northern New Mexico (2002) and with the Protestant meta-narratives that continue to shape the academic study of American religion (in press).

Jean-Joseph Goux is Lawrence Favrot Professor of French Studies at Rice University. He specializes in postmodern French philosophy, aesthetic theories, and socio-symbolic interpretation. Among his books translated into English are *Oedipus Philosopher* (1993) and *Symbolic Economies* (1990). He has published numerous articles on Bataille, Lacan, and Irigaray.

Diane Jonte-Pace is professor of religious studies and associate provost for Faculty Development at Santa Clara University. She is the author of *Speaking the Unspeakable: Religion, Misogyny and the Uncanny Mother in Freud's Cultural Texts* (2001) and has edited three books: *Teaching Freud* (2003); *Religion and Psychology: Mapping the Terrain* (with William Parsons, 2001); *Mourning Religion* (with William Parsons and Susan Henking, 2008). She is the author of dozens of articles and is the past general editor of *Religious Studies Review*.

Gregory Kaplan is the Anna Smith Fine Assistant Professor of Judaic Studies in the Department of Religious Studies at Rice University. He has written a book on hallowing daily life between the secular and the sacred in the writings of Martin Buber and Franz Rosenzweig. Other research he has published also covers Hermann Cohen, Eugen Rosenstock-Huessy, and Emmanuel Levinas—as well as the concept of divine immanence, moral psychology in Jewish thought, and antisemitism in the United States. A coedited book entitled *Race and Political Theology* is forthcoming. His current research projects extend his work on life and death through special consideration of biological tropes in religious thought and the notion of sacrifice in a secular age.

William B. Parsons is associate professor of religious studies at Rice University, specializing in social scientific approaches to religion. He is author of *The Enigma of the Oceanic Feeling* (1999) and coeditor (with Diane Jonte-Pace) of *Religion and Psychology: Mapping the Terrain* (2001) and (with Diane Jonte-Pace and Susan Henking) *Mourning Religion* (2008). He is the author of the "psychology of religion" entry for the *Encyclopedia of Religion*, and his articles have appeared in numerous journals and edited books, including the *Journal of Religion*, *The Annual of Psychoanalysis*, and *Vishnu on Freud's Desk: A Reader in Psychoanalysis and Hinduism*. He has served as chair of the Department of Religious Studies, director of the Humanities Research Center (Rice University) and is an editor (psychology of religion section) with *Religious Studies Review*.

Breinigsville, PA USA
22 July 2010
242125BV00002BA/1/P

9 780739 142127